THE
# SOCIAL ACHIEVEMENTS
OF THE
# CHRISTIAN CHURCH

I0160478

BY
## REV. PRINCIPAL EDMUND H. OLIVER
Ph.D., F.R.S.C.
*St. Andrew's College, Saskatoon, Saskatchewan, Canada*

REGENT COLLEGE PUBLISHING
Vancouver, British Columbia

First published 1930 by the Ryerson Press, Toronto and issued
by the Board of Evangelism and Social Service of the United
Church of Canada

Reprinted 2004 by Regent College Publishing
5800 University Boulevard, Vancouver, B C  V6T 2E4 Canada
www regentpublishing com

A catalogue record for this publication is available from the
National Library of Canada

ISBN 1-57383-293-6

# PREFACE

This study in Social Achievements was written originally for students in the Presbyterian Theological College (now St. Andrew's College in The United Church of Canada), to serve as the basis for class discussion in a weekly Seminar. It later formed the foundation of a course of lectures given before the Regina College Ministerial Conference in Regina, Saskatchewan, in August, 1924. The purpose was to ascertain just what each Age in the past owed to the achievements of the Christian Church, and what we owe to-day. It has been felt that the material gathered might serve a larger constituency, especially Study Groups interested in the Social Achievements of the Christian Church. A series of questions has been provided for each Chapter, and some of the more important books on the subject therein treated have been indicated.

What is the primary consideration in the whole task of social service from the modern point of view? It is the spirit of the man who renders the service. And the spirit of Christian social service means that such a man will be dominated by the spirit of the Christ. The second consideration is that social service requires empirical study, a detailed study, in the light of that spirit, of the actual situation where the service is to be rendered. There has arisen among the ministers and members of our Churches a social interest amounting to a passion. I believe that it will bring new life to our Church. But as faith without works is dead, so passion without knowledge is futile. This study aims to give a passing acquaintance with the history of the services of the Church.

I am indebted to my colleagues, Professor David S. Dix and Professor J. L. Stewart, for many suggestions of value.

The material in this study was gathered many months before the appearance of the two excellent volumes, "The Story of Social Christianity," by Francis Herbert Stead. In revising my manuscript I have had the advantage of perusing his work.

E. H. O.

St. Andrew's College,
Saskatoon, Saskatchewan, Canada.

# CONTENTS

# FOREWORD

Long ago an ancient sage reached the conclusion that: "God has so ordered that men, being in need of each other, should learn to love each other and bear each others burdens."

The best men in all ages have found their greatest pleasure in the life of service. They were willing to die, if need be, for a principle that those who came after them might benefit thereby. Nor have the efforts of such men been fruitless, for it is to such as they that the world's real honor is given.

As the years go on, men are seeing more clearly that true happiness does not lie in the possession of great riches, but in the joy of one who puts his shoulder to the wheel of progress and works for the removal of things which cause suffering and oppression.

The Church in our day has been startlingly awakened by voices like those of Studdert-Kennedy and Dean Shepherd. They remind us that what has been called the lost radiance of the Christian religion, need not remain lost if we are ready to pay the price demanded. This radiance can be found only in dangerous living or in the experience of triumph after dangerous living.

In "The Story of Social Christianity" Dr. Oliver calls us to face the task of our Church in the new Canada which has emerged before our eyes. No one knows the task better. No one has done more towards opening our eyes to see it and strengthening our purpose to meet it. Throughout the volume one feels the influence of the spirit of Christ. In all social progress during the Christian era one can trace the steps of the Great Emancipator and Minister. Jesus had to make his choice between the Primrose way where the crowd went and the Via Dolorosa which he trod alone. He chose deliberately. He pierced the sensuous and the seeming and found the secret of greatness in the life that serves. "For the joy that was set before him, he endured the cross." He had faith in the ultimate triumph of love. He risked all on the greatness of service, and he won.

> "Peace does not mean the end of all our striving,
>     Joy does not mean the drying of our tears;
> Peace is the strength that comes to souls arriving
>     Up to the height where God Himself appears.

> "Joy is the wine that God is ever pouring
>     Into the hearts of those who strive with Him,
> Opening their eyes to vision and adoring,
>     Strengthening their arms for warfare glad and grim."

D. N. McLachlan.

Board of Evangelism and Social Service,
        Toronto.

# CHAPTER I

# WHAT HAS THE CHURCH DONE?

The Church a Force. The Church a Pioneer. Complete Survey Impossible. Criticisms of the Church. The Problem. Service Related to the Age. Service Related to Growth of Church. A Study of Ministry, not Ethics. The Christian Contribution.

## The Church a Force

The Christian Church has rendered outstanding social service for mankind. The world is in debt to it at many points and all along the line of nineteen centuries. All eras, of course, have not witnessed the same vigilance nor the same high plane of social achievement. But even in this respect appearances may mislead. After the Reformation civilization became more largely secular, but this should not blind us to the fact that modern society has, for all that, come more and more under the influence of the Christian ideal. On the other hand, as in the first century, the kingdom of God is still only drawing nigh. But during the Christian era the Christian Church has done certain definite things that have constituted a distinctive social service. It has fought against certain wrongs, against sin and impurity, against sensuality and selfishness in every form. It has established certain institutions. It has introduced certain reforms. It has created a certain atmosphere both in life and legislation. It has made certain views of God, of man, of conduct, of society, of life here and hereafter, potent in the lives of men. It has been a Faith, a Fellowship, a Force. The Christian Church has achieved a certain something. It has made the world somewhat different. It is our purpose to outline not the teaching of the Church, nor the history of the Church itself as an institution, but to inquire what are some of the things that the Church has wrought for men here upon the earth.

## The Church a Pioneer

It must constantly be borne in mind that the kingdom of heaven "is like unto leaven which a woman took and hid in three measures of meal till the whole was leavened." Its deepest workings are in the souls of men and in the springs of human action. There is much that is potent now that traces its source back to a seed, Christian in character, planted by some humbler Paul or Apollos, that has sprung and grown up, we know not how. There can be no history of such service, for it has been silent and unobserved. And so it comes to pass that much that is Christian in character and inspiration has been achieved quite outside the pale of the organized Church. The Church created the atmosphere that made the achievement possible,

1

or handed on the torch of which the worker caught the gleam without himself detecting whose hand held it aloft. Thus a Board of Foreign Missions establishes hospitals in a Chinese province—a distinctive piece of social service rendered by the Christian Church. But in course of time the civil authorities of that Province become seized of the value of that work and themselves undertake to found hospitals which, with their ampler material resources, they are able to do on a larger scale. The Christian Church, finding that this work can now be adequately cared for, eventually withdraws from hospital work in this Province, and the State maintains a complete system of hospitals of its own. At length it is forgotten that it was the Christian Church that was pioneer and pathfinder in this service. Again and again the Church has blazed the trail along lines of educational and humanitarian effort, and has later withdrawn to explore still newer paths. In this way it teaches men to bear one another's burdens and so to fulfil Christ's law. But all this greatly complicates the task for him who would give a picture of the social service of the Christian Church. What will he say, for example, about the work of a modern university, the democratic movement, the operation of Associated Charities, the provision made by civil authorities for dependents and defectives, and a myriad of other matters, in which the Church can never cease to be interested, for the existence of which at the outset it was altogether or largely responsible, but with which in the present, except as a moderating or inspiring force, it has no manner of formal connection? He can only say that much of the work of the Church has been to drop fruitful seeds of truth and spiritual stimulus as the opportunity might present itself. The effectiveness and permanent worth of this method have splendidly justified themselves. The greatest social service of the Christian Church has not been itself to serve, far-reaching as has been its ministry in every generation. Its supreme achievement is that it has inspired and stimulated others to serve. It has created a kingdom of service wider than any institutional boundaries. In this respect even the kingdoms of this world become the kingdoms of our Lord and of his Christ, if only tardily and in part.

## Complete Survey Impossible

Moreover it must be remembered that the material is lacking for a complete appreciation of the social service rendered by the Church. The first three centuries subsequent to the Apostles afford the biography of not a single Christian man or woman. It must not be forgotten, also, that there are no chronicles for the good, but only for the exceptional. Unless one has been martyred, or founded an Order, or built a Church, his life of honest Christian service passes unmarked by the historian, however great his contribution may actually have been. There are few annals for the just. Many a kindly deed of helpful service has simply passed into oblivion. Our present discussion will disclose only the more obvious social achievements of the Christian Church and their effects upon civilization and society.

## Criticisms of the Church

The moment that an attempt is made to weigh aright the contribution made by the Christian Church critics spring up to recall this and that occasion wherein the Church failed or blundered, to point to its sins strewn all along the centuries and to its immature handling of difficult problems. "The Church," they cry, "has been a reactionary and hampering force thwarting the human kind in its struggle to be free." They point to Urban VIII's treatment of Galileo, to the Inquisition, to the Marian persecutions, to some of the severer phases of Puritanism, to acquiescence in, or espousal of, doubtful economic theories and systems, and proclaim the Church narrow, intolerant, cruel. They indicate the great Creeds as dogmas framed in a Hellenic environment, the Church's historic attitude towards science and new thought, and pronounce it conservative, unprogressive, even hostile to the advancement of learning. They remind us of the Papan alliance with the Hapsburgs, of the favor shown rulers in the Middle Ages, and criticize the Church as ever failing to espouse the people's cause. When German hordes crossed the Belgian frontiers and the passions of men were inflamed throughout the world they had a fresh argument to establish the impotence of the Church to abolish war. "In the face of such tremendous evils it has never been able to rise above national prejudices," was their stern indictment. It would be a mistake to deny that too great an admixture of truth adheres to these charges. But in the face of this heavy count against the Church not infrequently is to be found an explanation, if not a justification, for its conduct in the special conditions and views of the age or in the incompleteness of its own development. It is easy, though unfair, to find fault with the achievements of earlier centuries, and to forget that the Church was pioneer in many a field of service and pathfinder along an unblazed trail.

To have believed that love to God is love to man, to have been the first to establish hospitals, asylums, orphanages, homes for fallen women is great glory. It is unreasonable to demand that no mistakes should have been committed, that at the outset should have been known all that nineteen long centuries have since taught. It is something that the Church cared enough to exercise charity among the poor, and was not backward in loving, sacrificing and providing for the needy and unfortunate among the sons of men. We must not complain if it required time to learn to do so wisely. There still remain great and weighty contributions to human welfare even within the same sphere of learning, teaching, social, economic and political life as well as war, and no less great and weighty contributions quite apart from these areas of conduct and life. It will not be forgotten, in brief, that it was the Church that saved learning, that founded the universities, that kept alive intellectual life for centuries, that achieved all that was accomplished in the way of the scholary and the clerical for many a long year in Europe, and that furnished among its sons some of the very thinkers whose work was attacked. For if criticism emanated from the Church, the constructive efforts that were criticized were no less the work of its children. And if the

Church appeared, or was, intolerant, it may mitigate the offence to remember that it did so not with a view to conceal truth, but, as at any rate it thought, to defend and conserve it.   The Church has always maintained that the connection lies very close between wrong thinking and wrong doing.   From this point of view intellectual error and heresy assume a real importance.   They are not merely academic exercises for the intellect or subjects for philosophical speculation. To the Church truth has been something to be lived, to be incorporated within one's being.   That the Church has committed grave mistakes every one will now admit.   But that the Church, for all its faults, may have been much nearer fundamentals than those who readily carp at its intolerance or who fancy truth to be mere stuff for the exercise of one's wits, is a matter that at least will admit of debate.   At any rate the Church, however narrow, has not been indifferent to truth.   It has always believed that it does matter profoundly whether or not we attain to truth.

It will not be forgotten, either, that if the Church has favored rulers, this has been in particular periods.   Few will be so Bolshevistic as to demand that the Church should always oppose them.   Before Constantine the Church was not allied with the great and powerful. In the barbarian invasions it offered its churches and its monasteries as sanctuaries for all the destitute and oppressed.   If in the Middle Ages it was closely connected with rulers it must be remembered that this was not invariably so, that the Church often fought and restrained turbulent and oppressive nobles and princes, that it not infrequently championed the poor, and that its policy was dictated not by a desire to court kings and the mighty but to maintain order and to further justice.   The one scene at Canossa is permanent proof that the Church did not stand in awe of even the highest princes.   And in recent times it has been the Church that has awakened men to larger humanitarian efforts and to espouse the cause of the weak and afflicted.   And if the Church has not been able to abolish war, it will be recalled that, before the Church's efforts among men, war was more largely a normal experience than now, that it was the Church that did seek to check its ravages by humanizing its methods, by chivalry, by the truce of God, by the Red Cross, and by endeavoring to link it only to righteous causes.

### The Problem

It is worth while to consider whether the ground of the problem of social service has shifted since the foundation of the faith.   There are two points of view, one represented by Rauschenbusch in his *Christianity and the Social Crisis,* the other by Garvie in his *Studies of Paul and His Gospel.*   It will be necessary in the course of this study to bear these in mind.   Rauschenbusch holds that the essential purpose of Christianity was to transform human society into the kingdom of God by regenerating all human relations and by reconstituting them in accordance with the will of God.   He declares that the Christian Church has never undertaken to carry out this fundamental purpose of its existence.   He gives a series of historical explanations for this failure. Garvie doubts whether Paul, valiant worker for the kingdom that he was, ever sought to Christianize the social order in the sense that this is the conscious programme of the Modern Church. His primary interest was ever in the eternal. His citizenship was in heaven, from which he was waiting for a Saviour. His desire was to make men Christian, to impart to them the gift of the heavenly citizenship. He gave little thought to the existing worldly environment, to the political and economic order. He gave all his thought to the seed, and the planting of it in human life—"Ye are God's field to be planted, God's building." The primitive Church sought not to make a new earth in the Roman Empire. It sought to relate man to Christ, to lead him to live in touch with the Unseen and Eternal. As Garvie puts it—"Human society, how it is to be purified and perfected—that is our concern, and the Christian Church is value ' as it serves as a means to that end. It is no misrepresentation of Paul to say that his interest was exactly the reverse. The Church as the body of Christ was his primary concern, and the world appealed to him only as in need, and capable of being brought into the Church. . . . . . We run the risk of imposing on Paul ideas that were not present even to his mind, because we assume in him interests that had no place at all in his heart. How can the Christian be a saint in the world? is his problem, while ours is, How can society be Christianized?"

*Service Related to the Age*

The social service rendered by the Church in any age, the mode in which it was expressed, and the motives which inspired it, are not accidental in their character. They are related to, or dependent upon, the quality of Christian living and thinking in that same period. But they are related no less to the entire course of the whole stream of history, and, in particular, to the special conditions as a whole that existed at the time. Two illustrations will suffice. Even the superficial student will discern the distinction between the generous impulses and eager spontaneity of service before the crisis occasioned by Montanism on the one hand, and, on the other, the charity organized later under episcopal supervision. He will see this same transition manifested as the enthusiasm and inspiration of the general Christian movement pass over into the disciplined Church of the Bishops. Here we have an instance where the cause of the transformation is found *within* the Church. But when social service, in the change from the third to the fourth and subsequent centuries, ceases to be personal and congregational and becomes largely institutional, the cause is to be found *outside* the Church or in the external relations of the Church—Constantine has been making the Christian religion a department in, or an ally of, the State. To understand the Church's social service at any stage, then, one must be prepared to scan the whole field of history, in its economic, social and political aspects, no less than in its religious and ecclesiastical relations.

*Service Related to Growth of Church*

Christianity had many truths to impart. What it actually did impart in any age was determined not infrequently by the nature of the fight it had to wage, by the enemies it had to encounter. At the outset in the Mediterranean where many gods were worshipped, it taught with emphatic urgency its message of one God. The Christian Church did not shrink from this colossal task, to change the mind of a whole world, to induce the Roman Empire to give up pagan worship. Starting from an insignificant province at one end of the Mediterranean, from a despised and hated people, and with a message preached by fishermen, it conquered the State itself in less than three centuries. It succeeded because it had a message that challenged the heart of man concerning sin and the life to come. It spoke with great confidence about immortality and redemption. It brought to thousands of poor, ignorant, humble and greatly concerned folk the calmness and courage, the consolation and comfort that could come only from personal faith in a personal Saviour. On the part of individual men and women this faith found expression in a changed conduct that was no less than a moral revolution. It found expression in the establishment of the Catholic Church. It found expression later in what professed to be a Christian State. As has been frequently pointed out, in the first century the Government was ignorant of the very existence of Christianity except at a few points. In the second century it was responsible for the enforcement of local and temporary laws against it. In the third century the more aggressive and able emperors made definite attempts to turn back the tide by planning thorough-going imperial persecutions, for they looked upon the movement as an organized defiance of the law. Then came Constantine, who saw the significance of its organization, its fellowships, its power of concerted action as over against the leaderless and incoherent paganism of the Empire. The new hope was to be incorporated within the Roman Empire, which, had all been known, was without hope. Constantine set the Christian movement free to work in the world. As Paul had wrenched it loose from Judaism, so Constantine freed it from the shackles which bound a proscribed faith. Through the former it ceased to be tribal, under the latter it became imperial.

*A Study of Ministry, not Ethics*

In this study we must confine ourselves largely to the external. Down through nineteen centuries we behold kindlier deeds of helpfulness rendered, more numerous and unobstrusive acts of charity performed, social service institutions established on an ampler scale than ever before. These practical and external results flow, we believe, from the Christ,[1] from a new and more vital thought of God as Father and of man as brother, from a quickened sympathy, from the actuating motive of love, from the work of the Christian Church. A new

1. Brace, Gesta Christi, 270, says: "The victories of Christ are silent victories, won in the individual heart and life. No history chronicles them. Their fruits are seen later in the lessening or overthrow of great social abuses and in the gradual growth of justice, benevolence, purity, truth, and all those feelings and practices which specially result from Christian teachings."

spirit had been born. But it is not a history of motives that we are tracing. It is the story of the seen and the expressed. Seed needs time for germination and fruit-bearing. Social service, which is the fruit, ever lags behind the impelling thought-seed that gives rise to it, and sometimes far enough behind. This is not, then, a study of ethics but of ministry. Only we must not forget that teaching is itself a service rendered. In a sense all that nineteen hundred years have done, that has been Christian, was there in Jesus. Succeeding generations have simply endeavored to live out what in him was germinal. Jesus is the supreme social service rendered by Christianity—his teaching, his life, his ministry, his death and his resurrection. This is, however, not a history of the Christ in the hearts of men, but in their conduct. It is not the history of the Christian religion, not the story of the relationship between man and God, though to foster that and to give it meaning is the most splendid contribution made by the Christian Church. It is the story of the relationship between man and man as influenced by the Church. Through its confessors and martyrs, through its saints and disciples, the Christian Church has given an exhibition, in life and character, of fidelity to moral law, of personal allegiance to a heavenly Father. It has brought the message of the love of God to the debased, depraved, discouraged and discomfited. It has brought to human kind a power, hitherto unknown, to live a life of purity and helpfulness. It has taught the supreme need of God, the supreme value of the life of man. It has called into being a fellowship in which all men, whether bond or free, stand equal before the Head of the Church. It has given new life, new hope and new power to a sin-laden and burden-bearing world. A complete study of the fruits of the Christian religion would take all these achievements and contributions of Christianity into account, would estimate with exactness the full significance of the character of the Faith, would assess at their true worth the ideals and life and achievements of the last humble Christian worker. Our purpose is much more restricted, namely, to mention a few of the more patent and obvious and external things done in the communities of men by the Christian movement. Only the recording angel can tell the full story of the redeemed.[1] Perhaps it will not be without advantage, however, to contemplate even in a cursory way some of the apparent and practical things which the Christian Church has done in the way of service along with its task of bringing the message of salvation to the sons of men.

*The Christian Contribution*

In the *Gesta Christi* Brace, greatly daring, undertook to give a short summary of the contribution that is distinctively Christian. He stated: "There are certain practices, principles and ideals—now the richest inheritance of the race—that have been either implanted or stimulated or supported by Christianity, They are such as these: regard for the personality of the weakest and poorest; respect for

---

1. "The world has changed," says James Martineau, "and that change is historically traceable to Christ."

woman; the absolute duty of each member of the fortunate classes to raise up the unfortunate; humanity to the child, the prisoner, the stranger, the needy, and even the brute; unceasing opposition to all forms of cruelty, oppression and slavery; the duty of personal purity and the sacredness of marriage; the necessity of temperance; the obligation of a more equitable division of the profits of labor, and of greater cooperation between employers and employed; the right of every human being to have the utmost opportunity of developing his faculties, and of all persons to enjoy equal political and social privileges; the principle that the injury of one nation is the injury of all, and the expediency and duty of unrestricted trade and intercourse between all countries; and, finally and principally, a profound opposition to war, a determination to limit its evils when existing, and to prevent its arising by means of international arbitration." This statement, prepared in 1882, few students will find either complete or satisfactory. But it will be useful if it will challenge each of us to attempt to state for himself just what he finds that the Church has accomplished.

In his article on "Christianity" in the Jewish Encyclopedia, Rabbi Kohler pays the following tribute: "Christianity, following the matchless ideal of its Christ, redeemed the despised and outcast, and ennobled suffering. It checked infanticide and founded asylums for the young; it removed the curse of slavery by making the humblest bondsman proud of being a child of God; it fought against the cruelties of the arena; it invested the home with purity, and proclaimed . . . . the value of each human soul as a treasure in the eyes of God; and it so leavened the great masses of the empire as to render the cross of God the sign of victory for its legions in place of the Roman eagle. The 'Galilean' entered the world as a conqueror. The church became the educator of the pagan nations; and one race after another was brought under her tutorship. The Latin races were followed by the Celt, the Teuton, and the Slav. The same burning enthusiasm which sent forth the first apostle also set the missionaries aglow, and brought all Europe and Africa, and finally, the American Continent, under the sceptre of an omnipotent church. . . . Christianity is not an end, but the means to an end—namely, the establishment of the brotherhood of man and fatherhood of God."

Philip Schaff has eloquently expressed the achievement of Christianity thus: "Eighteen hundred years ago there lived, among a despised nation and in a remote country, a man by the name of Jesus, a carpenter's son, who had no political power, no social position, no secular learning or art, no wealth, no shelter to call his own, and who after a very brief public career was crucified in his youth by his own countrymen as an imposter and a blasphemer. Yet this humble Rabbi, by the force of his doctrine and example, without shedding a drop of blood, save his own, has silently accomplished the greatest moral revolution on record, founded the mightiest spiritual empire, and is now recognized and adored by the civilized nations of the globe as the Son of God and the Saviour of mankind."[1]

"Blessings abound where'er He reigns;
The prisoner leaps to lose his chains,
The weary find eternal rest,
And all the sons of want are blest."

### QUESTIONS FOR DISCUSSION

1. Is the social service that has been rendered by Christianity identical with that rendered by the historical Christian Church?

2. Discuss the following: "The Church that is seen and known of men represents often anything but his image. At times it is filled with bigotry and hate; it implants persecution in Roman law; it encourages frightful religious wars; it opposes liberty of thought, and the investigation of science; its skirts are stained with the blood of the Inquisition, and wet with the tears of millions of victims of the slave trade; it encourages war, and is often only an emblem of power and lust and ambition."

3. Have there been other great moral forces operating during the Christian era apart from the Christian Church? If so, what have they been?

4. "The Church has been a Faith." Has the Faith been the same in every age? What is the Faith of the Church now?

5. "The Church has been a Fellowship." Is it exclusive? Is it a benevolent society?

6. "The Church has been a Force." In what ways is the Church a Force in this day?

7. Has the Church the right to withdraw from certain kinds of social service? If so, under what conditions?

8. Has the Church failed in not abolishing war?

9. Is Garvie or Rauschenbusch right? Are both?

10. What determines the type of social service the Church will render in any one age?

11. If Jesus did not condemn slavery when here upon the earth, and if even in the nineteenth century there were churchmen opposed to the emancipation of slaves, what right have we to say that the liberation of the negro was an achievement of the Christ?

12. What social service has the Christian Church rendered in the sphere of International Law? Of Industrial Relations?

13. Stead says—"From the very outset the Gospel was a social message." Do you agree?

14. Is the criticism of some Labor leaders just, that the Church has been the chief support of Slavery, Feudalism, Capitalism, and, in general, of the *status quo*?

### BOOKS FOR ADVANCED STUDY

C. Loring Brace, *Gesta Christi, a History of Humane Progress under Christianity.* T. C. Hall, *History of Ethics within Organized Christianity.* Harnack and Hermann, *The Social Gospel* Translated by G. M. Craik. W. E. H. Lecky, *History of European Morals from Augustus to Charlemagne.* J. K. Mozley, *The Achievements of Christianity.* W. Rauschenbusch, *Christianity and the Social Crisis.* J. K. Ingram, *The History of Slavery and Serfdom.* J. S. Dennis, *Christian Missions and Social Progress.* Schmidt, *Social Results of Early Christianity.* A. B. Bruce, *The Kingdom of God.* Ernst von Dobschütz, *The Influence of the Bible on Civilization.* N. D. Hillis, *The Influence of Christ in Modern Life,* especially ch. ii. Ernst Troeltsch, *Protestantism and Progress.* Francis Herbert Stead, *The Story of Social Christianity.*

1. S. L. and E. L. Gulick, The Growth of the Kingdom of God, Foreword.

# CHAPTER II

# JESUS AND THE APOSTOLIC CHURCH

(a) JESUS

His Life a Social Ministry. His Field of Service. His Early Training. The Opening of the Ministry. His Purpose. The Kingdom. Jesus at Work. The Spirit of His Service.

(b) THE APOSTOLIC AGE

Social Service Based on Old Testament and Ministry of Jesus. Social Service Grew up With the Evangel. A Wider Field With New Forms. Social Service not yet Institutionalized. Appointment of the Seven. No Sustained System. Achievements. Sound Moral Judgments. Summary of Achievements. Confidence in Power of the Gospel.

## (a) JESUS

### His Life a Social Ministry

Social service was instinctive with Jesus, instinctive and deliberate. He came to minister. He lived under an inner constraint to do the works of him that sent him. As he worked, so he taught. Both his life and his message of a kingdom wherein God's will was done were, in the best sense, social, and they were not separate things. But the accounts given by the evangelists differ in their emphasis. Luke accentuates the social teaching of Jesus, Mark his social ministry. To the former we are indebted for the story of Zaccheus, the parables of the Good Samaritan, the Rich Man and Lazarus, the Lost Sheep, the Lost Coin, and, as I prefer to call it since the War taught us the poignancy of that adjective, the "Missing" Son. But it is to Mark we turns to see Jesus in the very business of service, thronged by crowds till he had not so much leisure even as for his meals, visiting the synagogues, walking the blazing, blistering paths of Palestine, healing, comforting, helping, mingling in the midst of men.

Though his spoken teachings constitute a social service of the highest significance, and serve as the basis and inspiration for all subsequent Christian doctrine and social achievement, yet it is our purpose here to examine action rather than words, ministry rather than message.[1] It will be helpful to inquire into the character of the field in which he worked, and the nature of the purpose which he cherished and pursued,

### His Field of Service

Practically the whole ministry of Jesus was spent in Palestine, a circumscribed land with a variety of governments—Judea and Samaria directly under the Roman procurator, Galilee and Perea

---

1. See F. G. Peabody, Jesus Christ and the Social Question, especially Ch. V, The Teaching of Jesus Concerning the Care of the Poor.

under Herod Antipas, and the north country, the tetrarchy of Philip, who was also a member of the Herodian family. Jesus belonged to and lived among a race that has given the world its most exalted conceptions of religion. Even the Pharisees, whose name has acquired sinister significance, had made a splendid contribution to man's acquaintance with God. In their best days they had built up religious individualism and purely spiritual worship; they had deepened belief in the future life and carried on a powerful missionary propaganda. But in addition to, or rather in conjunction with, the thought of drawing near to God and of finding in his service perfect fulness of life, the best thought of Israel had ever expressed a passion for social righteousness, an order of society in which the members stood in right and helpful relations to each other, not only walking humbly with God but loving mercy and doing justly. The great prophets had not divorced the religious and the social aims and principles of life. There was a rich background of deep religious intimacy with God and practical social idealism, even if there was no specific organization for charities, behind the life of his people when Jesus entered upon his service. Particularly in Galilee, the home of his boyhood, there had been a pronounced ethical development in religious thought and experience that had not faltered even when the prophets ceased. As compared with the conceptions and practices of Judea, religion in the north country was warmer, more kindly, more inward and spiritual, and more instinct with the thought of social obligation.

There was much of political and religious unrest in the time of Jesus. Roman rule was galling to the sensibilities of a patriotic folk. Tax-gatherers swarmed the land, exploiting the people. The rivalry of the religious sects was intense. The eager expectations of the faithful made them the easy prey of false Messiahs. The leaders of the nation were without sense of responsibility, and, as the barren fig-tree, without fruit. Social barriers based on religion divided the "sinners" from the "righteous," the Jew from the Samaritan.

*His Early Training*

Jesus' own training was not in orthodox Judea but in Galilee. There he had increased in wisdom and stature, in favor with God and with his fellow men. There in a home of piety he had dwelt with father and mother, probably the eldest of a considerable family. Mary did not need to attend the Passover at Jerusalem, but to the Remnant devotion left no option—she attended. In that home, moreover, the kindliness of Joseph insensibly moulded the conception of a heavenly Paternity. The child-mind bridges the transition from carpenter-father to our Father. In that hilltop village he learned the little lessons in the Scriptures and passed into the House of the Book. Joseph, as all wise Jewish fathers, taught him an honest trade—his own. At twelve years of age he had grasped with something of definiteness that it was in the Father's house or about the Father's business he ought to be. Yet he did not grudge nearly a score of years of meditation and training for that Father's work. Others saw in him only the quiet lad who helped Joseph frame the well-built houses.

Mary was pondering unspeakable things in her heart. He himself was seeing more and more that his mission lay beyond the hammer and the saw.

### The Opening of the Ministry

A revival swept across the land in his early thirties, not unlike the great awakening in America and the Wesleyan movement of England in the eighteenth century. A cousin preached a stern message of repentance and social righteousness and the coming kingdom, with lavish use of homely phrase, speaking much about axes and fire and shovel-fans. In the crowds that flocked to hear him was the Nazarene Carpenter, It proved to be a crisis in his life, a compelling spiritual experience that drove him forth from the haunts of men for an assaying of his soul. In those testing weeks in the inner wilderness, "with the wild beasts," he confirmed the lofty purpose of his life to do no deed that ministered to his own personal gratification, or that was for mere spectacular display, or that committed him to an allegiance other than God's. With this resolve fixed, the time for ministry was come. Over the hills from Nazareth to Capernaum he fared, from the secluded shelter of the shop to the busy haunts of men, from the flowers in the fields behind the village and the westward view of Carmel and the sea to the throngs along the lake, from the hillsides that he loved, the little synagogue and Mary's home out into the world of the weary and heavyladen, the toiling and distressed, the unclean, sorrowing and diseased, the world of swearing fishermen, greedy publicans and jealous scribes, of centurions, sinners and Sadducees. The ministry was begun. It would not end on earth till he had given his life a ransom for many.

### His Purpose

Jesus' purpose proceeds from the preaching of John. The Baptist had linked up his announcement of the approach of the kingdom of God and his call to a reformation of life with the rite of baptism. Jesus linked them to an inner fellowship with the Father. He so realized God in his life that he loved man and worked for him, His purpose was not destructive nor negative but positive—"I am come to fulfil." He had no social system to urge, but he had a social message to give. He taught God's Fatherhood and kingdom, and the life of service and brotherhood to man. He made the former the motive for the latter as he made the latter the test of our realization of the former. This was his supreme purpose—"I am come that they might have life." "Abundant life" was his mission, and he taught the message and fulfilled the mission by living that life.

### The Kingdom

Out of these fundamental principles grew his teaching about the kingdom and its social implications. If men but shared the Divine life and Divine love, the kingdom of God would be accomplished, and religious difficulties and social disorders would have an end. This lesson he drove home, now with poetic imagination in his teaching about the kingdom, with frankness, with winsomeness, with authority

—but not as the scribes—and always with seriousness. According to Jesus the kingdom was the greatest good for all and the supreme task for each. It involved a discipleship fraught with sacrifice and service. When at the last he was going up to Jerusalem, to the Cross, he knew —not to the Crown, as they thought—the throngs beset him. Again he laid down the terms of discipleship—"If any man come to me, and hate not his father and mother and wife and children and brethren and sisters, yea, and his own life also, he cannot be my disciple. And whosoever doth not bear his cross and come after me cannot be my disciple." It was characteristic of his method of teaching, as well as of his purpose of life, that this pronouncement should have been made as he "steadfastly set his face to go to Jerusalem." He knew the cost of achieving his purpose, but he never flinched.

*Jesus at Work*

It is not so much that Jesus proclaimed a social gosepl that interests us here as that he lived a social ministry. His life was marked with practical helpfulness. Chorazin, Bethsaida, Capernaum were the cities in which most of his mighty works were done. These were works calculated to cause men to repent, deeds of kindness that would have brought even Tyre and Sidon and Sodom to ashes and repentance. But when one seeks to catalogue the acts of social service performed by Jesus, it is not the number of them nor the nature of them so much as the spirit of them that compels our wonder and admiration.

Jesus did not begin his ministry till the arrest of John. Then he went back to Galilee to step into the breach made by his cousin's incarceration. He chose Capernaum, a crowded city, as the base of his operations. He had preached but a short time when he decided that he must persuade men to work *for* him and *with* him. He sought loyal, active individuals completely dedicated to his cause to cooperate with him for the kingdom. The first disciples chosen were brothers, Simon and Andrew. They were men of action—"casting into the sea, on this side and on that." A little further, and he spied another pair of brothers, "mending their nets." He needed that quality of patient mending for the kingdom, and he called them, too. Partners, brothers, fishers, these had been. He would make them more so in the days to come. His search for individuals had begun. For he also was a fisher of men, nay, also, a fisher for fishers of men.

"And *immediately* on the Sabbath he taught in the synagogue . . . . and *immediately* there was a man with an unclean spirit." That "immediately" reveals the crowded activity of his life. Teaching in the synagogues so long as that was permitted, but teaching at all costs, healing, when human need pressed in upon him—though not eager to found a reputation as a Doctor of Men—sometimes a man with an unclean spirit, sometimes the fever-stricken mother-in-law of his own Simon, sometimes with the whole town gathered at his door, and, again and again, early in the morning, when it was still dark, rising up and going away to a solitary place, and there praying— such was his life. He knew his purpose—to preach, not to one community alone, but to the villages of the land. When Simon came with the message to his hill-side fastness of prayer—"They are all looking for you"—he disclosed the aim of his mission—"Let us go elsewhere, to the *neighboring* country towns, I must preach *there* also; for that was what I came out for."

When lepers came to him he was moved with compassion and touched them. But he forbade publicity. When it came, he refrained from openly entering a town, but stayed in the country in uninhabited places. Even there they sought him out, When he stealthily entered Capernaum to return to his own home, the crowds gathered so that there was no longer room for them, not even before the door. Then he preached to them. When the paralytic was brought he pronounced the forgiveness of his sins, and, when his authority for this was disputed, he healed him of his disease.

His call of Matthew is suggestive. In the account given by Mark it appears as if the call of Matthew were the main feature of the story, with the feast an accompanying incident, a sort of farewell feast, at which it happened that Jesus was present. The fact probably is that the feast was the main thing, and the call of Matthew a part of a carefully conceived plan of action. Jesus was aiming at a mission to the reprobated classes. He wanted to win the outcasts. How could he establish some contact with them? How could he get into touch with them?

Jesus carefully laid his plan. The first step was to secure the confidence and co-operation of one of the outcast class. Doubtless he discussed the affairs of his own kingdom more than once with this representative of the Roman Empire. As his plans matured, to reach the outcast, I can imagine him saying—"That Matthew there, at the Customs House, he is the man I need for this work." The next day he would discuss the matter with Matthew, and Matthew would say— "I have a sure income here, but there is something in what you say. A man's life *is* more than finance. You can have my answer as you pass this way to-morrow." The next day Jesus came, and, looking at him with steady eye, said—"Follow me." And he arose and followed him. He had made the great acceptance. Then they would plan together how the Master might reach the other outcasts. The farewell banquet would be suggested. It was not to be so much for Matthew's honor, though given in his name, as a part of Jesus' campaign. A social entertainment was to be used as a spiritual means. And the affair was a great success. Mark mentions the size of the crowd twice. So it was a success. Some of the straight-laced, long-faced religious leaders shrugged their shoulders and wagged their heads and said—"Look now. It is just as we thought. This Jesus is keeping company with the outcasts. What do you think of that? And he is feasting. You know how often we fast. And the Baptists, they fast, too. This Jesus isn't fasting. He is feasting." And Jesus replied—"We just can't fast yet. We must feast. It is a time of joy and cheer. We are all together yet. It is like a wedding. Everyone rejoices there. Some day we shall have our sorrow, but never in the Master's presence. The Master's presence means joy."

Then come the parables about patching with unfulled cloth, and putting new wine into old and stiff leathern bottles. I take it that the main point here is that the Gospel is not only one of joy, it is also one of freedom. It has life in it. It tends to move and grow. Joy and freedom are marks of the kingdom, but the kingdom does not exist for these ends. The kingdom exists to save Matthew and his associates, to give them an ampler life, to lead them out into a fuller service and to enable them to realize the Bridegroom's presence and the Master's purpose.

So Jesus lived in Joy and Freedom, but in Service too. He had twelve men in discipleship, at school, constantly with him. The religious authorities of the nation ranged themselves against him. His own family declared, "He is out of his senses!"[1] But he pressed forward with his task in brave confidence. Though difficulties confronted him, and men fell away, he was certain of success, for "some fell on good ground and bore fruit as it grew up and increased and yielded." And all the time he was training the Twelve, "in private giving interpretation of everything."

It is not necessary to follow him through his whole career of service, to learn the faith, the bravery, the seriousness of his life. "Why are you such cowards?" Why do you not have faith? with these words he reproved his faint-hearted followers on the Sea. He gave woman a new place, healing Jairus' daughter and the woman with the hemorrhage. After him a woman as a chattel or a mere drudge was forever unthinkable. That one scene at Bethany where Mary sits at his feet and bustling Martha's complaint is rebuked has legitimized for woman for all time other spheres than the Kitchen and other occupations than preparing meals. He gave childhood a new dignity, welcoming the little ones "to the crook of his arms." He remembered that his disciples returning from their trial mission needed rest, that the crowds who had journeyed around the north end of the Lake were in hot pursuit of him needed food, spiritual food and not merely material nourishment, that fathers and mothers suffered lack while Elders insisted upon Corban. He felt that it was conduct rather than external contact, thoughts rather than food, that determined character and made men either clean or unclean.

Occasionally we glimpse him in the very act of ministry, digging his fingers into the ears of the man who was deaf and imperfect in speech, and touching his tongue with saliva. We see him in the distribution of bread to the multitudes, making the feeding like unto the Lord's Supper. We behold him at Bethsaida curing the man by stages so that he first saw men "like trees, walking," then able to take a steady look, and finally restored and able to see everything clearly. In all this work he was, as we have said, averse from publicity. Not once but constantly "he forbade them to say so about him to any one." He was not an oriental fakir seeking advertisement. As the Inner Three came down from the Mountain

1. Mark 3: 21.

of his Glory "he enjoyned them not to tell any one what they had seen."

Though the shadow of the cross fell athwart his pathway with growing intensity he did not shrink, he pressed forward.

Nothing is more remarkable than the forces upon which Jesus did not count or which he did not employ. He did not count on wealth or position or force or any external influence, nor did he use them. But he was ever confident of the ultimate issue. He appreciated the humble, the childlike, the constructive, the helpful, the disciplined, the eternal, the divine. To be rich towards God was the true wealth, and this wealth he abundantly employed. The Kingdom of Heaven was "of such," of little children, and he would not suffer them to be thrust forth from his presence. As he conceived his Messiahship, it had nothing to do with war or politics or secular kingship, and not even with religion, as then authoritatively interpreted. And yet he purged the Temple with scourges. He bravely withstood the Jewish parties face to face, parrying their questions about Tribute, giving personal and spiritual content to the thought of the Resurrection, and attaching social obligation to the Chief Commandment. In the latter instance he was not asked the second greatest Commandment, but it is characteristic of him that he gave it. The first, without the second, did not satisfy his high outlook upon the destiny of man. He could not divorce devotion to God from service to man. He did not hesitate to denounce the Scribes for their pretensions, nor fail to appreciate the widow's mite for all the smallness of the gift. He recognized that a period of trial and suffering awaited his followers and endeavored to hearten them and to arouse them to an alert watchfulness. At his anointing at Bethany, when the group about him spoke cant about the constant presence and need of the poor, he reminded them that, though it was well never to forget the needy, and though he himself enjoined his followers to sell their possessions and to give alms trusting that the Father would provide, yet there was room in life for other generous impulses.[1]

## The Spirit of His Service

It is possible to find lives of longer service than that of Jesus, though none more packed with helpfulness. It is not the length of service but the spirit and quality of it that will forever mark the contribution of Jesus. He gave *all*. One sees this at Calvary. One sees this in the Lord's Supper as he instituted it. In our Communion Services the custom is to follow Paul. Paul was impressed with the conception of the bread and wine as the symbol of broken body and shed blood. But the writers of the Gospels view what happened from a different angle. They do not compare his body with the loaf in respect that both were broken. It is possible that Jesus did not on that night either eat the bread or

1. One of the most deplorable features in the history of social service is that, through long centuries, the Church believed in poverty as a fixed social condition, the incurable and necessary lot of a certain proportion of the human kind. The Church had no thought for growth or for science. It might alleviate but never cure nor prevent.

drink the wine. He simple *gave* it. He was a generous host. They
were welcome guests. He was not thinking about something broken
or something spilt, but about something *given*. He explicitly stated
that he would not drink of the wine yet, not till he might drink it
new in the Kingdom. It is a gift for others even to the utmost
sacrifice. It is not for himself, though by him and from him.
This is his own interpretation of his life, a willing giving, a complete and voluntary offering, forever spent here, but assuring a
glad reunion later when once again the fellowship will 'be complete.
He gave all, his work, his life, and he gave it in service, gladly,
ungrudgingly. He gave all, linking his life to God, giving his life
to and for man, loving and sacrificing and inspiring, and with a
happy looking forward to a glad reunion. It was his social service
to deepen life here, making it more abundant, and to extend it to the
hereafter, making it more glad.

What did Jesus mean by the Kingdom? Did he seek to
found a new Society in the world, or did he endeavor to bring the
world into his new Society? Did he aim to quicken individual
hearts through spiritual regeneration or did he desire to "Christianize
the social order"? It would be more nearly correct to say that
he sought to make the hearts of men more spiritual by rendering
them at the same time more social. He wanted them to rethink
life in terms of love to God and service to man. He had every
confidence that once spiritual forces were awakened in men's souls
they would find their proper expression, and Christ-touched men
would create Christian societies, and ultimately, in God's own good
time, the Kingdom would come.

The Christian Church will in its long career render many a
social service of surpassing worth. Many a social achievement
will make its name glorious. But nothing will manifest forth its
glory as radiantly as did the life and character and ministry of its
Carpenter Founder himself. Jesus not only taught service, he
himself served, and he inspired others that, leaving all and following him, and they too should give their lives in service. In his picture
of the Grand Assize he places on the right hand of the Judge all
who failed not in service with the cup of cold water, all who
ministered unto him that was "an hungred or athirst, or a stranger,
or naked, or sick, or in prison." In all that Jesus was, in all that
*he* taught, in all that he did, in all that he prayed, in all that he
suffered, he served. In the villages of Galilee, beside the Lake, on
the road to Jerusalem, on the lonely mountain-side, by Lazarus'
grave, at the Last Supper "taking a towel and girding himself,"
and, supremely, on the Cross, he served. The Christian Church
derives its inspiration and power, its very life, from Jesus the
Christ who came not to be ministered unto but to minister, who
gave his life a ransom for the many.

## (b) THE APOSTOLIC AGE

*Social Service based on Old Testament and Ministry of Jesus*

The social service of the Apostolic Age found its inspiration in the writings of the Old Testament and in the life and teachings of Jesus. In the former, compassionate love exhibits itself in the land-laws, in regulations regarding the shaking of olive-trees, the manner of gathering the vintage, the leaving of sheaves of corn in the fields, in the prohibition of usury, in the care of widows and orphans, and in the second-tithe. There was a considerable restriction of obligation that was national, and undoubtedly there was a development of charity that was Pharisaic and altogether legal and formal. But there was never lacking a deep current of social helpfulness and a warm charity that provided for the poor and needy. The Jewish conception of charity, with the thought of alms as service, and the belief that "the poor would not cease out of the land" passed into the Christian Church by way of the Apostles, though not through Paul.[1]

But it was particularly to the social ministry of Jesus that the Apostles turned for guidance and inspiration. They never turned to his *teaching* as to a code. They felt, somehow or other, because they had been with him, and because he still lived with them, that it belonged to that atmosphere of the Kingdom to serve. They could not but remember that to Jesus the "weightier matters of the law" were justice, mercy, and faith. His was a social Gospel that would seek the good of all in love. But they knew that he had not come merely as a "social reformer." His aim was not formally to banish poverty for, looking facts in the face rather than prescribing the existence of the destitute as a moral or economic necessity, he had specifically declared, "The poor ye have with you always." His aim, they clearly understood, was to bring all men, not excluding the poor, into the Kingdom. Where he led, they would follow.

*Social Service grew up with the Evangel*

It is, therefore, Christ's Kingdom, and not an itemized programme of social reform, that his Apostles sought to realize. And that Kingdom was not of this world. It was ampler and wider in scope, they believed, than the betterment of the conditions of life on this earth. And yet the Kingdom and its life were not to be altogether postponed to the hereafter. It was the Middle Ages, not the Apostolic Age, that made the mistake of doing that. It was the higher life, not the future life, nor the easier and more comfortable life, that the Apostles sought to implant. They, too, would go out to bring in the Kingdom, a Kingdom wherein men are brethren and God is Father. They would feel the Master's compassion for the sick, the deaf, the dumb, the blind, the leprous, and, above all, they would bring to the sons of men victory over sin. Social service in the first instance grew up alongside of, not instead of, the preaching of the evangel. The practice of charity went hand in

---

1. To Paul the Christian group formed the "body of Christ," existing by love, and manifesting it in service. To him charity is love.

hand with the proclamation of the Cross. Only their resources were more abundant for the latter than for the former. "Silver and gold have I none," declared Peter, suddenly confronted with human need, "but such as I have give I to thee: In the name of Jesus Christ of Nazareth rise up and walk." Such practical helpfulness was felt to be consonant with the mind and ministry of Jesus.

### A wider Field with new Forms

The range of social influence was greatly widened under the Apostles. Jesus had tilled a small field intensively. But the Apostles were witnesses unto him both in Jerusalem, and in all Judaea, and in Samaria, and unto the uttermost part of the earth. This meant that the Gospel overleaped the petty confines of Palestine and was given to the Roman Empire and the Mediterranean world. It was inevitable that social service should take on other forms. For instance, hospitality assumed a new significance when the missionaries of the faith and fellow Christians began to journey as far afield as the Capital of the Empire itself, and Aquila and Priscilla might be found, now at Corinth, now in Ephesus, and now again in Rome, and the Apostle of the Gentiles moved with eager enthusiasm from one strategic point to another to plant his churches. Little wonder that it became a qualification in a bishop to be "given to hospitality. . . . not a lover of money, able to manage his own household."[1] The entertainment of strangers became a burden, gladly borne but one which weighed heavily, upon both individuals and the churches.

### Social Service not yet Institutionalized

Social service in the Apostolic Church did not become institutionalized. It never can so become in a pioneer or mission church. Even in the matter of property the relations of Christians to each other were those of members of a family, "The multitude of them that believed were of one heart and of one soul: neither said any of them that ought of the things which he possessed was his own; but they had all things common."[2] This is far from being the communism in the accepted sense. It is rather the voluntary dedication of one's property to the members of a common family. It is a recognition in the way of social service of a common brotherhood, a relation that was recognized also in the common meal or love-feast.

### Appointment of the Seven

With the growth and expansion of the Church the labors of the Apostles themselves soon proved too varied and onerous. The Hellenists complained that their widows were neglected in the daily ministration. But the very complaint itself shows that the Apostolic Church had a mind for the dependent and the destitute, and perhaps Jesus' example, if not his words on the cross addressed to the

1. 1 Timothy 3: 2.
2. Acts 4: 32.

disciple whom he loved concerning his own mother, inspired a special care for the widowed. The Twelve believed that their first duty was not Social Service, but Witness, "It is not reason that we should leave the word of God, and serve tables." As a result seven men were "appointed over this business." They served tables. To them was intrusted the social service of Jerusalem. The cleavage between Evangelism and Social Service, never manifest in Jesus himself, and so disastrous in the centuries that lay ahead, thus early appeared in the very heart of the Apostolic Church, and, unfortunately, it arose in connection with a racial, or at least linguistic, cleavage.

*No Sustained System*

There was no extensive official organization of charity in New Testament times, no permanent system of poor relief. There were individuals, a growing number of them, who rendered deeds of kindly helpfulness. Tabitha of Joppa was such, a "woman full of good works and alms deeds which she did." She made coats and garments for poor widows. But she did not establish a neighborhood settlement. Such also was Phoebe, "a servant of the Church which is at Cenchreae. . . . a succourer of many, and of myself also," according to the account of Paul. Paul had collections taken in the churches of Galatia, Macedonia, Corinth and elsewhere for the poor saints in Jerusalem, seeking by generous deeds of sacrifice thus to unite in a common Christian fellowship, Jew and Gentile, the more prosperous and the destitute, the new and the old, the communities he had founded and the Church that persecuted and pursued him. But this was no sustained system of poor relief. Both individuals and churches were engaged in deeds of charity. But just as the organization of the Christian communities themselves was simple and far from formal so the work of social service was largely personal and occasional, according as the need rose.

*Achievements*

It would be possible to reconstruct in a fairly detailed manner a picture of the social service rendered in the Apostolic Age. But to do so would give an impression of organized effort which would be untrue to the facts. It will suffice to say that alms-giving, the care of orphans and widows, and hospitality were some of the more conspicuous forms which this assumed. It was recognized that within the Church God had set not only Apostles and Prophets and Teachers, but also Speakers, Administrators, Healers and Helpers.[1] But many helped who were not "Helpers." And the New Testament affords many a glimpse of some kindly deed done in the name of the Lord, the cup of cold water; the reproof of the selfish rich who are exploiting the poor, or defrauding workmen;[2] the aiding of a brother or sister ill-clad and destitute of daily food;[3] the visiting of orphans and widows;[4] the care of the sick and dis-

1. 1 Corinthians 12: 28.
2. James 5: 1-6.
3. James 2: 15.
4. James 1: 27.

tressed;[1] widows over sixty years of age with a reputation for service, who had brought up children, had shown hospitality, washed the feet of saints, relieved distress, and interested themselves in all good works;[2] the "Agape" with food provided by the well-to-do and of which the poor partook, sometimes, too, unsparingly; hospitality to strangers—sometimes a Paul, sometimes a nameless brother who must be helped on his journey, for travel was growing apace;[3] and, above all, many a gentle courtesy and kindly consideration in those early communities by which, although the Church did not attack slavery as such, yet it was breaking down the barriers between the bond and free in Christ Jesus,[4] for the free was the servant, nay the slave, of Christ, and the slave had become Christ's free man.

### Sound Moral Judgments

In his letter to the Ephesians,[5] Paul lays down three points that were to prove of the utmost significance for the future social activities of the Church and of Christian men, "Let him that stole steal no more; but rather let him labor, working with his hands the thing that is good, that he may have whereof to give to him that hath need." There are three matters here that claim his attention, property, work, charity. It is a Christian's duty to work. So the new Faith gave a moral dignity to labor. It is a Christian's duty to have respect for property. Paul bound it up closely with respect for labor. It is a Christian's duty to minister "to him that hath need." To have had sound moral judgments on these matters was a fundamental contribution which the Apostolic Church made to the world. The foundations were laid for future social service and achievement. To these principles the primitive Church adhered. Its members labored to serve their brethren,[6] and this labor of compassionate love commended the Gospel to those who were without the Church. By this all men knew that they were his disciples because they had love one to another. The Church began to conquer through the ministry of its loving social service.

### Summary of Achievements

What, in belief, was the achievement of the Church of the Apostolic Age? That Church took the Faith from the seclusion and exclusiveness of a small Province and placed it in the heart of every major city of the Empire. It committed to writing the oral tradition of those who had seen the Lord, and the *memorabilia* of wandering missionaries concerning the Christ, laying the basis for a Scripture to rank in dignity and authority alongside the Old Testament. It heartened believers in the times of persecution, giving them courage to face death in the crises under Nero and Domitian. It rebuked the glaring sins of Corinth and attacked with frankness her ethical

1. James 5: 13-15.
2. 1 Timothy 5: 10.
3. Romans 12: 13; 1 Peter 4: 9; 3 John.
4. Epistle to Philemon.
5. 4: 28.
6. McGiffert, The Apostolic Age, 508, believes that love among the early Christians lost something of the meaning which it had for Jesus. He finds a growing tendency to narrow the circle, to confine it to the brotherhood, to one's fellow-disciples.

problems. It confirmed the freedom of Galatia and Antioch. It encouraged the social ministry of Philippi. It proclaimed, and created of Jew and Gentile, a new spiritual Humanity in Christ, "of twain one new man," depicting for Ephesus and the Churches of Asia Minor the Ideal Unity of the Divine Commonwealth and the Living Temple, and making Christ's message of the Kingdom to be forever comprehended in the vision of the Church as "His Body." It expressed in Gospel and Epistle, in "Acts" and Apocalypse, the spiritual significance of Jesus, his death, and the out-working of his endless life. It called men back from vain speculations to which the Greeks were ever prone. It experienced and preached Pentecostal Power to a world hungrily craving Redemption, and brought courage and new life to despairing men "having no hope and without God in the world." It made the personal Fellowship of a group that had known Jesus into a growing Church that, believing, confessed his Name. It took the Jewish Messiah and proclaimed him as the world Saviour, telling men everywhere that "God hath made that same Jesus. . . . both Lord and Christ." These notable services of the Apostolic Age were to constitute the basis of all future social achievements of the Christian Church.

### Confidence in Power of Gospel

In June, 17 B.C., were celebrated in Rome the Saecular Games for which Horace composed his well-known festal hymn. These games commemorated the new and better order of things at home and abroad, the reorganization of the provinces, the work of domestic reform, inaugurated by Augustus. The diffusion of Caesar-worship was another feature of the new Empire. Side by side came into being a new administration and a new cult. The imperial authorities themselves associated the new order with a new religion. But slavery persisted, and many another phase of the old order, sensual, selfish, corrupt, cruel. Was Christianity, another new religion, equally ineffective in changing the old order? Wherein differed Jesus and Paul from Seneca and Burrhus in their social efforts? When Hadrian assumed the purple in the second Century his legislation exhibited a marked humanity towards slaves, none were to be sold by their masters for immoral purposes nor for fighting as gladiators. He did not shrink from direct legislation. But there is no legislation against, no condemnation of, slavery in the New Testament. There appears to be a complete acceptance of the present political and social arrangement. To what did the Pioneers of the Faith trust? They did not seek immediately to transform society as such. They trusted to the leaven of the Gospel, the secretly growing seed, the quiet radicalism of a new spirit, the divine power working from within they trusted to the living Christ. Such was the patience of the saints.

QUESTIONS FOR DISCUSSION

1. How did Jesus' early life and training in Nazareth fit him for a life of social service?

2. Is the ministry of Jesus, exhibited in the restricted area of an

obscure Province and under the temporary conditions obtaining in the first Century, normative for all believers in all times and at all places?

3. Were Jesus' social service ideals original with him or borrowed from the social teachers of his race? If they were already in possession of his race, what new contribution did he make?

4. Mark 1: 21-38 is a single day in the life of Jesus. Study the service rendered.

5. Study Jesus' social teachings regarding the following: The neighborly attitude, Luke 10: 30-37; the limit of service, Matt. 25: 14-30, Luke 17: 7-10; the significance of a life, Matt. 5: 21-22, 8: 1-4, Mark 10: 13-16, Luke 15: 1-10, 19: 10, John 8: 2-11; love as of prime and final importance, Matt. 22: 35-40, 25: 31-46; the sufferings of the poor and lowly, Matt. 9: 35, 10: 1, 11: 28; the use of wealth, Luke 12: 13-21, 16: 1-13, 19-31.

6. What is the relation of suffering to service? Read Matt. 11: 7-10, 16-19, 16: 21-25, 23: 29-36; Mark 12: 1-9; Luke 13: 31-34.

7. Study Macedonia from the viewpoint of service in the following matters: The summons to Paul, Acts 16: 9-10; the exhibition of hospitality, Acts 16: 15; the support of the Apostle, Phil. 4: 10-20; charity, 2 Cor. 8: 1-5; problems that hindered work, 1 Thess. 4: 9, 5: 11.

8. Discuss the causes, character and organization of Gentile charity to the poor in Jerusalem. The following passages are helpful: Gal 2: 10; Romans 15: 25-31; 1 Cor. 16: 1-4; 2 Cor. 8 and 9.

9. Study the social service obligations mentioned by Paul in the following Epistles: Gal. 5: 7 to end; Eph. 4 to end.

10. What attitude towards slavery does Paul exhibit in Philemon?

11. Is James' conception of Christianity merely social service and purity of life? Read the following passages in James: 1: 21 ff., 25, 27; 2: 8 ff., 14 ff.; 4: 11. Then read also 1: 6 ff.; 4: 7; 4: 8; 4: 10; 4: 15.

12. Make a list of some less well-known saints of the New Testament, who are mentioned for their social service. Examples are to be found in Luke 8: 3; Acts 5: 32, 10: 36, 11 27-30, 12: 12, 16: 15, 21: 16; Romans 16: 2, 6, 23; 1 Cor. 16: 15; 2 Timothy 4: 11.

### BOOKS FOR ADVANCED STUDY

C. F. Kent, *The Social Teachings of the Prophets and Jesus.* A. B. Bruce,. *The Kingdom of God.* A. C. McGiffert, *The Apostolic Age.* T. R. Glover, *The Jesus of History.* W. Manson, *Christ's View of the Kingdom of God.* J. W Jenks. *The Social Significance of the Teachings of Jesus.* Shailer Mathews, *The Social Teachings of Jesus.* Walter Rauschenbusch, *Christianity and the Social Crisis* and *The Social Principles of Jesus.* F. G. Peabody, *Jesus Christ and the Social Question.* H. C. Vedder, *The Gospel of Jesus and the Problems of Democracy.* G. B. Stevens, *The Teaching of Jesus.* Francis Herbert Stead, *The Story of Social Christianity.*

# CHAPTER III

# UNDER THE PAGAN EMPIRE
## (SAY TO A.D. 313)

(a)  THE CHURCH UNDER THE PAGAN EMPIRE

The Spread of the Christian Movement. The Growth of the Catholic Church. The Equipped Church Making its Way in the World. Accommodation to the World. Persistence of old Panganism. The Enlarging Sphere of Social Service.

(b)  SOCIAL ACHIEVEMENTS UNDER THE PAGAN EMPIRE

Original Sources,—The *Apology* of Justin Martyr and the *Apologeticus* of Tertullian. Types of Social Achievement. Alms-giving. Care of Fatherless and Widows. Poor Relief. Care for Prisoners and Captives. Burial of the Dead. Testimony of Inscriptions. Church and Slavery. Persecutions and Calamities. Provisions for Unemployed. Hospitality towards Strangers. Assistance to Sister Churches. The Church and Business. Social Order. Martyrdom a Service. Imperial Patronage.

(c)  CHARACTER OF SOCIAL ACHIEVEMENT

The Church survives in the World. Social Service Congregational. The Larger Vision. Not Scientific Study but Generous Impulse. A Communion of Saints Knit Together in Service.

## (a) THE CHURCH UNDER THE PAGAN EMPIRE
### (SAY TO A.D. 313)

*The Spread of the Christian Movement.*

We have seen how in the Apostolic Age Christianity had come to make its appeal to a larger world than the land of its birth. Paul translated Jesus' thought of the true inwardness and spiritual nature of religion into an aggressive missionary campaign that carried the Gospel throughout the Levant and along at least the northern coasts of the Mediterranean Basin. The Faith had become a Fellowship, perhaps, even a Force, in the world whose foci were no longer Jerusalem and Antioch but Ephesus and Rome. But at the time even a close observer might have failed to note the progress of the movement that, in less than three centuries, the wily Constantine would be glad to summon to his assistance as a bulwark of Empire. Many things pass unnoticed that transpire among the lower classes. And this Religion, founded by a Carpenter, preached by fishermen, tentmakers and suchlike, was able, so ran the sneer of Celsus—to win the allegiance only of "the baker and the fuller." "Not many wise, not many mighty, not many noble" embraced the faith, according to the observation of Paul. And this remained true at least to the time of Commodus. Its appeal met with favor most largely among slaves, freedmen, and laborers. For, naturally enough, "the wise and the prudent" scorned a message which did not exclude the publican and adulterer.

## The Growth of the Catholic Church

The close of the Apostolic Age marks a real, though not a sudden, transition. Christianity, losing the shelter of Judaism and the advantage of operating through the synagogues of the Diaspora, became a *religio illicita,* an illegal Faith. The Apostles had passed away, and the growing Church was forced to look elsewhere for guidance. How heavily the Church had leaned upon these companions of its Lord, few could have realized at the time. But within little more than two generations the early Christian enthusiasm, in spite of the fervor of Ignatius and the heroic martyrdom of Polycarp, had suffered decline. Competing creeds, heresies, superstitions and philosophies with not a little of quackery, the arbitrary selection of Writings for Scripture, an overstimulated enthusiasm of the spirit, a cosmology parading as a rational religion, all these threatened the Faith. A rival church under the organizing genius and subsidies of the Gnostic Marcion struck at the most precious elements in the Christian tradition. In those critical years, the generation following the middle of the second century, the "Catholic" Church was born. It came into being on the basis of an authoritative Canon, an authoritative Rule of Faith, and an authoritative type of ecclesiastical organization, the monarchical episcopate. And Church, Canon, Rule of Faith, Episcopate, all, with a view to the preservation and progress of the Christian movement, were invested with apostolic sanction and designated "Holy, Apostolic, Catholic." Members of the Church, who knew little of history, were taught that what had come to pass at the end of the second century had been even so in the days of the Apostles. But change there had been, inevitable perhaps, but, none the less, of profoundest character. Christianity had once been a life. It now became a discipline. Enthusiasm was duly organized, set under a Bishop. What had been an inspiration could, with the opening of the third century, be read out of a book. To be a Christian had once meant to be a loyal follower of the Nazarene and to put one's trust in him. It now meant to be a member of a Church, to accept a sacred Scripture, to believe at least the rudiments of a Creed, and to submit to a Bishop. It is the glory of the Faith that its primary, and essential, significance was never entirely obscured. Men always knew that it linked them with the Christ.

## The Equipped Church Making its Way in the World

No one can deny that this transformation involved much of loss. But those who regard the change as entailing only loss must remember that the century that lay ahead was the Age of Decius, Valerian and Diocletian. In the face of the fierce persecutions that assailed the faithful only a well organized Church could have survived at all. Upon this transformation was reared a federation of

Churches, a "Catholic" Church, that withstood the calumnies of Celsus and Porphyry, met with courage the hideous cry that rose from the Flavian Amphitheatre, "Christianos ad leones," and worshipped its God with a glad faith in the Catacombs under the Appian Way. It waged war against pagan polytheism, interpreted the significance of its Founder to the Hellenic world in terms of the Logos Christology, and inspired the literary productions of Cyprian and Tertullian, of Pantaenus, Clement and Origen. It was this Catholic Church, fully equipped with institutions, orders, and the beginnings of credal statements, and becoming daily more powerful with its increasing membership, that became the hope of the Roman Empire after being the object of its unmitigated persecution. Neo-Platonism, the last spiritual effort of an expiring world, could not save the Empire. Caracalla was not able to save it by the gift of citizenship to the freemen. The organizing genius of Diocletian, with all his plans of devolution, proved unavailing. There was no help in rude Barbarians, already on the frontiers and soon to be at the gates. But all the while, from Commodus to Constantine, in spite of persecution from without and peril from within, there had been proceeding the consolidation of the Church. The Faith had made enormous strides along the high-roads of Roman trade and intercourse. It had shared the effort to satisfy religious cravings with a swarm of Syrian and Persian faiths and superstitions that had likewise journeyed westward. Its organization had taken, in some measure, the form or recognized municipal associations for charity and burial. And, above all, it preached a Redeemer to a world that vastly needed, and was beginning to understand that it needed, redemption.

*Accommodation to the World*

It is impossible to overestimate the impression made upon its members under the Pagan Empire by this growing Church with its developing doctrine, its defined Scripture, its orderly worship, its duly appointed officers, its new standards of purity, its active charity and social service. No biography has come to us out of this period to illustrate the significance of all this in the lives of individual Christians. From the time of Commodus the work of the Apologists and of others made itself felt for the first time in the higher and more enlightened ranks of society. The Church more and more definitely forsook its pristine simplicity to speak in terms of Hellenic philosophy and to organize itself after the pattern of the Empire in which it lived. It began to think not only of its own faithful, but of the great unleavened mass of men and women it had not yet reached. As its position became secure, as its mission gained headway, it began to accommodate its message and its life to the surrounding pagan polytheism. Festivals, saints, sacraments and relics made the transition easier for those to whom a too rigorous monotheism would have proved repellent. It was a social service of the first magnitude that it rendered in the mere spread of the faith and the growth of the Church. How necessary, or how spiritual, this accommodation of the Christian message to the world of its environment may have been, opinions will differ widely. It is sufficient to remind ourselves that the Church was competing with other eastern religions that exhibited similar powers of syncretism. In the next period that comes under review this insidious process will continue with increasing vigor, only to yield what Harnack has happily designed "Christianity of the second rank."

### Persistence of Old Paganism

It would be a mistake to underestimate the persistence of the old paganism in the sphere of family religion, particularly in the rural communities. Christianity was still a religion of towns and cities. Though the upper classes were widely tinged with scepticism and religious indifference, on the whole it was a religious age. The old State worship could not satisfy. Men turned now to the new Imperial worship, now to the cults of other nations, and leaned more and more heavily on the old domestic gods of their ancient faith. The worship of the Emperor was an instrument of State. It fostered a spirit of loyalty, promoted order, and was of unquestionable police value. But if men gave their allegiance to the Augustus, and their worship to the dog-headed Anubis, their hearts still went out to the family deities of the house, the store-closet and the hearth. For the family rites of the family had a greater sanctity, as well as a greater antiquity, than the more gorgeous official State religion. This worship of the Lar Familiaris, the Di Penates, and Vesta held no mean place in the life of the Mediterranean folk, particularly among the humbler classes, long after Jupiter and Mars had yielded to the Christ on the worship of the people. The worship of the household gods was associated with every family event from the cradle to the grave. About 200 A.D. Tertullian was still authorizing Christians to participate in the innocent family festivals of their pagan friends. In fact, at the end of the fourth century Theodosius constrained to issue his famous edict against the practice of the old pagan family religious rites.[1] There is a little doubt that in the country places this domestic worship persisted for centuries longer.

### The Enlarging Sphere of Social Service

It is a far cry from Christ to Constantine. A wide gulf separates the former's declaration, "My kingdom is not of this world," from the latter's policy of making Christianity an ally of Empire. In this period of the Pagan Empire the Church won its way in the world, and the world won its way more and more in the Church. However disastrous this development may have been for Theology and Church Government, unquestionably it operated to enlarge very considerably for the Church its sphere of service, and to change the character of its social achievements.

1. Cod. Theodos, XVI, 10, 2 (A.D. 392).

## (b) SOCIAL ACHIEVEMENTS UNDER THE PAGAN EMPIRE
### (SAY TO A.D. 313)

*Original Sources—(a) Apology of Justin Martyr*

It is to the writings of Justin Martyr and of Tertullian, in each case to an *Apology* of the Christian Faith, that we turn for a review of the social achievements and service of the Church in the period of the Pagan Empire. The former after describing Christian Worship, and in particular the Eucharist, states (*Apology*) i, 67):

"But we henceforth continually put each other in mind of these things, and those of us who are wealthy help all that are in want, and we always remain together. And for all things that we eat we bless the Maker of all through His son Jesus Christ, and through the Holy Spirit. And on the so-called day of the Sun there is a meeting of all of us who live in cities or the country, and the memoirs of the Apostles or the writings of the prophets are read, as long as time allows. Then when the reader has ceased, the president gives by word of mouth his admonition and exhortation to follow these excellent things. Afterwards we all rise at once and offer prayers; and as I said, when we have ceased to pray, bread is brought and wine and water, and the president likewise offers up prayers and thanksgivings to the best of his power, and the people responds with its Amen. Then follows the distribution to each and the partaking of that for which thanks were given; and to them that are absent a portion is sent by the hand of the deacons. Of those that are well to do and willing, every one gives what he will according to his own purpose, and the collection is deposited with the president, and he it is that succors orphans and widows, and those that are in want through sickness or any other cause, and those that are in bonds, and the strangers that are sojourning and in short he has the care of all that are in need."

From this passage we learn the following facts with reference to the social service performed by the Christian Church:

(a) The Eucharist was regarded as an incentive to Social Service.

(b) Wealthy Christians were accustomed to help the needy.

(c) Freewill offerings were made at Sunday Services for the purpose of Social Service.[1]

---

1. The Roman *Collegia*, or clubs, also had contributions. The collections of the Christians differed from these in that the contributions of the *Collegia* constituted obligations of membership in the *Collegia*, but the collections of the Christians were given by members as an act of worship to God and a means of social service to men. The former were obligatory; the latter, free-will offerings. The former were monthly; the latter, weekly.

(*d*) This voluntary collection was deposited with the President of the Congregation who devoted it to the following forms of service.
1. Care of orphans and widows.
2. Care of the sick.[1]
3. Care of prisoners.
4. Care of strangers.
5. Care of all in need.

(*b*) *The Apologeticus of Tertullian*

Tertullian, after contrasting the customs of Christian worship with the disorderly heathen clubs, states (*Apologeticus, 39*) :

"We pray also for emperors, for their ministers and for them that are in power, for the welfare of the world, for peace therein, for the delay of the end. We meet together for the reading of the divine writings, if the character of the times compels us in any way to forwarning or reminder. However that may be, with the holy words we nourish our faith, lift up our hope, confirm our confidence, and no less make strong our discipline by impressing the precepts. At these meetings we have also exhortations, rebukes, and a Divine censorship. For judgment also is executed with much gravity, as before men who are sure that they are in the sight of God; and it is a notable foretaste of judgment to come if a man has so sinned as to be banished from the communion of our prayer and meeting and all holy intercourse. Our presidents are the approved elders, obtaining that honor not for a price, but by attested character; for indeed the things[1] of God are not sold for a price. Even if there is a sort of common fund, it is not made up of money paid in fees, as for a worship by contract. Each of us puts in a trifle on the monthly day, or when he pleases; but only if he pleases, and only if he is able, for no man is obliged, but contributes of his own free will. These are, as it were, deposits of piety; for it is not paid out thence for feasts and drinking and thankless eating-houses, but for feeding and burying the needy, for boys and girls deprived of means and parents, for old folk now confined to the house: also for them that are ship-wrecked, for any who are in the mines, and for any who, in the islands or in the prisons, if only it be for the cause of God's people, become the nurslings of their own confession."

Tertullian has here established the following facts with reference to the service of the Christian Church:
1. Prayer was offered up in its assemblies for all civil authorities, for the peace and welfare of the world, and "for the delay of the end."
2. Within the Church itself Christians used the Scriptures for their own mutual strengthening and comfort.

---

1. There were as yet no hospitals.

3. For its own members it had a system of discipline enforced by excommunication.

4. Churches had a common fund (arca), made up of free-will offerings, to which members made, each month or oftener, such contributions as they pleased or were able.

5. These *"deposits of piety"* were devoted to the following forms of service:

(a) Feeding the needy.
(b) Burying the poor.
(c) Care of orphans or other poor boys and girls.[1]
(d) Care of the aged who were confined to their homes.
(e) Care of the shipwrecked.
(f) Care of those in the mines.
(g) Care of exiles—whether in prison or in the islands —who were suffering for the Christian cause.

The distinctively Christian feature in all this is not that collections were made, for such was the practice also in the Roman *Collegia,* or clubs. What is new is that the funds were devoted to social service, to the care of the poor and needy. Under the system in vogue in the *Collegia* the money was spent in social features, or devoted to some such purpose as the erection of honorary statues.

*Types of Social Achievement*

The passages that have been quoted indicate some of the outstanding forms of social service rendered by the Church and its members under the Pagan Empire.[2] That service during this period was in the main congregational. According to the testimony of ancient literature, of inscriptions, of papyrus finds, the chief types of service were: Almsgiving, Care of Fatherless and Widows, Poor Relief, Care of Prisoners and Captives, Burial of the Dead, a new Thought for the Slave, Provision for the Unemployed, Hospitality towards Strangers, Assistance to Sister Churches, Promotion of social order, and the Challenge to a Better Life through martyrdom and ordinary Christian conduct. All this was apart from the social contribution made by the Church in effecting a reconciliation between the New Faith and the Roman State in the beginnings of organization made after the patterns of municipal life and the Imperial system, and the reconciliation effected between the New Faith and Hellenic thought in Apologies and in the beginnings of creedal discussion and formulations. These creedal utterances, however, contained no statement in regard to either social service or the idea of the Kingdom of God. But it was no mean social achievement that the Church should be feeling its way

1. It should not be forgotten that from the time of Nerva the Romans themselves began to establish *alimentationes,* or endowments for the education of poor children. More than one Emperor founded such institutions, notably Antonnius Pius and Septimus Severus, but private individuals, e.g. Pliny at Comum, made similar provision for poor boys and girls.

2. The Apostolic Constitutions (IV, 2) describe the whole scope of Christian charity as similar to that indicated by Justin Martyr and Tertullian, an indication that the work of social service did not differ greatly in Rome, Africa and the East.

to voicing a belief in a Catholic Church, and, in its doctrine of the Trinity, at that time in' the very throes of being born, a faith in a social God.

## Almsgiving

Almsgiving was regarded not only as a means of grace for individual Christians but also as a public duty for the Church.[1] The Second Clementine letter, dating from the middle of the second Century or later, says of almsgiving that it "lightens sin," "Almsgiving is good even as penitence for sin: fasting is better than prayer, but the giving of alms is better than both."[2] The Didache encourages almsgiving: "Be not one that stretches out his hands to receive, but shuts them when it comes to giving."[3] The president of the congregation supervised public alms-giving although it was dispensed at the hand of the deacons.

## Care of Fatherless and Widows

The Church did not forget the fatherless and the widows in their affliction. From the beginning Christians attached high value to child life. They were never guilty of that enormity of ancient classical civilization, the exposure of infants. "They do not cast away their offspring," says the author of the Christian apologetic pamphlet addressed to the Diognetus.[4]

The Roman world without compunction exposed the little ones, for, as the classical poets repeatedly inform us, luxury had degraded the natural instincts of the rich and misery had perverted the impulses of the poor. The Roman world reared foundlings to be prostitutes or gladiators. Exposure and child-murder and the sale of children were far too common. The Christians trained those whom others exposed, that they might lead useful and industrious lives. To them *all* human life was sacred. From the time of the Apologists onward they uttered protest after protest against such enormities as abortion and exposure of children. To anticipate, it was under the influence of the Church that Constantine issued a proclamation against the practice of child-exposure, and at the same time made provision for supplying food for the newly found infant, and for his adoption. In the three following Centuries Church Councils condoned holding these children either in servitude or in adoption in order to save their lives. No Council, however, was bold enough to insist upon the emancipation of the abandoned little ones. It was Justinian, the great Christian Emperor, of the sixth Century, who insisted that the exposed child should, even if a slave, be considered free. This care for the young was prompted by Jesus' love for children. These first efforts for the little ones are forerunners of many a helpful institution and enterprise to come: Crêches, Schools, Reformatory Institutions, Foundling

---

1. Cyprian, De Opere et Eleemosynis, I, speaks of "thus opening a way to obtain salvation, so that by means of alms we may wash away any stains subsequently contracted."
2. 2 Clem., XVI, 4.
3. Ch. I.
4. Auct. Ad Diogn., 5-7.

Hospitals, Establishments for the Defective and Deformed and Handicapped and Outcast.

The Life of Barlaam and Joasaph indicates the settled policy of Christians towards widows, orphans and the poor, "They despise not a widow, and an orphan they grieve not. He that hath given help ungrudgingly to him that hath not."[1] Bishop Cornelius wrote that on one occasion the Roman Church was supporting fifteen hundred widows and poor persons,[2]—"All of them the Master's grace and lovingkindness support." In a papyrus from Oxyrhynchus, now in possession of the Egyptian Exploration Fund, discovered and published by Grenfell and Hunt, dated June 17th, I B.C., we get a glimpse of the family of Hilarion, an Egyptian laborer.[3] This gay dog, as his name implies, writes to his wife Alis who is expecting her confinement shortly—"If thou art delivered, if it is a male child, let it (live) ; if a female, cast it out." Set over against this, "Suffer little children to come unto me." These two attitudes towards childhood were pitted against each other in that far-off Age of the first century.

How great was the social ministry of sympathy in bereavement ushered in with the Christian faith we realize only when we see the helpless despair that was found outside the pale of the Christian Church. In the Yale Library is an original letter addressed in the second Century by Irene, an Egyptian, to the mourning Philo and Taonnophris on the death of their departed son, Didymas, "Against such things one can do nothing. Therefore comfort ye one another. Fare ye well."

Ignatius in his Epistle to the Church at Smyrna points out how un-Christian is the behaviour of heretics. He inveighs against their shortcomings. The obverse of this picture should give a faithful delineation of the social service of Christians in the time of Trajan, "For love they have no care, none for the widow, none for the orphan, none for the distressed, none for the afflicted, none for the prisoner, or for him released from prison, none for the hungry or thirsty.[4] The same writer has a number of precepts to urge in his letter to Polycarp, and among them, "Let not the widows be neglected."[5] And the recipient of this communication, in laying down the duties of presbyters, includes "caring for all the weak, neglecting neither widow, nor orphan, nor poor." The Shepherd of Hermas enumerates among the acts of social service, "To minister to widows, to look after orphans and the destitute."[6] The same writer associates with the Ninth Mountain, which was desert, those ministers "who ministered amiss, and devoured the living of widows and orphans and made gain for themselves from the ministry which they had received to administer," but associates with the Tenth Mountain, with its foliage and its flocks of sheep, "bishops and

1. H. M. Gwatkin, Selections from Early Christian Writers, 47.
2. Eusebius, H. E., VI, 43.
3. A. Deissmann, Light from the Ancient East, 154.
4. Ignatius, To the Smyrnaeans, VI, 1, 2.
5. Ignatius to Polycarp, IV.
6. Mandate VIII.

hospitable men who at all times received the servants of God into their houses gladly and without hypocrisy; and the bishops who ever ceaselessly sheltered the destitute and the widows by their ministration."[1] The care that Christians gave to the fatherless was rewarded in a conspicuous instance. The great theologian of the Alexandrian School, Origen, was adopted by a Christian woman.[2] Bishops brought up orphans at the expense of the Church, provided Christian husbands for marriageable girls, and had boys taught useful trades and provided with suitable tools.[3]

*Poor Relief*

The Church had a policy of poor relief that was not confined to its own members. It derived its means for rendering this assistance from these sources—(a) Eucharistic offerings; (b) Freewill offerings, first-fruits and voluntary tithes brought to the Bishop; (c) Collections in Churches on Sundays and week days. The Didache encouraged Christians to give the first fruits of their produce and stock to the prophets.[4] Failing these, their share was to be given to the poor. Justin Martyr tells us that the sick were assisted out of voluntary Sunday offerings.[5] We know that women were engaged in visiting the sick and afflicted. For Tertullian complains that one of the inconveniences caused by mixed marriages between Christians and pagans was just this, that the Christian wife was precluded from going on her charitable errands and visting the poorer people in their cottages, because the pagan husband interposed exacting household duties.[6] This social service to the poor was only in keeping with the advice tendered by Clement to the Church of Corinth, "Let the strong care for the weak. . . . and let the rich man bestow help on the poor."[7] Of course, only the necessaries of life were given, and the poor were enjoined to be content with frugal fare.[8]

An elaborate theory of the way in which the rich and poor may be mutually helpful is given in the Shepherd of Hermas:[9] "Therefore," he concludes, "the two together complete the work, for the poor works in the intercession in which he is rich, which he received from the Lord: this he pays to the Lord who helps him. And the rich man likewise provides the poor, without hesitating, with the wealth which he received from the Lord." Undoubtedly a large part of the work of poor relief fell directly upon the deacons. The Apostolic Constitutions say of these: They are to be doers of good works, exercising a general supervision day and night, neither scorning the poor nor respecting the person of the rich; they must ascertain who are in distress and not exclude them from a share in the church funds, compelling also the well-to-do to put money

1. Sim. IX, XXVI.
2. Eusebius, H. E., VI, 2; See also V, 17; de mart. Palaest. c. 11.
3. Const. Apost. IV. 2.
4. Didache, XIII.
5. Justin Martyr, 1st Apol., 67.
6. Tertullian, Ad Uxorem, II, 3-6.
7. Clement, Ad Corinth, XXXVIII.
8. Cyprian, Ad Corinth, I, 38.
9. Sim., II.

aside for good works."[1]  The active charity rendered by the Church
to all alike wrung from the Apostate Julian, in the years immediately
following this period, this tribute in a letter to Arsacius: "These
godless Galileans feed not only their own poor but ours: our
poor lack our care."[2]  Lists of the poor were drawn up lest any be
forgotten in the distribution of food, and relatives of the necessitous
were encouraged to attend to the wants of their funds to prevent
excessive burdens from resting on the church.[3]

### Care for Prisoners and Captives

Among those to whom the presidents of congregations dispensed assistance from their voluntary collections, as Justin Martyr
informs us, are "those that are in bonds."[4]  The prisoner and the
captive always appealed strongly to the sympathy of Christians,
especially when these suffered for the faith.[5]  They were equally
prepared to render aid to the persecuted and the exiled.  The discoveries of non-literary papyri lay bare kindly acts of service
rendered in the crises of persecution.  Psenosiris is a long-forgotten
Christian presbyter in the Great Oasis.  Little is known of him or of
his friend, the presbyter Apollo.  But a papyrus in the British
Museum records how, when Diocletian attacked Christians,
Psenosiris wrote Apollo in the interests of a banished Christian
woman.[6]  Among the "deeds of goodness" enumerated in the Eighth
Mandate of the Shepherd of Hermas is "to redeem from distress
the servants of God."  Christian brethren in prisons and the mines[7]
were visited and cared for.[8]  Imprisoned debtors were redeemed and
prisoners of war ransomed—and of these, thanks to the severity of
the Roman laws and the growing frequency of contests with the
barbarians, there was an increasing number.  The Roman bishop,
Victor, had a list of all Christians who had been sentenced to the
mines in Sardinia.  He was instrumental in procuring their release.[9]
The very last of all the emperors who persecuted the Christians,
Licinius, passed stringent legislation with severe penalties against
those Christians who supplied prisoners with food when starving.[10]
The Christians of Egypt went to mines as remote as those of
Cilicia to encourage those condemned to hard labor, and that those
in the mines were actually sustained in their terrible trials is
abundantly proved by the fact that cases are known where regular
congregations were actually organized in these difficult places.[11]

1. Harnack, The Mission and Expansion of Christianity, I, 161.
2. Sozom., V, 16.
3. Const. Apost., IV, 2.
4. 1st Apol., 67.
5. Const. Apost., IV, 9; V, 1: "If a Christian is condemned to the combat, or to be
thrown to the wild beasts, or sent to the mines for the sake of his faith and love to God, you
are not to despise him, but to send to him of your labor and of the sweat of your brow,
wherewith to live and to pay the soldiers their fees, that he may obtain some alleviation
and be cared for."
6. Deissmann, Light from Ancient East, 37, 202.
7. The lot of those in the mines was hardest of all for most of those so condemned soon
succumbed.
8. Harnack quotes Acta Perpet., IX; Eus., H. E., IV, 23.
9. Harnack quotes Hippolytus, Philos., IX, 12.
10. Euseb., H. E., V, 8.
11. Harnack, The Mission and Expansion of Christianity, I, 164, n.

## Burial of the Dead

Among the earliest official societies established under the auspices of Christianity was the burial society.[1] This was not a new type of society in the world, but it was undoubtedly under different ideals of charity and a larger sense of brotherhood that it was organized among Christians.[2] They found this the easiest way to secure recognition from the civil authorities. The government allowed certain important legal privileges to *collegia tenuiorum*, particularly to burial societies. Christians in this way not only secured protection but also rendered notable social service. During plagues both in Carthage and in Alexandria, Christians cared for the corpses and prevented infection.[3] The Apostate Julian pays tribute to the careful attention which Christians paid to the burial of the dead.[4] We have seen that Tertullian speaks of this as one of the services paid for out of the common fund, although Aristides make it a matter of private generosity. The whole ancient world viewed with apprehension the prospect of being forced to lie unburied. The Christian view of immortality enforced this feeling and insisted on giving proper burial. Deacons were especially charged with this duty.[5] Christians would not have the image and workmanship of God exposed to wild beast and birds even though the dead were unknown to them.

## Testimony of Inscriptions

Inscriptions on tombstones bear witness to the social service rendered by the Church and its members. In an inscription from the end of this period the duties of a presbyter are declared to include "the help of widows, orphans, strangers, and poor." The inscriptions speak of Christian orphanages for foundlings, and church funds used for the liberation of slaves and for the care of aged people, prisoners, and exposed infants.[6] When we remember that pagan families reared foundlings to sell for immoral purposes we can appreciate the significance of this rescue work carried on by the Christians. In the pre-Constantine Christian inscriptions of Phrygia we find a love for the stranger and outcast that is very Christlike.[7]

## Church and Slavery

The Christian Church did not wage war against slavery as an institution, but it was careful for slaves as individuals.[8] Within the Church itself there was neither bond nor free. They were all brothers, or, as Paul wrote of Onesimus, "no longer a mere slave but something more than a slave, a brother beloved." Christianity

---

1. Cobern, The New Archaeological Discoveries, 275, 427.
2. Uhlhorn, Christian Charity in the Ancient Church, 23, has shown that there was nothing in the guilds which reached the height of actual charity.
3. Vita Cypr., Ch. 9.
4. Soz., V, 15.
5. Aristides, Apol., XV; Lactantius, Inst., VI, 12.
6. Cobern, The New Archaeological Discoveries, 427.
7. Cobern, The New Archaeological Discoveries, 429.
8. Clement Alex. assumes that Christians as well as others should possess slaves. The Apostolic Constitutions (II, 62) regard slaves as necessaries which Christians might purchase in the market.

created the spirit that ultimately undermined slavery. To the slave no less than to the free the Church was open.[1] It recognized the slave's personality as no longer "res" but "persona." The Church began to emancipate and to treat kindly certain individual slaves. The Apostolic Constitutions reckon the liberation of slaves as a work of love.[2] In his letter to Polycarp,[3] Ignatius has seven precepts to urge, among them the following: "Do not be haughty to slaves . . . let them not desire to be set free at the Church's expense that they may not be found slaves of lust." Servile status was not believed to be inconsistent with the Christian life. The slave had no right to claim emancipation, but he was, nevertheless, in many instances, emancipated. Christianity joined its liberating impulse to the social revolution that was in progress under the early Empire.[4] Even where a formal emancipation did not take place the relation between Christian masters and Christian slaves was essentially more humane than in the case of pagans.[5] And in the Church itself no distinction was made in general between bond and free. The slave might become a Bishop, or, better still, a martyr.

*Persecutions and Calamities*

Cyprian and others have testified to the practical social service and genuine sympathy manifested during periods of plague, persecutions and calamities.[6] There is little doubt that Eusebius is right in asserting that this spirit of self-denial in times of stress was of great practical influence in the extension of the faith.

*Provision for Unemployed*

The Church sought to provide for the unemployed by finding work. Travellers were entertained hospitably but encouraged to pass on. They were not to live upon the kindness of Christian brethren. This was 'trafficking in Christ.'[7] The Church had no encouragement to offer to idlers who would exploit the generosity of its members.

*Hospitality Towards Strangers*

There was a deal of travelling in the early Christian Church. The movement spread over a large area. Many cities established a reputation for hospitality. Rome was conspicuous for its care of the traveller and the stranger. In the letter of Clement, addressed to

---

1. In the third century the consent of the master was under certain circumstances required for the admission of the slave to the Church. Uhlhorn, Christian Charity in the Ancient Church, 194.
2. IV, 9.
3. Ignatius to Polycarp, IV.
4. Uhlhorn, Christian Charity in the Ancient Church, 192, declares that manumissions were not so frequent among Christians as among heathens, for the latter often "freed their slaves from impure motives, for the sake of fame, or pomp, that very many might follow at their funeral with the hat, the token of manumission, and even for the sake of gain, that they might get more profit out of freedmen than they get out of slaves. . . . Christian masters had a special motive for keeping their slaves, viz. that they might have the opportunity of exercizing a religious and moral influence upon them, and of winning them for Christ."
5. The Bishop could receive no oblation from those who ill-used their slaves. The Church punished such severely. The Synod of Elvira, 305, excluded from communion a woman who struck her slave in anger so that she died within three days—for seven years if it was intentional, for five if accidental.
6 Harnack, Mission and Expansion of Christianity, I, 172.
7. Didache, XII.

the Church of Corinth, A.D. 95-6, he draws a picture of the past prosperity of the Corinthian Church, and reminds it of its splendid reputation for kindness to strangers: "who did not publish abroad your magnificent disposition of hospitality?"[1] Polycarp in his Epistle to the Philippians warmly commends their hospitality: "They have helped on their way . . . . . those who were bound in chains."[2] The Didache contains stringent regulations for the treatment of travelling Christians[3]: "If the comer is a traveller, assist him, so far as ye are able; but he shall not stay with you more than two or three days, if it be necessary. If he wishes to settle with you, being a craftsman, let him work for and eat his bread. But if he has no craft, according to your wisdom provide how he shall live as a Christian among you, but not in idleness. If he will not do this, he is trafficking in Christ. Beware of such men." "If they see a stranger," says Aristides, "they bring him under their roof, and rejoice over him as over a brother of their own, for they call not themselves brethren after the flesh but after the spirit."[4] Justin Martyr tells us that the "strangers that are sojourning" received voluntary Sunday congregational offerings.[5] Tertullian complains bitterly that marriage between Christian women and pagan husbands operate to prevent hospitality to a "brother on a journey."[6]

The writer of a Didache impresses upon his hearers that due hospitality should be given to Christian missionaries, and yet he takes care that the Church's hospitality should not be traded upon by imposters or false prophets or lazy persons: "No prophet who orders a meal in a spirit shall eat of it; otherwise he is a false prophet; whosoever shall say in a spirit, 'Give me money or something else,' you shall not listen to him."[7] The abuse of the privilege of hospitality became so great that travelling brethren had to carry with them authenticating documents with mystic letters representing the Trinity. Hospitality especially devolved upon the officials of the Church.[8] The Shepherd of Hermas places hospitable bishops in a special class among the saints.[9] Houses for the reception of strangers did not come into existence till the next period. In case the bishop's house was not large enough strangers were cared for in the houses of church members. In the fourth century the practice of hospitality was extended to the erection of hospices in waste places along the roadside.[10]

Harnack has pointed out that the Roman Church owed its rapid rise to supremacy in Western Christendom not simply to its geographical position, but also to the fact that it did not shirk the special obligations of hospitality that fell to it as the Church of the Imperial Capital.[11] There is little doubt that in the days before Constantine,

1. Clemens Romanus, Ad Corinth., 1.
2. Ch. 1.
3. XII.
4. Vita Barlaam et Joasaph, p. 252.
5. Justin Martyr, 1st Apol., 67.
6. Tertullian, Ad Uxorem, II, 3-6.
7. XII.
8. Melito, Bishop of Sardis, wrote a book on Hospitality, Euseb., H. E., IV, 23.
9. Sim., IX, 27, 2.
10. Harnack, Mission and Expansion of Christianity, I, 179; Euseb., H. E., IV, 23.
11. Harnack quotes Acta Archelai, Ch. IV.

when the ties of government were slender, the exercise of hospitality towards travelling Christians aided greatly in binding the Church together as one Church throughout the Empire.

### Assistance to Sister Churches

Not only did individuals and churches minister to travelling brethren. They also followed the example of the primitive church, which had remembered the poor in Jerusalem, by granting support and succor to distant churches. In this work the Church of Rome won a well-merited reputation. Towards the end of the second century, at the very time the Catholic Church was becoming something like a federation of Churches, Dionysius of Corinth could write to the Roman Christians:

> "From the very first you have had this practice of aiding all the brethren in various ways and of sending contributions to many churches in every city, thus in one case relieving the poverty of the needy, or in another providing for brethren in the mines. By these gifts, which you have sent from the very first, you Romans keep up the hereditary customs of the Romans, a practice your bishop, Soter, has not merely maintained but even extended."[1]

That Rome should be, as Ignatius described her,[2] "the leader of love," was of untold benefit to the growing Church. She had her reward. It made her the leading Church of Christendom in the days to come.

In an elaborate and important letter Cyprian records that, when wild hordes of robbers had invaded Numidia and carried off many Christians of both sexes into captivity, one African Church extended financial aid to another:

> "We transmit to you a sum of a hundred thousand sesterces collected and contributed by our clergy and people here in the church over which by God's mercy we preside; this you will dispense in the proper quarter at your discretion . . . . Should the like occur again for a test of love and faith, do not hesitate to write of it to us; be sure and certain that while our own church and the whole of the church pray fervently that this may not recur, they will gladly and generously contribute even if it does take place once more. In order that you may remember in prayer our brethren and sisters who have taken so prompt and liberal a share in this needful act of love . . . . . . I add herewith the names of all. Further, I have subjoined the names of my colleagues (the bishops) and fellow-priests, who like myself were present and made such contributions as they could afford in their own name and in the name of their people ; I have also noted and forwarded their small sums along with our own total. It is your duty—faith and love alike require it—to remember all these in your prayers and supplications."[3]

1. Eus., H. E., IV, 23, 10.
2. Ign., ad Rom., prooemium.
3. Ep., LXII. Cf. also Ep., XII

But it was particularly when a Church was subject to persecution or exposed to pestilence,[1] that sister churches sprang to its aid. As Lucian remarks, "On such occasions no expense is grudged." One needs only to read the letters of Ignatius to see the intercourse and solicitude that existed between sister churches. Letters of peace were sent from one Church to another. The bishop of Rome sent out such communications to compose difficulties. Thus, in an important crisis, he sought to allay the difficulties caused by the Montanist prophecies of Asia Minor.[2]

*The Church and Business*

In what he regards as the oldest Christian autograph letter extant, Deissmann has shown that the Church rendered a social service, hitherto unknown to us, even in the matter of business.[3] It was, however, not by way of engaging in business itself but in facilitating it for others that this was accomplished. The letter is written on papyrus and dates from the period 264-282 A.D. It was sent from an Egyptian Christian to his fellow Christian in the Arsinoite *nome.;* It shows the Christians of the generation before Diocletian going about their work in the world, buying and selling. This letter clearly indicates that the provincial Christians of Egypt employed the highest ecclesiastic in the land as their confidential agent in trade and money affairs. The Papas of Alexandria, Bishop Maximus, served as go-between for the Christian corn-sellers in the Fayum and their agent in Rome. This bit of Christian service helped to hold together the scattered churches in a social and economic, and therefore also in an ecclesiastical, way. And the great church leaders of Alexandria are shown to have thought it not unbecoming to help even the worldly affairs of their humble fellow Christians. It is impossible, of course, at this distance of time to estimate the extent to which the Church rendered informal service of this character, but that it must have been deeply appreciated can hardly be gainsaid. It is not improbable that the immediate absorption of the churches of Alexandria in the Arian controversy prevented any great development of this financial service on their part, and headed off a movement that might have made out of the Christian Churches a banking system after the model of the ancient pagan temples.

*Social Order*

In addition to specific social services rendered by the Church and its members it must not be forgotten that the Church always made a general contribution to social order, simplicity of living, and even domestic harmony. It instructed women to manage the affairs of their households "in seemliness with all discretion."[4] The leaven of Christian lives was bound to make itself felt in the communities in which they were found. Pliny informed Trajan that they "bound themselves with an oath, not for any crime, but not to commit theft or

1. Euseb., H. E., VII, 22; IX, 8.
2. Tertullian, Adv. Prax., 1.
3. A. Deissmann, Light from the Ancient East, 195.
4. Clemens Romanus, Ad Cor., I.

robbery or adultery, not to break their word, and not to deny a deposit when demanded.[1] Although Christians frequently were unpopular through setting themselves against the pleasures of their pagan friends, yet they bore themselves "in all things as Christians."[2] In the Paedogogus Clement declared—"It is not right that one should live in superfluity, while many are in want. How much better to be a benefactor to many than to possess a splendid house."[3]

*Martyrdom a Service*

Nor can we forget that the testimony of the martyrs was a conspicuous social service. No one can read the record of the persecution at Lyons and Vienne in 177 without being thrilled at the heroism of the noble Sanctus and the brave slave-girl, Blandina.[4]

*Imperial Patronage*

By the beginning of the fourth Century the Empire was casting about for some new means of safety. It had little resource within itself. Neither Diocletian nor Plotinus had saved the State. Roman arms, which had only too often in recent decades been turned against themselves, were to find new foes pressing across the Danube and the Rhine. The contribution of the Mediterranean world was not yet made in its totality. But the strength of Rome was ready to break beneath its burden. Strong though the Empire was, it was not strong enough. As Constantine scanned the horizon he recalled how the palace at Nicomedia had been struck by lightning after the edict of persecution against the Christians in 303. The dream on the eve of the Battle of the Milvian Bridge was the product, not the cause, of his decision to turn to the followers of the Galilean as an ally of Empire. Hitherto the Christian Church had rendered its social service, under the suspicion, or even the persecution, of the State. Henceforth the Church was to work under imperial patronage. The scope of its service and the character of its social achievements would, as a consequence, be profoundly altered.

## (c) THE CHARACTER OF SOCIAL ACHIEVEMENTS

*The Church Survives in the World*

During the whole of this period Christianity was, in large measure, on the defensive. It was not to be expected that it should heal all the social ills of the Empire. If the movement was aggressive, it was aggressive to establish itself, and to express its social ideals chiefly within its own community. In the face of persecution it remained true to its beliefs, it shrank not to assert its spiritual aspirations, its new social standards. It had social service to render to the persecuted, to those for whom in these days of conflict the adoption of the Christian faith entailed poverty or imprisonment, or a loss of property or occupation or even life itself. "What the Christian

1. Pliny, Ep., X, 96.
2. Auct., Ad Diogn., 5-7.
3. II, 12; III, 7; I, 2, 3, etc.
4. Euseb , H. E., V, 1, 37-42.

Church could do during these centuries was," says Mozley,[1] "in the face of organized persecution, to bear repeated and magnificent witness to its beliefs, and to impress its own members with new moral, spiritual and social ideals, that in the dark ages which were to come there might be forces strong enough to counteract and to tame the savagery of the northern invaders, and to build up on the ruins of the old a new and more vital civilization." Christianity had problems to solve within its own development. It could scarcely be anticipated that at the same time it should leaven the whole Roman Empire, which was itself the product of a thousand years. It was achievement enough that Christianity should have survived as a vital force itself and should have captured in Constantine the head of the State. Had Montanism triumphed the Christian movement could never have become the Church of the Empire. Montanism sought to withdraw the "perfect" and the "spiritual" from the world that they might live "above the thunders," free from contact and pollution. But the Church chose to live *in* the world, with the masses, performing social service and leavening the whole lump. There was herein an acceptance of a "lower standard" of Christian living, but, nevertheless, a pressing forward to a wider sphere of social Christian achievement. But in the hour of the Church's choice ascetic impulses were greatly quickened with all their train—celibacy, a double ethical standard as between the holy and the imperfect, faith as a Rule of Faith, and that corrupting but persistent thought of social service as meritorious almsgiving. This last conception conspired both to stimulate the amount of charity, as conferring greater advantage, and to organize and institutionalize social effort, thereby making it, even if less personal, at any rate more comprehensive and, it was hoped, more effective.

*Social Service Congregational*

There was much yet to be accomplished. Arius was to be reckoned with. The great mass of the people were yet to be won to the way of the Galilean. The new folks on the frontier were still to descend with devastating might upon the sacred soil of Italy, and then to be evangelized. In the days that were to come we shall see the Church active in a Christian Empire. There will be the establishment of charitable institutions and the definite organization for social work. But under the Pagan Empire the work of social service, of practical help, of brotherly sympathy was carried on by the *Congregation* as a free and independent institution. It was the Congregation and, of course, as ever, individual Christians, that helped the unfortunate and unemployed, for the question of unemployment was no less vital then than now. The sources of inspiration were from congregational worship. Contributions, at any rate to the time of Cyprian,[2] were largely spontaneous, not the outcome of public exhortation as with Ambrose or Chrysostom in the next period. The revenues were derived from the monthly contributions to the congregational chest, or from the collections and obligations at the congregational Eucharist.

1. J. K. Mozley, The Achievements of Christianity, 31.
2. Cyprian wrote the first book on alms—itself an indication that a change was in process from the first generous enthusiasms.

The giving of alms was a part of public worship. The circumstance that some of these offerings were in kind, bread and wine,[1] indicates how circumscribed in sphere was this Christian activity. Though individuals like Marcion and Cyprian made large gifts, yet the main givings were congregational. They were generally dispensed by congregational officials and to congregational members and adherents. In this social service, revolving around the sharing of the fund of charity, were contained the germs of the development of the parish and diocese on the one hand, and, on the other, of the whole hierarchial system of bishops, presbyters and deacons.

The motive of social service was to be found in the sense of congregational brotherhood and fellowship. Congregations were small, like enlarged families.[2] Harnack quotes an ancient document[3]: "To the sick, give relief; to the sound, work." This was, doubtless, a congregational maxim. We know that the teaching and ethics of the period were congregational, or, as Hall calls them, group ethics.[4] Thus the Shepherd of Hermas warns, praises and punishes the household or congregation.[5] The Church was consolidating itself in congregations. Its activities were parochial. It was girding itself against the world as the Roman legion girded itself against the Northern Barbarians. The virtues of both were the virtues of obedience and co-operation. Organization virtues, qualities, activities and services received emphasis.

### The Larger Vision

Yet, while the social service was in the main congregational there was already a vision of a larger service. The impulse to bury the dead even of those outside the congregation, the care of other congregations for which the Roman Church established an enviable reputation, the building of hospices in dreary or dangerous stretches of the roads, the entertainment of strangers who were travelling, the poor relief which Julian noted as reaching even to the pagans, all this was suggestive of the wider outlook that was to drive the Church in the next period to send its missionaries to our own Teutonic forefathers.

### Not Scientific Study but Generous Impulse

The Church made no scientific study of the causes of poverty, nor did it deal with them. It had no theory about charity. It did not reflect to whom alms should be given or why they might be withheld.[6] There was simply the spirit of brotherly love alive in the congregation, and that sufficed. Social service institutions did not exist, nor was the need for them felt as yet. In fact there were not even large Church buildings in existence. Leaders in the congregation became

1. This was more especially the case with the so-called oblations given at the celebration of the Lord's Supper. The sacrificial character was prominent here.
2. Uhlhorn points out that both Cyprian in Carthage and Victor in Rome knew all the members of their Churches.
3. Harnack and Hermann, The Social Gospel, 28.
4. Hall, History of Ethics within Organized Christianity.
5. Vis., I, C, 3, Sim., 7.
6. "We communicate to all, and give to every one who is in need," Justin, Apol., I, 14; Shepherd of Hermas, Mand. II.

leaders in social service tended to become leaders in the congregation. There were comparatively few rich Christians. Alms and charity came for the most part from those who labored with their hands. Doubtless the giving was generous, and sometimes even impulsive, but it may well be doubted whether in the whole history of the Church gifts have ever been more wisely bestowed.

### A Communion of Saints Knit Together in Service

It remains true that the social achievement of the Church lagged behind the sweep of its Catholic outlook, and the universal character of its organization, but it was on a far sounder basis. The Church took the forms of Hellenic thought and of Roman government. She took them ready-made, complete. She came to think that her dogma was vastly more important than her social service. She rested the Catholic Church on her Episcopate, her Rule of Faith and her closing Canon. But the real communion of saints lay in the democracy of the congregational life of the Church, and in its social service. The humble, the oppressed, the toiling, the persecuted, were being knit together in actual fact, not by Cyprian's theory of unity nor by his belief in the episcopate, but by the kindly deeds of her people. The world has never fully appreciated the contribution made by the social service of the Church towards its Catholicity and its victory. Here was a humble, but mighty, leaven working from beneath, and from within, in the world of poverty, of need, of paganism in the pre-Constantine Empire.

### QUESTIONS FOR DISCUSSION

1. Under the Pagan Empire the Church first stated its belief in the form of Rule of Faith, it decided on the character, and, in the main, on the extent, of the Canon of the New Testament, and it adopted the monarchial episcopate as the main feature of its government. Were these social services? If so, why?

2. The Christians of the period endured martyrdoms for the Faith, wrote Apologies to establish the truth of their beliefs, and repelled such heresies as Gnosticism. Were these social services? If so, why?

3. Marcion published a mutilated New Testament, declared that the good God was not the God of the Old Testament, and organized a confederacy of Churches. Were these social services? If so, why?

4. To what extent has the Christian Church of the twentieth century advanced in social service beyond the Church as pictured by Justin Martyr and Tertullian?

5. Is almsgiving social service if regarded as a means of grace to the bestower?

6. Why has hospitality always been a duty inculcated by the Church?

7. Under the Pagan Empire the social service was largely congregational in character and extent. What are the advantages and disadvantages of this type of social service?

8. Christians of this period were warned against "trafficking in Christ." What would you consider as the modern equivalent of this sin?

9. During this period the Christian Church was growing in little voluntary associations of believers unconnected with the civil power,

and with a simple organization. At the end of the period the Church formed a union with the State under Constantine. Was this a blunder? Would it have been wiser, and might it have rendered a greater social service, if it had limited itself to the reforming of manners and morals, and abstained from directly influencing legislation?

10. In the second century there is a distinct loss of the early Christian enthusiasm and at the same time an eclipse of the prophetic ministry but a better organization of the Church. Is such a change calculated to increase or to decrease the efficiency of social service?

11. Is the Lord's Supper regarded to-day as in the second century as an incentive to social service?

12. Mixed marriages with pagan husbands interfered in this period with the social service rendered by Christian wives. Name some things that similarly interfere to-day.

BOOKS FOR ADVANCED STUDY

A. Harnack, *The Mission and Expansion of Christianity in the First Three Centuries,* translated by James Moffatt, Vol. i. G. Uhlhorn, *Christian Charity in the Ancient Church,* translated by Sophie Taylor. Kirsopp Lake, *The Apostolic Fathers.* Hastings, Encyclopaedia of Religion and Ethics, Article on *Charity.* Hatch, *The Organization of the Early Christian Church.* T. M. Lindsay, *The Church and the Ministry in the Early Centuries.* R. Rainey, *The Ancient Catholic Church.* G. Uhlhorn, *Conflict of Christianity with Heathenism.* H. M. Gwatkin, *Early Church History to 313, and Selections from Early Christian Writers.* Francis Herbert Stead, *The Story of Social Christianity.*

CHAPTER IV

# UNDER THE CHRISTIAN EMPIRE AND AMONG THE BARBARIAN TRIBES

(SAY TO A.D. 800)

(a) THE CHURCH UNDER THE CHRISTIAN EMPIRE AND AMONG THE BARBARIAN TRIBES

Transition From Old Empire to New Peoples. Consolidation of Church. Readjustment for Middle Ages. Larger Resources and Responsibilities. Privilege instead of Persecution. A Large Task. Constructive Period. The Church in the World and the World in the Church. The Church Equipped.

(b) SOCIAL ACHIEVEMENT

More Compact Organization. Types of Service Rendered. Enhanced Value of Human Life. Child Exposure. Suppression of Gladiatorial Shows. Influence on Legislation. Influence on Administration. Philanthropy and Poor Relief. Tribute of Julian. Testimony of Chrysostom. Ambrose, A Social Worker. Social Service Work in Rome. The Bishop, a Social Worker. Alms. Social Service Institutions. The Church and Slavery. The Colonus. War Prisoners. Social Significance of Monasticism. Evidence of a Papyrus. Evidence of Ostraca. Financial Transactions. Hospitality, Charity, etc. The Leadership of Rome. The New Peoples. Law-giving and National Organization. Moral Culture. Education. Position of Woman.

(c) CHARACTER OF SOCIAL ACHIEVEMENT

World Conquest and World Flight. Unity of the Church. Service better than Theory. For Merit. Institutionalized Service. No Scientific Study.

## (a) THE CHURCH IN THE CHRISTIAN EMPIRE AND AMONG THE BARBARIAN TRIBES

*Transition From Old Empire to New Peoples—Consolidation of Church*

This period begins with the capture of the Roman Empire for Christianity. It ends with the evangelization of the Barbarian Tribes. The Church completed its conquest of the ancient world,·and began its education of the modern nations. It watched beside the death-bed of the old age—for in the end Christianity failed to save the Empire—and witnessed the birth-throes of the new Day, bringing comfort to the one, and to the other, guidance and strength. The impact of the Teutons which broke up the Roman State consolidated the Roman Church. In the process of the disintegration of the Empire the Church became one, one in creed, and largely one in government. In the same period the Hellenic spirit exhausted itself in its victories. The fundamental dogmas of the Church were fixed in the seven General Councils. They began their work by settling the orthodox faith on such high matters as the Trinity and the Incarnation, and concluded it by sanctioning the use and worship of images.

### Readjustment for Middle Ages

The period was one of reconstruction. The relation of the Church to the State under the conditions of civil patronage was determined. The development of its doctrine and constitution took place within an Empire whose peace was rudely shattered by a prolonged struggle for supremacy in Western Europe on the part of successive waves of Teuton Invaders. The Empire was not only broken in many of its parts, but also rent in twain between East and West. The Church itself felt the first symptoms of that same cleavage that time has never healed. It was the period of transition to the Middle Ages. National Churches were established in the Northern Tribes in an epoch of intense missionary activity. The foundations of mediaeval life and order were laid in institutions, piety, thought and culture. The great Fathers of the Church made each his own peculiar contribution to the common ecclesiastical life and thought. Monasticism competed with the Papacy and Missions as the creative product of the Church in this period. But the Bishop of Rome emerged supreme over Western Christendom. He had his way in the great controversies that tore the bosom of the Church, and Gregory made him heir to that Patrimony that was both lost and regained within the memory of men now living. In the East arose the portent of Islam, and in the North the new forces of the new peoples. Under the leadership of Charles Martel the Franks at Tours saved Western Christendom from the menace of Islam and gave Europe a chance to become European. The Teuton King and Christian man. In him first Christianity, Teutonism and Classicism coalesced. In him the past converged, and the future was born.

### Larger Resources and Responsibilities

The changed circumstances of the period, as contrasted with the days before Constantine, enormously increased the resources of the Church, but increased, no less, the need which the Church must meet and the scale upon which it must operate.[1] The life of a State Church could not be confined either to congregations or to congregational activities, even though those congregations were federated and shared Catholic views. The Church had to organize itself on the scale of the Empire, even if the Gospel failed to penetrate every phase of national life. And when the Empire waged war with the Barbarians, the Church, too, felt the necessity laid upon it to wage holy war against their paganism. That the spiritual warfare against the Tribes issued not from Rome alone, but also from the East, is seen in the circumstance that all the Barbarians, save the Franks only, were tainted with Arianism before they were finally won over to orthodox Catholicism. It is no accident that the northern missions should arise during the period of the struggle with the Tribes. Nor yet is it an accident that, though the Empire succumbed to the Barbarians, the

---

1. The characteristic of the Age was an increasing impoverishment extending to larger numbers. Uhlhorn, Christian Charity in the Ancient Church, 118.

Barbarians in turn succumbed to the Church. In both cases it was a victory for life and spirit.

Such is the general character of the transition to the Middle Ages. But it is necessary to indicate some phases in greater detail if we would understand the nature of the social achievements of the Church in this period.

## Privilege Instead of Persecution

The reign of Constantine inaugurated a new epoch for Christianity. The things of God became the things of Cæsar. The religion of the Galilean was no longer exposed to persecution, though it could not escape the more subtle, but no less serious, danger of persecuting. Under the wing of the State the Church acquired legal rights, favours and immunities and the doubtful advantage of imperial patronage and material endowment. Constantine awarded the Church a portion of the corn contributions.[1] He ordered fifty splendid copies of the Bible to be prepared at his expense for the churches of his new Capital.[2]

It was not deliberately nor through ingratitude, but owing to the inherent qualities of its spirit and leaven that the Christian Faith repaid the State by gradually undermining and loosening the whole fabric of Empire. Paganism had identified Religion and State, but the Kingdom of God was ever for Christians more than the Roman Empire. This conception in itself had elements of disruption of vast political import. The life of the Christian needed no longer to be shut within a closet, his worship hidden in a Catacomb, nor the Church's activity and organization confined within the congregation. The power of the Bishop became greatly extended in the days when the Church became not merely Catholic, but Roman as well.

## A Large Task

In the sphere of the purely pagan and classical there was much of decadence. Population was steadily decreasing, trade was growing less active, burdens of debt and taxation were becoming daily more intolerable.[3] Intellectual power, imperial patriotism and actual courage declined. Christianity drew into its current much of the intellectual strength of the fourth century and thus checked any distinctive pagan progress.[4] Attempts were indeed made, as under Julian and Justinian, to restore the grandeur of the Empire, with or without the pagan religion, but the ancient world had no hidden resources of inspiration. Even on the economic side of life the citizens of the Empire were becoming enslaved. Every one was bound to his position, whether in an office or on the soil itself. Only in the Church was there liberty. What there was of new power came from the vigor of the Barbarians or the vital forces of the Christian movement. It was a large task that confronted the Church—to recast an ancient civilization, to develop its own thought upon the high prob-

1. Theodoret, H. E., I, 10.
2. Dobschütz, The Influence of the Bible on Civilization, 28.
3. Zosimus, Hist., II, 38, tells how parents sold their sons and sacrificed their daughters' honor to pay taxes.
4. H. O. Taylor, The Classical Heritage of the Middle Ages, Ch. 3.

lems of the Person of its Founder, and to carry its evangel to the new peoples of the North. That Christianity failed to save the Roman Empire is not surprising, but it is no small achievement that what was saved in the Empire was saved through and in the Church. The very throes of the struggle brought forth the great spirits whom the Church has always lovingly designated the Fathers. They undertook their task of interpreting the Faith to the Roman world the more readily inasmuch as even they had little understanding of how rapidly the Roman world was rushing to its ruin.[1]

*Constructive Period*

It was a constructive period. This was the case even in the matter of building. Constantine himself founded churches, many of them imposing and costly, and St. Sophia, or the Church of Holy Wisdom, dates from the reign of Justinian. Creeds were formulated on great points of doctrine that satisfied the faithful for centuries. These have remained so long a rigid and unalterable legacy that it is difficult to think back across the centuries to a time when the full and eternal deity of the Son and of the Holy Spirit had not yet been established as the Catholic faith. After a career full of vicissitudes and not a little of court favor Arianism was proscribed. Athanasius suffered five exiles, but his cause conquered. St. Hilary in Gaul and the Cappadocians in the East left the cause of Arius prostrate. Theodosius, following the line marked out by Constantine, required all subjects of the Empire to hold the orthodox view of the Trinity. He would chain citizens to the Christian faith, and the Christian faith to that expression of it which his Century had evolved. Unity was achieved by Constantine through enactment. Theodosius would secure uniformity in the same way. Speculation was to be the speciality of experts. Common men must believe as instructed. Accordingly they turned to rest their religious life in the Sacraments, to which the Incarnation controversies had given a new impulse. In them they found the divine. Piety was associated with the prevailing thought of the God-man and its implication of mystery and the supernatural. Those who were not theologians were content with a syncretism of the old polytheism, now partially christianized, the thought of the divine forever entering the human, and the memory of the martyrs of the persecution period that a pious affection would not allow to die. Worship grew up that had much to do with relics, martyrs, saints, masses—the mysterious and supernatural manifested in the sensuous. Helvidius, Jovinianus, Vigilantius might protest—it was Jerome that triumphed. The religion that proclaimed that the Divine had once appeared in Palestine now found the divine in all the paraphernalia of its worship, its emblems, its thought and life. It even tended to ascribe the divine to its organization. It obscured the fact that it had accommodated its organization to the imperial constitution. The hierarchy patterned after the higher civil service was deemed to be celestial.

1. The problems of the clash of Christianity and Paganism, of the Roman Empire and ancient Civilization with the new Barbaric influence and peoples called forth as intense a discussion of the ways of Divine Providence as ever in the history of the world. Augustine, Orosius, Salvian, all discuss this mighty theme.

*The Church in the World and the World in the Church*

The success of the Church in the world exposed the Church to worldliness. This manifested itself in what was perhaps its grossest form in legacy-hunting on the part of clerics. So great did this evil become that Chrysostom was constrained to advise Olympias and other wealthy persons not to lavish their gifts too promiscuously on the clergy, but to be their own almoners. Augustine also expressed his disapproval of persons disinheriting their children in order to make wills in favor of the church and the poor. The abuse had to be corrected by the enactments of civil law.[1] But the Church never entirely forgot its spiritual character and purpose. It built up a penitential discipline and enforced it by private confession. This was the Church's substitute for the testing fires of persecution which had been so effective to purify its members in the days of Decius. In earlier days Christianity had been able to impose something approaching an adequate training upon its catechumens. But the favor of the State caused many to flock to the Church. Under Constantine the Christians formed but a minority of the population; before the end of the fifth Century they vastly outnumbered what was left of the Pagans. In the North the too abrupt conversion of the masses followed hard upon the changed allegiance of some doughty warrior. A lowered moral tone was everywhere discernible. The Church had won the heathen Empire, but heathenism was entering the Church. The Barbarians did not slough off all their barbarism with their group baptisms. To these conditions the Church opposed a definite creed invested with mystery rather than accompanied with explanations. In actual conduct and worship it accommodated itself not a little to the practices, ideas, festivals of the heathenism it sought to overthrow. Its converts imported their morals with them into the Church. The Church dressed up much in Christian guise. This explains the fight of the West for images and emblems, this and its resentment against spiritual autocracy on the part of the eastern civil ruler. But all the while the Church relaxed not at all its governmental hold upon its subjects. It strengthened the privileges of its clergy and magnified the office of the Bishop. It built up the Papacy as the great arbiter of the West and a curia for counsel. It extended its jurisdiction to Purgatory and thus stimulated the generosity and spiritual interests of the faithful. It laid the foundations of mediæval culture and of schools. It brought the Vulgate to the nations. And it established in Monasticism its most effective protest against worldliness—in the East its most potent weapon against error, in the West its keenest agent to extend the faith.

*The Church Equipped*

When Christianity entered the Middle Ages it entered equipped and furnished, determined to work out the programme of St. Augustine's City of God. The Church had become an institutional system highly organized. It had a body of doctrine formulated in seven great World Parliaments. It had evolved a distinct type of piety and

1. Codex Theodosianus, XVI, 2, 20; Ayer, Source Book for Ancient Church History, 381. Hieronym. Ep., XXXIV, ad Nepot.

religious life, and had made up its mind as to what was "holy." Much that great teachers like Augustine had taught, it had heard, but had not absorbed; but it was all there ready to be revealed. And the Church had accepted a form of morality that praised the ascetic, but did not exclude the worldling. It is our object to enquire what types of social service the Church evolved in this transition period.

(*b*) Under the Christian Empire and Among the Barbarian Tribes

*More Compact Organization*

The union of Church and State enlarged at once the material resources of Christianity and the scale of its benevolent operations. The disorders of the Invasions gave ampler scope for social service. To meet the changed conditions the Church brought to its task somewhat less of spiritual enthusiasm—such was the price it paid for its allegiance with the world—but it wielded its power in a closer and more compact organization. Though it was not till the Synod of Macon, 583, that obligatory tithes opened to it a steady and sufficient source of revenues, its funds were ampler from the day when Constantine gave it the right to receive testamentary endowments.[1] It became the residuary legatee of many a treasure stored in heathen temples. Its position in the world was secure. For the same Emperor had legalized Christian corporations, and this lent an impulse to hierarchical jurisdiction. Much that was formerly spiritual in life, custom, and activity became statutory. Sunday became a legal festival. Bishops were no longer merely spiritual leaders in their community. They were also the recognized ecclesiastical governors of extended dioceses with proper subordinate officials, each set aside for some specific religious or charitable function.

*Types of Service Rendered*

The Church was active to modify the legislative enactments of the State, and at the same time by its teaching it strove to raise the whole moral tone of society. Thus it contributed its great influence to increase the sense of the value of human life, to punish abortion, to prevent the exposure of infants, to restrict gladiatorial contests, to temper the administration of law particularly in the matter of capital offences,[2] to lessen the evils of slavery, to forbid concubinage, to increase the sanctity of marriage, to restrain licentiousness, to promote Sunday observance,[3] to care for prisoners, to guard public morality, to protect dependants, and even to deal with questions of property and wills. It labored to improve the lot of women. It condemned suicide. It mitigated the evils of war, particularly during the Barbarian Invasions, by ransoming prisoners and affording havens of refuge, even at the cost of sacrificing the sacred vessels. It made effective in word and act and institution a larger conception of brotherhood. Its poor relief wrung a testimony of praise from even the Apostate Emperor Julian. It carried its missionary enter-

1. Uhlhorn, Christian Charity in the Ancient Church, 256-8.
2. A Canon of the Synod of Orleans prescribes that an archdeacon should visit prisoners every Sunday and that the Church should provide necessary foods.
3. Spectacles were forbidden on Sundays.

prise to the New Peoples, established schools, saved learning, and, in the case of England, laid the foundation of the nation-wide organization of the State. It promoted almsgiving and found therefor a new motive. It encouraged social order and fostered social justice. And in Monasticism it exemplified the Catholic Faith and transmitted to the Middle Ages more than one feature of the civilization of Rome. In an eloquent passage Lecky has described the social service rendered by the Church in this period: "The high conception that has been formed of the sanctity of human life, the protection of infancy, the elevation and final emancipation of the slave classes, the suppression of barbarous games, the creation of a vast and multifarious organization of charity, and the education of the imagination by the Christian type constitute together a movement of philanthropy which has never been paralleled or approached in the pagan world."[1] Little wonder that Lactantius saw the superiority of the Christian over the heathen world in the matter of social and charitable enterprise: "Compassion and humanity are virtues peculiar to the righteous and to the worshippers of God. Philosophy teaches us nothing of them."[2]

*Enhanced Value of Human Life*

In the eyes of the Church a human life was an eternal soul. Accordingly the Church lent its great weight to every movement to enhance a sense of the value of life. It believed that life received its tremendous and sacred significance even before birth. Therefore the Church condemned and punished abortion. The ancient world had not regarded this practice as an offence of such grave seriousness. At the most it was simply inhuman. But the Church considered abortion as plain murder. The guilty mother was excluded by the Council of Ancyra from the privilege of the sacrament up to the very hour of death. Even though the years of penitence were reduced first to ten, and then to seven, the Church never looked upon abortion as other than a crime of the utmost sinfulness. For it meant the destruction of an unbaptized human life.

*Child-Exposure*

The Church dealt a death-blow to the old system of child-exposure, and it waged an unremitting warfare against infanticide.[3] Though it is not certain that exposed children were received into them, the Church established homes for the care of infants and orphans. These received the names of Brephotropheia and Orphanotropheia and were under the care and administration of the Bishops. Nuns collected foundlings and reared them to baptism. From the sixth Century Foundling Hospitals grew up under the supervision of religious workers. Later the Church invited unmarried mothers to leave their little ones at the doors of the Church. In these measures the Church struck an effective, though unfortunately, not a complete,

1. History of European Morals, II, 43 a.
2. Lact. Inst., VI, 10.
3. The Synod of Toledo, 589, Can. 17, states: "The clergy and the secular judges must unite in extirpating the widespread and terrible crime of parents' killing their children to escape the trouble and cost of bringing them up."

blow at prostitution, which had recruited its victims from among the foundlings.

## Suppression of Gladiatorial Shows

"There is scarcely any other single reform," says Lecky, "so important in the moral history of mankind as the suppression of the gladiatorial shows, and this fact must be almost exclusively ascribed to the Christian Church."[1] The Pagan Empire had a passion for these contests.[2] "Panem et Circenses," was the degrading cry of the Roman mobs, the counterpart of the terrible "Christianos ad leones." Even in the last days of the third Century amphitheatres were still rising in more than one part of the Empire. It is interesting to note the change of attitude in this respect in Constantine himself. At one time he had condemned barbarian captives to combat with the wild beasts of the arena. Then he adopted the expedient of sending criminals to the mines instead of forcing them to become gladiators.[3] But finally it was the same Constantine who issued at Beirut the first edict in the Roman Empire to suppress and restrict these terrible games—"Bloody spectacles in our present state of civil tranquility and domestic peace do not please us, wherefore we order that all gladiators be prohibited from carrying on their profession." They were never introduced into his new Capital of Constantinople. Nearly a century later, such was the influence of Christianity, they largely disappeared, the passion for chariot racing supplanting what even the best of the Pagans themselves recognized as a degrading and brutal exhibition, and the Church ever stigmatized as the most inhuman and shocking murder. Theodoret tells the story of how the ascetic Telemachus endeavored to stop the contests at Rome:

> "He had set out for the East and for this reason had repaired to Rome. There, when the abominable spectacle was being exhibited, he went himself into the stadium, and stepping down into the arena endeavored to stop the men who were wielding their weapons against one another. The spectators of the slaughter were indignant and, inspired by the mad fury of the demon who delights in these bloody deeds, stoned the peacemaker to death. When the admirable Emperor (i.e., Honorius) was informed of this he numbered Telemachus in the army of the victorious martyrs, and put an end to that impious practice."[4]

Against these bloody shows the Christians waged unceasing warfare. At the end of the fourth Century Symmachus, a Prefect of Rome, sought to celebrate the birthday of his little son by exposing a large troop of Saxon prisoners to the slaughter of wild beasts in the arena. To cheat the populace of their festival our kinsmen of that

1. Lecky, History of European Morals, II, 15.
2. In his Confessions (VI, 8), Augustine tells how a Christian was carried to a spectacle by his family, but carefully covered his eyes. A shout from the multitude caused him to open them in the midst of a bloody scene. The old savage pagan thirst for blood was aroused, and he became as eager for the slaughter as the Romans. Henceforth he was an outcast from the Church.
3. Codex Theodosianus, XV, 12, 1.
4. Theodoret, Hist. Ec., V, 26.

early Age, on the very day of the Show, strangled each other. It was a Christian who on this occasion rebuked Symmachus with the words: "No one should perish in the city whose punishment is an amusement."

*Influence on Legislation*

The Christian Church succeeded in implanting a more humane spirit in Roman legislation. To begin with, it inevitably undermined the rigor and tyranny of the old *Patria potestas* by which the head of the household exercised absolute control over the lives and fortunes of its members. From the time of Constantine only might a father killing his son be punished. Under Justinian the father's powers were still further curbed. Henceforth he could himself inflict only moderate penalties. He could indeed bring the son into the civic courts, but his jurisdiction was now restricted to suggesting the kind of punishment to be meted out. In the same way the rights of a son in his own property were also considerably extended. Under Justinian the son was given full control. Thus the paternal tyranny was being undermined, and the ideals of the old Roman *familia* were being displaced by those of the Christian family. Christianity was showing its interest in, and throwing its protection around, the child. The Roman father could no longer "expose," buy or sell or, except through the courts, imprison, his son. He could not abuse or kill him. He could not force him into a marriage, although he might still veto one that he regarded as undesirable. He could not adopt him into another family contrary to his wishes. All this the Christian Church was doing for the independence, social and legal, of the child. At the same time the laws of succession were altered so that henceforth property tended to follow the natural bonds of family life. These reforms, says Brace[1], "are an indication of the tendency everywhere of the Christian Faith to introduce equality of rights among persons, to elevate the individual, to control arbitrary power, to substitute self-command, consideration and the influence of the affections for tyranny and unchecked power in the family."

A new conception of woman found expression in Roman legislation. Her relation to her husband, her interest in her dower, assumed new significance. Under Justinian the absolute control of the husband ceased. The mother acquired equal rights with the father in the matter of the property of deceased children. She was competent to determine the choice of husband for her daughter.

The marriage tie was strengthened in Roman law by the influence of the Christian Faith. Fidelity became a sacred obligation to both husband and wife. From 340 A.D. a married man was prohibited from keeping a concubine. Adultery was made a capital crime. This subject of marriage and divorce is very complex as the legislation fluctuates from reign to reign. In spite of the impetus given to celibacy by the Roman Church Justinian's *Novellae* tells us that nothing in human affairs is so much to be venerated as marriage. The Church, then, while attributing special holiness to virginity,[2] put

1. Gesta Christi, 18.
2. Jerome, Adv. Jovinianum, I, 7.

a new emphasis upon marriage. It sought to make divorce less easy than under the Pagan Empire, and in the matter of marriage succeeded in considerably modifying the legislation of the Empire.[1]  It emphasized two principles:
(a) That the marriage bond was indissoluble;
(b) That there was no double standard of morality for the sexes.[2]
Christianity was putting a new kindliness and consideration, a fresh religious influence, and a deepened sense of social stability into the statute book. Of this there are many traces from Constantine onward. In an ordinance of Theodosius it was required that a Bible be present in every court-room.[3]  The granting of liberty of conscience to Christians, the right of the poor and weak to appeal to the emperor, laws upon Sunday observance forbidding on that day all labors other than those in the fields and all civil acts saving only emancipation, the better care of prisoners, the insistence that cells should have air and light—these are among the achievements of the Christian spirit operating in the domain of Roman law. In the life of the Empire the contribution was no less important—licentious and cruel games were checked, the exposure of children ended, unnatural vices rooted out, a new sanctity given to marriage, and a new day begun for the outcast, the slave, the prisoner, the child and the woman. At the same time that this claim is advanced for the influence of the Christian Church it must not be overlooked that Stoicism was responsible for a more humane conception of slavery, and that other influences were operating to promote better conceptions of marriage.[4]

*Influence on Administration*

The Church also assisted the State by means of the administration of justice in its episcopal courts of arbitration,[5] and thereby set in motion a process that was to continue to our own day—the Christianization of legislation, the tempering of justice by mercy. And particularly was the Church's right of sanctuary recognized—a right which did no little to check violence and tyranny.[6]  The Church claimed the right to inspect the conduct of, and to discipline, those of her members who became magistrates, a right actually exercised by Athanasius,[7] Ambrose, Chrysostom and others. Its officials exercised a supervision over civil officials in the expenditure of funds for public improvements,[8] as illustrated by the following law of the Emperor Justinian, A.D. 530:

"With respect to the yearly affairs of cities, whether they concern the ordinary revenues of the city, either from funds

1. Codex Theodosianus, III, 16, 2.
2. Jerome, Epist. ad Oceanum, 78.
3. Evon Dobschutz, The Influence of the Bible on Civilization, 31.
4. Ibid., 32.
5. Cod. Just., I, tit. 3, de episcopali audientis; Ayer, Source Book for Ancient Church History, 380-2.
6. Not all could find sanctuary. Those with arms, murderers, adulterers, public debtors, carriers-off of virgins, the acknowledged criminals were excluded. The sojourn was limited to 30 days.
7. Basil, Ep. 61.
8. Codex Just., I, 4, 26; Ayer, Source Book for Ancient Church History, 383.

derived from the property of the city, or from legacies and private gifts, or given or received from other sources, whether for public works, or for provisions, or public aqueducts, or the maintenance of baths or ports, or the construction of walls and towers, or the repairing of bridges and roads, or for trials in which the city may be engaged in reference to public or private interests, we decree as follows: The pious bishop and three men of good reputation, in every respect the first men of the city, shall meet and each year not only examine the work done, but take care that those who conduct the jobs, or have been conducting them, shall manage them with exactness, shall render their accounts, and show by the production of the public records that they have duly performed their engagements in the administration of the sums appropriated for provisions, or baths, or for the expenses involved in the maintenance of roads, aqueducts, or any other work."

In general, the period furnished exceptional opportunities for social work and influence. The Church elevated the tone of society[1] and the position of women. By its institution of private penance it enforced its moral instruction upon individuals[2]. It protested against the exploitation of the poor and humble on the part of the rich and powerful. In the cathedral of Milan Ambrose thundered forth his sermon on Ahab and the vineyard of Naboth[3], while Chrysostom, both in Antioch and Constantinople, described in unforgetable phrases the luxury of the rich and the grinding poverty and beggary of the poor. When the Church interposed in the matter of legislation, it was in favor of the oppressed.

*Philanthropy and Poor Relief*

The Church also rendered social service of outstanding importance through works of philanthropy and poor relief and in the encouragement of generosity towards these ends. It became on a large scale the refuge of all the oppressed and suffering, at times even against the emperor himself. In this period social service came to be organized and institutionalized, equipped with officials and establishments. The Church could now act openly and with more abundant resources. For individuals, almsgiving might still possess the most praiseworthy merit. It was considered good in itself, apart from its social purpose. It contributed to salvation. "If there were no poor," declared Chrysostom, "the greater part of your sins would not be removed; they are the healers of your wounds."[4] It is a postulate of the penitential system that almsgiving is good for the penitent. The teaching current in the time dwelt rather upon spiritual advantage to be received in the next world, than upon

1. According to the Canones Ecclesiastici no catechumen could be a painter or sculptor, go to the theatre, nor train men for pugilism or war. No Christian was allowed to be a soldier. No Christian could wear lascivious clothes or ornaments, or wear phylacteries or drink magical potions. These regulations come from the beginning or middle of the fourth century, but the Apostolic Constitutions are an enlargement of the Didache.
2. Leo the Great, Epist., 168, Ch. 2.
3. De Nabuthe, C. 1.
4. Chrysostom, Hom., XIV. Timothy.

social good to be accomplished in this. According to Ambrose, whose teaching and example became normative for the whole Middle Ages, almsgiving is the second bath of the soul, baptism being the first. For Augustine alms and fasting constituted "the two wings of prayer which must fly up to God."

But poor relief was not left to the voluntary action or gifts of either individuals or congregations.[1]

For the first time in the history of the world there was organized a definite scheme and system of charity. The ancient world and the Pagan Empire had witnessed sporadic acts of mercy, but compassion and kindness had never been institutionalized. Now there was to be something approaching a constant oversight of the poor. A diocesan arrangement for dispensing charity was brought into being, for the distress was now far too great, in face of the suffering of the times, for individuals to alleviate. The Bishop,[2] who had already exercised supervision over poor relief, now became the Patronus of the poor and dispenser of alms. Great dignitaries of the Church with duly appointed officials exercised their charity on a lavish scale. The State itself made no serious effort to assist the poor, abandoning to the Church the whole business of relief.[3] Bishops who not infrequently devoted their personal estates to the poor might well be trusted by the State as its trustee for administration of poor relief.[4] In the disorders of the times ecclesiastical property was not seldom respected even by the rudest Barbarians, and the Church as a privileged landowner possessed exceptional means and resources for carrying on charitable activities. Uhlhorn says: "In the midst of this chaos stood the Church as the sole power which survived the universal ruin, and continued to perform its office of being the refuge of all the oppressed and suffering. In these times of confusion, when every other support failed, she alone held out a helping hand to the poor, pursued, and alarmed people . . . . The Church could not save the old world, but she sat at its death-bed with help and comfort."[5] Side by side, from this time on, we may witness the Church's system of relief through institutions, and, confined largely to the parish, the giving of alms and charitable activity on the part of individuals. In the Middle Ages, except perhaps in England, it was the former that came more and more to predominate, the parochial giving way to the institutional.

*Tribute of Julian*

Illustrations might be multipled from this period to show the scale and character of this diocesan charity. The general

1. Moeller, History of the Christian Church, I, 483, has pointed out that rich offerings were still brought to the church only on high festivals, the martyrs' days and the commemorations of the dead. From 500 A.D. these offerings lose their special destination for the poor and become the emoluments of the bishop and the priest who reads mass.
2. In those days a diocese was not a group of small churches, so often as a large church. It was one Church even when there were several places of worship in a town, and one administration.
3. The State, however, provided the Church with its means for the work through donations and contributions of corn.
4. Uhlhorn, Christian Charity in the Ancient Church, 264.
5. Uhlhorn, Christian Charity in the Ancient Church, 393.

economic tendencies of the time had created a poverty of the direst kind and of well nigh universal extent. Julian the Apostate recognized that the Church was gaining support and strength through its practical charity. In his letter to Arsacius he endeavored to awaken the same sense of social responsibility and the same benevolent zeal within a revived paganism. To him of course, Christianity is atheism, and paganism is Hellenism. He writes:

"Hellenism does not flourish as we would have it, because of its votaries. The worship of the gods, however, is grand and magnificent beyond all our prayers and hopes. Let our Adrastea be propitious to these words. No one a little while ago could have dared to look for such and so great change in a short time. But do we think that these things are enough, and not rather consider that *humanity shown strangers, the reverent diligence shown in burying the dead, and the false holiness as to their lives* have principally advanced atheism? Each of these things is needful, I think, to be faithfully practised among us. It is not sufficient that you alone should be such, but in general all the priests, as many as there are throughout Galatia, whom you must either shame or persuade to be zealous, or else deprive them of their priestly office, if they do not come with their wives, children, and servants to the temples of the gods, or, if they support servants, sons, or wives who are impious toward the gods and prefer atheism to piety. Then exhort the priests not to frequent the theatres, not to drink in taverns, nor to practise any part or business which is shameful or menial. Honor those who comply; expel those who disobey. Establish hostelries in every city, so that strangers, or whoever has need of money, may enjoy our philanthropy, not merely those of our own, but also those of other religions. I have meanwhile made plans by which you will be able to meet the expense. I have commanded that throughout the whole of Galatia annually thirty thousand bushels of corn and sixty thousand measures of wine be given, of which the fifth part I order to be devoted to the support of the poor who attend upon the priests; and the rest is to be distributed by us among strangers and beggars. For if there is not one among the Jews who begs, and even the impious Galileans, in addition to their own, support also ours, it is shameful that our poor should be wanting our aid."[1]

*Testimony of Chrysostom*

Chrysostom indicates the higher character of the service which the Church rendered in his day to the needy in Antioch:

"If both the wealthy and those next to them were to distribute among themselves those in need of bread and raiment, scarcely would one person fall to the share of fifty men, or even a hundred. Yet, nevertheless, though in such great abundance of persons able to assist them, they are wailing

1. Julian, Ep., 49, ad Arsacium; Ayer, Source Book for Ancient Church History, 332.

every day. And that thou mayest learn their inhumanity, recall that the Church has a revenue of one of the lowest among the wealthy and not of the very rich; and consider how many widows it succors every day, how many virgins; for indeed the list of these amounts to the number of three thousand. Together with these she succors them that dwell in prison, the sick in the caravansaries, the healthy, those that are absent from their homes, those that are maimed in their bodies, those that wait upon the altar; and with respect to food and raiment, those that casually come every day; and her substance is in no respect diminished. So that if ten men only were willing thus to spend, there would be no poor."[1]

## Ambrose, a Social Worker

No more splendid type of social worker can be found in this period than Ambrose of Milan. He gives us a picture of his own work and of Church workers of his day in his "Duties of the Clergy" (De officiis Ministrorum). He reckoned among the duties of an ecclesiastic the care of the oppressed and suffering.[2] His duty was to hinder the oppression of widows and orphans, to esteem the command of the Lord more than the favor of the rich or great or powerful. "The possessions of the Church," he declared, "are the maintenance of the poor. Let them (i.e. the Pagans) count up how many captives the temples have ransomed, what food they have contributed for the poor, to what exiles they have supplied the means of living."[3] He could fling this taunt, for under his guidance the Church of Milan had not failed in duty. Nor was he blind to the evil of indiscriminate charity. In his "Duties of the Clergy" he warned them against the lying imposture of mendicants."[4] "A method in giving is necessary," he declared. And yet he would have the giver "hard towards none, but free towards all." He would have discrimination in the amount, but not as to the recipient—one should give to all the needy. Farrar has drawn for us a fascinating picture of the social activity of this great Father of the Church.[5]

"When men were unjustly persecuted, he extended to them the rights of asylum. When multitudes were taken prisoners in the incessant battles against rebels and invaders, he unhesitatingly melted down the sacred vessels to purchase their ransom. Nobody spoke more boldly against vice. He denounced the custom of drinking toasts, and put down the vice of revelling on the feast days of martyrs. He rebuked the perfumed and luxurious youths; the women who reclined on silver couches and drank in jewelled cups; the men who delighted in porphyry tables and gilded fretwork, and cared more for their hounds and houses than for their fellow-

1. Chrysostom, Hom., 66 in Matt. 20: 30; Ayer, Opus, Cit. 394.
2. Ambrose, De offic. ministr., II, 29.
3. Ambrose, Ep. 18.
4. Ambrose, De offic. ministr., II, 15.
5. Farrar, Lives of the Fathers, II, 200.

Christians. Nor did he less faithfully denounce the idle multitude who patronized the madness of the circus and the vice of the theatre. To the rich he said: "You clothe the walls of your houses and leave the poor unclad; the naked wail at your gates, and your only thought is of the marble with which you shall overlay your floors; he begs for bread, and your horse has a golden bit. Costly apparel delights you, while others lack food. The very jewel in your ring would protect from hunger a mass of people." To the poor he preached: "Be sober, be diligent, awake to worthier efforts and nobler aims."

When the profiteer and the hoarder were abroad in the land and even Theodosius failed to reprove, it was a magnificent contribution which the Church made through Chrysostom, Basil, and Ambrose, in rebuking the greed of the rich, in forcing them to disgorge the food from their granaries.

## Social Service in Rome

The need of relief had now come far to outstrip the resources of separate congregations. The methods of the previous period no longer sufficed. Almsgiving became well-nigh wholesale. A complete machinery of charity arose in the form of special officers as deacons, and of special institutions as hospitals and monasteries. It is at Rome itself that we see the social service of the Church most highly organized, and most efficient in its methods. For a considerable portion of this period the work was carried on through endowed deaconries as established at the end of the fourth century by Pope Anastasius. Under Gregory the Great the system was reorganized and perfected. He divided the city into seven eleemosynary districts,[1] each under a deacon with a Diakonia, or special house[2] for the care of the poor and distressed. The deacons were under the supervision of an archdeacon, but had to assist them, in addition to voluntary workers, each an oeconomus or steward. A register, or *matricula*, was kept of the needy who were in constant want of relief. At the hospitals food was dispensed, the infirm and sick were fed, and waifs and orphans were maintained. To support this work the Church at Rome drew revenues from its large estates in Italy and in nearly every country bordering on the Western Mediterranean.[3] It is clear that charity and social effort were ceasing more and more to be congregational in character and extent. Dean Milman has described the method of its distribution: "The shares of the clergy and of the papal officers, the churches and monasteries, the hospitals, deaconries or ecclesiastical boards for the poor, were calculated in money, and distributed at four seasons of the year, at Easter, on St. Peter's day, St. Andrew's day, and that of the consecration of Gregory. The first day in every month he distributed to the poor in kind, corn, wine, cheese, vegetables, bacon, meat, fish, and oil. The

1. Rome adhered to this number, but in other cities the number was much greater.
2. Also called Ptochia, or even matriculae, because the poor whose names appeared on the matricula were there fed.
3. In Alexandria the matricula contained at one time 7,500 names; it was a stout volume in Rome in the days of Gregory the Great.

sick and infirm were superintended by persons appointed to inspect every street. Before the Pope sat down to his own meal a portion was separated and sent out to the hungry at his door. A great volume containing the names, the ages, and the dwellings, of the objects of the papal bounty, was long preserved in the Lateran with reverential gratitude. . . . So severe was the charity of Gregory that one day, on account of the death of an unrelieved beggar, he condemned himself to a hard penance for the guilt of neglect as steward of the Divine bounty. . . . He authorized not merely the alienation of the wealth of the clergy, but even the sale of the consecrated vessels from the altar for the redemption of captives—those captives not always ecclesiastics, but laymen."[1]  In view of this elaborate system of charity and poor relief one is not surprised that the Agape was in this period entirely abolished. At an early date it had ceased to express the family unity of the entire Church. It had become a regular meal for the poor members of the congregation. By the Council of Laodicea the Agape was now altogether forbidden in churches, and Ambrose and Augustine put an end to the institution in the West. Congregational social service was disappearing with congregational life itself.

### The Bishop as Social Worker

"The former Church care of the poor," says Uhlhorn," was such no longer. The beneficence of the bishop, distributing with open hand to the needy, had, on the contrary, an unmistakable likeness to what the ancient world also was acquainted with, viz., the distributions of the emperors and the Roman nobles. When Gregory the Great had corn, oil, wine, meat distributed every month, when he had carts full of provisions driving through the town for the relief of the poor, this looks more like a revival of the old distribution of corn than the relief of the poor by the Christian Church. The Bishop of Rome had come into the place of the Emperor, the bishops into the place of the Roman nobles; Christian *caritas* has assumed a suspicious similarity to the ancient *liberalitas*. Still it was a splendid sight to see a bishop daily in the midst of the hungry as the open-handed dispenser of alms, from whom every one expects assistance and receives as much as possible, the poor Roman driven from house and home by the Barbarians, and the Germans, whom the mild breath of Christian love now for the first time touches, awakening in his heart the feeling of the Divine mercy therein reflected; a bishop with whom the stranger finds an asylum, and the sick attendance, who sells the church furniture, the golden and silver vessels for the Lord's Supper to ransom prisoners, and leads in his home the life of a poor man, to let the poor find that the Church possesses what is hers only for the poor; a Basil himself attending upon the sick and leprous; a Chrysostom in the midst of Byzantine luxury himself living simply and modestly and daily feeding seven thousand poor; an Ambrose, a proud Roman, but at the same time a humble

---

1. Milman, History of Latin Christianity, Book III, ch. VII.  Gregory was promoter of the scheme whereby church property was quartered--one quarter for the bishop, one for the rest of the clergy, one for the maintenance of the church fabric, and one for the poor.

Christian, encountering the Emperor and condescending to the poor; an Augustine desiring no other garment than such as he can give to any poor brother; a Gregory taking so deeply to heart the whole misery of the times and yet fretting when an individual dies of starvation in Rome."[1]

### Alms

Benevolence was the chief *active* virtue of the Christian Church. Two circumstances served to emphasize this kind of social service in the Church:

(*a*) The increasing distress of the times and the sufferings due to the Invasion.

(*b*) The growing tendency for Christians to express their religious aspirations in retirement from the world. For the Christian who did not seek safety or consolation in world-flight his religious life found expression in almsgiving, in which he found sin-atoning power.

Never were alms more frequently or more eloquently preached. Chrysostom, Ambrose, Augustine, Basil, the three Gregories and Leo the Great poured forth their persuasive eloquence in an untiring appeal for compassion and for bounty in almsgiving.[2] And they did not hesitate to appeal to the motive of reward. As Ambrose expresses it,—"Alms bring forgiveness as often as given." It was lamentable indeed that the impulse to almsgiving should have been corrupted in motive by the thought of its power to erase and cancel sin, and also at the same time encouraged through the rising doctrine of Purgatory which enabled the donor through his gifts to afford relief even to the departed.[3] This latter custom had risen through the offering of obligations, particularly on the anniversaries of deaths. Men believed they could still commune in love and prayer with the departed. Tertullian says that the husband offers oblations for the wife "to procure for her eternal repose and a share in the first resurrection."[4] With the development of the doctrine of purgatory this custom became in the Middle Ages the chief inspiration and object of Christian charity.

### Social Service Institutions

Between the fourth and sixth Centuries social service institutions were established to assist the poor and destitute and infirm of every type. On all sides arose monasteries, deaconries, hospitals, hostelries, orphanages, poor-houses, refuges, homes for the aged, for infants, and infirmaries. These establishments were created and supported by the Church, and, as need arose, elaborated by the Church. This type of institutionalized social service was unknown in the pagan world.[5] For the ancient world had no hospitals. It had

---

1. Christian Charity in the Ancient Church, 270-1,
2. Uhlhorn, Christian Charity in the Ancient Church, 274-6.
3. Augustine, Enchir. ad Laur., 26, 110, says: "It is not to be doubted that the dead are assisted by the prayers of the Church by the saving sacrifice, and by alms, which are offered for their souls." See also Ibid., XVI, 70.
4. De Monog., C. 10.
5. Uhlhorn, Christian Charity in the Ancient Church, 14-15.

simply houses of refuge, not institutions for care and attendance. They had been restricted, moreover, largely to the sick,—slaves, gladiators and soldiers. The hospital is a Christian development from the hospice or hostel. The house for the stranger and infirm became on the one hand a shelter for the poor and needy, on the other a hospital for the sick.

In the fourth Century Fabiola established a hospital in Rome as an act of penance, and, says Lecky, "the charity planted by that woman's hand overspread the world and will alleviate to the end of time the darkest anguish of humanity." In Fabiola's hospitals sufferers with the most frightful disfigurements and diseases found care and shelter. "The poor wished to be sick," says Jerome, "if only to come under her care." Basil, in addition to founding the first asylum for lepers, established a hospital—called *Basilias* from his own name—in Caesarea about 370 A.D. that became the model for similar institutions both in the East and West. The friends of Jerome were especially active in founding hospitals. Pammachius established one in Portus, and Paulinus and his wife Theresia another in Nola, and Chrysostom, two in Constantinople.

Some hospitals were supported by private benefactions or received legacies;[1] others were maintained by the Church. The value of these institutions was quickly recognized by the State, though none existed in Milan in the time of Ambrose, and Augustine found them still a novelty. The State enacted legislation in 475 A.D. permitting donations to be made to Nosokomeila, or infirmaries, and to Ptocheia, or poor-houses. About a half century later the law allowed property to be given to "churches, hostels, poor-houses, infant and orphan homes, to homes for the aged, or any such community." This was the beginning of endowed charities. Deaconries were district kitchens for the feeding of the poor, who were the peculiar charge of the deacon. The Theodosian code mentions as eleemosynary institutions the following: Guest-houses, Xenodocheia; Poor-houses, Ptocheia or Ptochotopheia; Orphanages, Orphanotropheia; Homes for infants, Brephotropheia. By the time of Justinian these institutions had become common. He mentions also Cherotropheia, houses for widows; and Gerontomocia, houses for the aged. There were also about the same time houses for the reception of women for child-birth and Homes of penance for fallen women. Refuges for strangers, or Inns, Pandocheia, were erected, particularly along the path by which pilgrims must travel. There was one at Ostia. Paula and Melania erected one in Jerusalem. They must have been fairly numerous. The council of Nicaea ordered one to be placed in every city.

The number that received food and poor relief daily was excessive in the great cities. Chrysostom mentions about three thousand widows and virgins as being cared for in Antioch; and seven thousand persons in Constantinople. Larger numbers are recorded for a later time in both Alexandria and Rome. Those in immediate charge of the Church's establishments were given clerical

---

1. Donations and bequests were made valid from 475 A.D.

rank and lived a disciplined life under a Rule. They were appointed on the nomination, and subject to the supervision, of the Bishop. Apart from the deacon the chief helpers were the eleemosynarius, or almoner, and the oeconomus or steward. But even the orderlies, Parabolani, and the buriers of the dead, Copiates, were reckoned as belonging to the clerical order, even if to the lowest rank. These hospitals and similar establishments were called into being on account of the great misery of the times and the "institutional impulse," to quote Uhlhorn, which then prevailed, and which alone could cope with the enlarged needs of the extended Christian community.

*The Church and Slavery*

It is interesting to observe the attitude of the Church in this period towards slavery. The Church accepted slavery as an institution of the State, as St. Paul accepted it, as the Fathers accepted it, as George Whitefield accepted it. It was itself a slave-owner.[1] The Canons of Councils reckon slaves among the Church property which the Bishop is bound to protect and preserve. None the less no little part of the resources of the Church was devoted to ransoming individual slaves. And its teaching of a universal brotherhood, wherein was neither bond nor free, was a leaven that was surely, if slowly, working for the emancipation of all the sons of men. Its influence was on the side of the slave, even though it did not assail slavery. It maintained the lawfulness, even though it contributed to the ultimate abolition of slavery. It was not till the ninth century that St. Treodore of Studium, Constantinople, put forth the command—"Thou shalt possess no slave, neither for domestic service, nor for the labor of the fields, for man is made in the image of God."[2]

An Edict of Constantine permitted manumission to take place in Churches, and granted certain rights to the clergy in the liberation of slaves. Thus emancipation was associated with the Church:

"Those who from motives of religion shall give deserved liberty to their slaves in the midst of the Church shall be regarded as having given the same with the same legal force as that by which Roman citizenship has been customarily given with the traditional solemn rites. But this is permitted only to those who give this liberty in the presence of a priest. But to the clergy we concede more, so that, when they give liberty to their slaves, they may be said to have granted a full enjoyment of liberty, not merely in the face of the church and the religious people, but also, when in their last deposition of their effects, they shall have given liberty or shall direct by any words whatsoever that it be given, on the day of the publication of their will, liberty, without any witness or intervention of the law shall belong to them immediately."[3]

1. Monasteries in the West, but not in the East, possessed slaves.
2. Brace, Gesta Christi, 42.
3. Codex Theodosianus, IV, 7 ,1.

At a later time a slave-child held over the font of baptism by the master, his wife, or son, became free in the act. The mode of manumission was associated with the Church. The master led the slave with a torch around the altar, then, grasping the horns of the altar, he spoke the words of liberation: "For fear of Almighty God, and for the cure of my soul, I liberate thee, and may the angel of our Lord Jesus Christ, deem me worthy of a place among his saints." In many of the forms employed the act is said to be done "for lessening" my sin," "for the benefit of the soul," or "divine compassion inspiring."

Though the intervention of the Church in the matter of legislation in behalf of slaves seems all too slight, yet some real contribution was made. It excommunicated all those who cruelly maltreated their slaves or killed them without judicial sentence.[1] It afforded sanctuary to runaway slaves. Thirty-seven Church Councils passed Acts favorable to slaves. Crucifixion was abolished. The Church had in mind not only the exquisite torture that it involved, but also the sacred associations that this manner of death recalled to every believer. Increasing restrictions were placed on the use of torture in general. The breaking-up of families was forbidden.[2] The great Church Councils thundered their anathemas upon all who dared to re-enslave those freed under religious forms. And Jews were prohibited from owning Christian slaves[3]—a prohibition that was not always observed. This circumstance called forth the care of the Church for the unfortunate Christian slave.

Bishops were not permitted to manumit slaves belonging to the Church except under regulations adopted by the Synod of Agde, 509 A.D.[4] They were regarded as valuable property held in trust, and could not be lightly alienated. The Church more than once asserted its rights as slave-owner.[5] The regard for property was greater in official circles than the regard for life. Nor could slaves be ordained to the priesthood, without the consent of their masters. But they might be ordained if their masters first granted them their freedom.[6] Male and female slaves might not be married by the Church without the will of their owners. The rights of slave owners were recognized.[7] It was not wrong to own slaves. It was wrong to fail to treat them in a Christian manner.[8]

Under the inspiration of the Church Justinian took a bolder course. That Emperor made effective the moral power of Christianity—"We have much at heart," he declared, "to raise slaves to liberty." He gave additional facilities for manumission. He

1. Uhlhorn, Christian Charity in the Ancient Church, 374.
2. Codex Theodosianus, II, tit. 25.
3. Euseb. Vit. Const., IV, 27. Uhlhorn, Christian Charity in the Ancient Church, 378-9.
4. Ayer, Source Book for Ancient Church History, 386.
5. Though the Bishop could give freedom to individual slaves, the abbot could not free the slaves belonging to a monastery.
6. Apostolic Constitutions, IV, 6.
7. The Council of Gangra declares: "If any one under the pretence of piety advises a slave to leave his master and run away from his service, and not to serve his master with good-will, let him be anathema." Uhlhorn, Christian Charity in the Ancient Church, 376.
8. Augustine (Enarr. in Ps. 124: 7) declares: "Christ did not make slaves free masters, but bad slaves good slaves."

abolished the old class of freedmen, and granted immediately the privileges of citizenship to the emancipated. This was no slight contribution to make to the democracy of the future and to the great task of assimilating the peoples of Europe. With the consent of his master a slave might now marry a free woman, and a free man might marry a slave woman by first freeing her. Henceforth the same punishment of death was held for the rape alike of a female slave and of a free woman. Justinian's code declared its purpose "to have the Republic frequented by freemen rather than liberated slaves."

But it was not in the field of legislative enactment that the Church made its influence most felt for freedom. In its teaching, in its ceremonies of church worship, in its penitential discipline, all men were brothers in Christ Jesus. Distinctions of class were repudiated within the Church. Moral dignity and responsibility were attributed to all alike. "This slave," says Chrysostom, "is thy sister in Christ. Has she not an immortal soul like thyself? Is she not honored by the Lord himself? Does she not sit at the same table of grace with thee?[1] The teaching of the Church was bound ultimately to stifle slavery, even if, for the moment, it had no expectation of abolishing it. The word "slave" seldom occurs on a Christian epitaph. The Christian slave frequently declared to his judge: "I am not a slave: I am a Christian—Christ has freed me." The Church of St. Vitale which Justinian dedicated at Ravenna was in memory of a martyred slave. It came to be an act of piety, particularly at Easter, to free slaves.[2] "To buy a slave is to gain a soul," became a proverb. It was regarded as especially fitting to grant freedom as an act of thanksgiving for the birth of a child, for recovery from sickness, for any signal blessing. And, of course, the Church always sought to mitigate the hardships of slaves as it endeavored to alleviate the suffering of the poor and distressed. And it made all bondmen free who entered the service of the Church or State.

In two other ways the Church raised the position of the slaves. The inmates of the great monastic establishments assumed the lot of humanity and obedience, of labor and poverty. And in this they were not despised, but honored. In the world's history labor and poverty had never before been revered. It was a new standard. In the epitaphs Christian men and women are praised for being good workers. Men were beginning to regard more and more the character and worth of a man. It gave a new opportunity to the slave whose whole life had been simply poverty, labor and obedience. "The legal weakening of slavery," says Brace, "proceeded by various steps such as the forbidding the sale of new-born infants; the introducing new modes of emancipation by the Christian Church; the delay afforded in proof of liberty and the legal presumption in its favor; the privileges granted in reclaiming it; and many precautions taken to prevent slavery from being used for purposes of unchastity

---

1. Chrysostom, Hom. 15 in Ep. ad Eph.
2. Gregory M. Ep., V, 12.

and of crime." After 922 A.D. no Christian was permitted to enslave a fellow Christian.

*The Colonus*

The lavish gifts of charity on the part of the Church undoubtedly made paupers. But in the economic situation of the times this was a step in the march upward to freedom. It was a period of economic transformation. The Colonus, the laborer or hereditary tenant who paid rent in kind, or, as he was often called, the serf, was displacing the slave. In him, also, the Church took an interest, for he groaned beneath oppressive taxation and heavy usury. But the pauper was a superior to the Colonus as the Colonus was superior to the slave. The charity of the Church during many long years made easier this transition from slavery to freedom through serfdom.

*War Prisoners*

In keeping with the work of the Church, in the interests of slaves, was the noble sacrifice of many of its great leaders in the task of redeeming captives from the servitude which resulted from war. The Barbarian Invasions imposed this obligation upon the Church of Western Europe through a long series of devastating wars. Ambrose, Bishop of Milan, sold the rich Church ornaments to ransom captives who had fallen into the hands of the Goths. His example was emulated by a splendid line of generous Churchmen in this period, Bishop Deogratias of Carthage, St. Augustine, Gregory the Great, St. Caesarius, St. Hilary of Arles, and Paulinus of Nola. Acacius, Bishop of Amida, expressed the spirit of this social service, when he sold all the rich ornaments of his diocese, rescued seven thousand unbelieving Persian prisoners, and sent them back to their king. "God had no need of plates or dishes," he declared.[1]

*Social Significance of Monasticism*

Contemplative Christianity was the ideal of the period. And Monasteries grew up to illustrate the blessings and to further the opportunities of personal piety. The secular clergy performed the ceremonies of the Church, guarded its property, and won souls by the ordinances that had been evolved. But the monks, especially those who lived under the rule framed by Benedict of Nursia, while renouncing the world to "found a school for the Lord's service," nevertheless rendered the world of that distant day a notable service that was not contemplated when in 529 the first Benedictines planted their picturesque settlement on Monte Cassino. The rule of life was obedience and humility. The walls of the monastery became a refuge for the tempted, the studious, the persecuted, the disconsolate, the disgraced, as well as for the holy. Private ownership was not permitted—"He should have absolutely not anything; neither a book, nor tablets, nor a pen—nothing at all. For indeed it is not allowed to the monks to have their own bodies or wills in their own power." The monasteries did much to hold before the world

---

1. Uhlhorn, Christian Charity in the Ancient Church, 388 seq.

a better ideal than force[1] and to save the dignity of labor—"Idleness is the enemy of the soul. . . . They are truly monks if they live by the labors of their hands." "The monasteries," declares Uhlhorn, "were the birthplaces of free labor." Says Lecky: "The monastic bodies, that everywhere arose, formed secure asylums for the multitudes who have been persecuted by their enemies, constituted an invaluable counterpoise to the rude military forces of the time, familiarized the imagination of men with religious types that could hardly fail in some degree to soften the character, and led the way in most forms of peaceful labor. When men, filled with admiration at the reports of the sanctity and .the miracles of some illustrious saint, made pilgrimages to hold him, and found him attired in the rude garb of a peasant, with thick shoes, and with a scythe on his shoulder, superintending the labors of the farmers, or sitting in a small attic mending lamps, whatever other benefit they might derive from the interview, they could scarcely fail to return without an increased sense of the dignity of labor."[2]  In this matter of elevating the value and dignity of labor the monasteries were making the same contribution as the Church at large had been making since the days of its Founder. The *operarius* was held in esteem only in the Church. Only among Christians under the Roman Empire was work honored. It was made a reproach by the enemies of the Faith that Christ was born of a "working mother" (operariae matris). The Church undoubtedly gave a great impulse to free labor and went far towards alleviating the lot of slave labor. It won to lives of diligent industry and usefulness not a few members of Roman society who were its bane—"the parasite, the pimp, the circus rider, the gladiator, the debauched actor, the representative of indecent amusements, the servant of idols, the object of disgusting and unnatural pleasures, the low and obscene comedian and prostitute."

The monasteries served also as the inns of the time for travellers—"All guests who come shall be received as though they were Christ. When, therefore, a guest is announced, the Prior or the brothers shall run to meet him with every office of love. And first they shall pray together, and then a kiss of peace." Those who had special crafts were encouraged to practise them, "with humility." The Rule of St. Benedict says practically nothing of the pursuit of learning, and nothing at all of the missionary and civilizing activity of the monks. And yet herein lay not the least important contribution which Monasticism made in the way of social service.

It was the Monks who preserved the great part of the Latin‧ literature of antiquity, and both sacred and profane Manuscripts.[3] They cleared the forests, tilled the fields, rescued manual labor from

1. The Church neither condoned nor consecrated war. It needed the terrors of Mohammedanism to inspire the Crusades, and to commit the Church to a policy of war.
2. Lecky, History of European Morals, II, 102. One of the most potent causes of the impoverishment of the Empire is to be found in the prevailing contempt for labor. Uhlhorn, Christian Charity in the Ancient Church, 107. It is notable how little the Church Fathers themselves have to say about work. Clement found even hard labor with the spade to be an honor. Paedagogue, III, 10. Labor that ministered to heathen worship, the theatre, the circus, etc., was disapproved.
3. H. O. Taylor, The Classical Heritage of the Middle Ages, 45.

disrepute, dispensed charity,[1] taught children, entertained travellers, ransomed prisoners, tended the sick, protected the poor, overawed turbulent nobles, made roads, built bridges, converted many of the barbarous tribes, teaching them the civilization of Rome and the faith of the Catholic Church. They were the schools, hospitals, hotels, and libraries of the transition centuries. "The way in which Jerome, Ambrose, Gregory of Nursia, and Cassiodorus Senator," says Hall, "made the monastery a refuge for learning and linked religion with life and scholarship atones for much of the fundamentally unsocial character of the monastery ethical ideal."[2] And again, "It was not the least of the services that the monastery rendered to Europe that the monks worked with their hands and taught better methods of farming, gardening, fruit-growing as well as household management."[3] The monks were not infrequently a great bulwark for the Papacy. But above all they stood as the type and challenge of the holy life. The monk was regarded as the true and perfect Christian.[4] Social service was not the primary aim of Monasticism. It is none the less to its credit that while seeking to give an interpretation of Christianity in the way of personal life, it was surpassed by no other institution of the time in exhibiting Christianity as a ministry of social helpfulness.[5] In Western Monasticism work was ever combined with meditation. And that institution which grew up out of the abandonment of the endeavor to introduce Christian ideals and life into the world often succeeded most effectively in achieving the very aim it had abandoned.

*Evidence of Papyrus*

As fine a piece of social service as one can meet, and one that recalls St. Paul's letter to Philemon, comes from a papyrus of 346 A.D. written by the village priest of Hermupolis. Paul, a soldier of the garrison, has been entrusted by his commanding officer, Abinnaeus, with some commission. But he deserts. He knows that he is already posted as "Absent without leave." He soon tires of his freedom and wants to rejoin the garrison. How will he proceed? He knows that the Orderly Room is awaiting him. Then he comes to Caor, village Papas, and unburdens his soul. The good priest intercedes in the following letter:

> "To my master and beloved brother Abinneus the Praepositus—Caor, Papas of Hermupolis, greeting. I salute thy children much. I would have thee know, lord, concerning Paul the soldier, concerning his flight. Pardon him this once, seeing that I am without leisure to come unto thee at this present. And, if he desist not, he will come again into thy hands another time. Fare thee well, I pray, many years, my lord brother."[6]

In the year 314 A.D. the Council of Arles had prescribed for

1. The presence of the monastery tended to cause the almoner to disappear.
2. T. C. Hall, History of Ethics within Organized Christianity, 271.
3. T. C. Hall, History of Ethics within Organized Christianity, 329.
4. "The central conceptions of the monastic system are the meritoriousness of complete abstinence from all sexual intercourse and of a complete renunciation of the world." Lecky, History of European Morals, II, 43 *b*.
5. For rule of St. Benedict, see Henderson, Historical Documents of the Middle Ages, 274.
6. A. Deissmann, Light from the Ancient East, 205.

the Church the discipline that was to be meted out to deserters—
"That those who throw down their arms in time of peace shall be
excommunicated." But Caor, village priest of Hermupolis, in the
south west of the Fayam, knows more of social service than of
ecclesiastical, or for that matter, of military discipline. But we
shall not think too hardly of Caor for that.

### Evidence of Ostraca

The Church was on the side of social justice. A Coptic
ostracon of about 600 A.D. from Bishop Abraham of Hermouthis in
Egypt gives an episcopal letter of excommunication addressed to his
clergy against a certain Psate who had been guilty of oppressing the
poor. This was in keeping with the best traditions of the period,
with the eloquent discourses of the magnificent Chrysostom, or with
the splendid conduct of Ambrose towards Theodosius after the "Bath
of Blood" at Thessalonica.

### Financial Transactions

The private and official letters of the Christians of the period
show that they were expected to help each other in financial matters.[1]
Their Churches served as banks and loaned money to deserving
members.[2] There survive business letters from business men, one of
these involving a transaction of 51,000 talents written by Zacharias
and Silvanus, "head men" of the village of Demetrios near Hermo-
polis, to Tyrannos "deacon of the Church there."[3] Among those that
have survived on Egyptian ostraka are many begging letters
addressed to the Church and its ministers. The common requests are
for such articles as vinegar, flax, oil, rope, clothing, vegetables, and
especially bread and corn. Some ask for books to read; in one case
a medical book is specified. One Christian has cause to complain
that his minister has not visited him. One letter says in part:[4]

> "Never have I suffered trouble greater than this present.
> Do not fail to come to me in the trouble that I and my children
> are in . . . If thou hast compassion on me, thou wilt have
> redeemed six souls from death. No man gives me wherewith
> to cover me. . . Thy heart will grieve for me if I die with
> children. . . If I can find two loaves a day I shall not die;
> if I find one I shall not die. I have little ones and they . . .
> weeping to me and break my heart."

### Hospitality, Charity, etc.

The monuments[5] and letters of members of the Church show
that the Christians were not deficient in hospitality, the care of

1. The Christian Church of the time regarded the taking of interest as a sin. Since
the State allowed interest, the Church prohibited it entirely only in the case of ecclesiastics.
For Church members, also, it was a moral duty to lend without interest. It was a work
of piety to deliver debtors from the hand of usurers. Uhlhorn, Christian Charity in the
Ancient Church, 384.
2. Amherst Payri, II, p. 28-30.
3. Cobern, the New Archeological Discoveries, 323.
4. Ibid., 331.
5. In numerous epitaphs of the time we find love to the poor, benevolence, abundant
almsgiving commemorated. Uhlhorn, Christian Charity in the Ancient Church, in 321.
"Lover of the poor" is a common designation. In an inscription on Bishop Namatius of
Vienna, 522, we read, "The poor went away from him happy, the naked left him clothed
the prisoner rejoiced that he was ransomed."

widows, orphans, strangers and poor. They show, too, that the reward of eternal salvation was ever kept in view. Orphanages were established and men of means used their funds for the liberation of slaves and the care of prisoners.[1] The sermons of the period are uniformly orthodox, and heavily larded with scriptural quotation, but a familiar theme is "charity," and Gregory closes one of his most eloquent discourses with an insistent exhortation to benevolence.

### The Leadership of Rome

We have already observed that the Church at Rome gained a splendid reputation for hospitality, for affording relief to suffering and distress, for acts of charity and social service. It never faltered in its orthodoxy at a time when every variety of heretical teaching assailed the East. It became a natural arbiter of disputed points of faith, and its will was decisive to determine doctrinal standards at Chalcedon. There is no indisputable evidence that it was outstandingly active in the direct work of Christian missions, but its other services were so notable, and its natural position at the Capital so pre-eminent that its supremacy was but a matter of time. The Petrine tradition may have been without foundation in fact, but it gained credence, and the mere belief made its Bishop a power in Christendom. Its leadership in benevolence, a succession of capable bishops like Innocent, Leo, and Gregory, the political situation which led to the eclipse of the civil governor in the West and made "lordship" equivalent to "rule of a city," the reputation that came to the Roman Bishop through the retreat of Attila, the freedom from local rivalries such as plagued Constantinople, Alexandria, Ephesus, Corinth and Antioch in the East, the circumstance that from the fifth Century the growth of Christianity was almost exclusively in the West, the fact that the West did not foster a patriarchal constitution, and above all the unequivocal attitude to their own claims of the successors of Peter—all conspired to give to the Bishops of Rome both moral and doctrinal superiority and governmental supremacy. The rise of the Papacy at a period when all the world rocked and reeled through the cataclysms of the times was a steadying force and an assuring fact that was in itself, at the time, a social service of the greatest magnitude, and was to prove, in the subsequent development of the Church, an element the importance of which not even a Leo or a Gregory could have forecast. The significance of the supremacy of the Bishop of Rome was tremendously enhanced by the fact that, although the final formal rupture was postponed, yet virtually from the close of the fifth century Christendom ceased to be one Church.

### The New Peoples

If the Church of Rome was not pre-eminently missionary before the time of the Invasions, still, thereafter, it was not behind others in its zeal for the souls of the Barbarians. In fact, the foundation of the Tribal and National Churches of the West during these centuries was, perhaps, the greatest social service that was rendered. To the

---

1. Cobern, The New Archaeological Discoveries, 427.

success of this great evangelizing effort, both the Papacy and Monasticism made magnificent contributions. In teaching the tribes, the Church christianized them, and in christianizing, subdued. It is no part of our task to give a detailed account of the spread of the Gospel in the West, but much of the subsequent social service of the world rests on that very basis. Celtic Christianity and the work of Columba with his colonizing monks, the conversion of Clovis to the Catholic faith, and the significance of that both to the Franks and to the march of events in Europe, the contribution of Gregory the Great and Augustine in the conversion of the Anglo-Saxons, the missionary enterprise of Columbanus and Boniface in Gaul and Germany—all these, although their influence was impaired through being mass movements and the conversion of tribes *en bloc,* nevertheless meant the gift of civilization and the spread of Christianity, and constituted a social service as brilliant as the lives of some of the great missioners, like Alban and St. Patrick, were heroic and self-sacrificing.

*Law-giving and National Organization*

But profoundly important as were the spiritual results of the evangelizing movement it must not be forgotten that the directly social consequences were no less noteworthy. One point alone will suffice to make this clear. In the break-up of the Western Empire order itself was menaced, and chaos threatened to envelop Europe. On the soil of Italy itself Authari, Rothari and Liutprand did evolve a Lombard Code, but elsewhere local tribal customs seemed the only bulwark between the peoples of the West and complete disorder. Here the Church had a noble function to fulfil, and fulfilled it nobly. This was over and above the service it rendered through its control of feudalism. It laid the foundations of an ecclesiastical order with parish and diocese and an organized Church. It kept alive the thought of order, justice, rule and responsibility, and, at a time when, on all sides, men were appealing to brute force, it insisted on reverence and respect for things divine. Men saw episcopal government and church order, and little guessed that Roman law was still speaking justice to the nations through the Church that had displaced the Empire.[1] No more marvellous illustration of the contribution which the Church made to national organization and government can be cited than the case of England. There Theodore of Tarsus, Archbishop of Canterbury, achieved a political work of unification in his organization of Canterbury with national synods and ecclesiastical canons. His synods were the precursor of the Witenagemot. For the Church was the one unifying force of the time.

*Culture*

The Church stood both for righteousness and for education, at any rate for that education which was necessary to equip the youth of the land for the clerical office. It felt itself to be responsible for

---

1. After the establishment of the Germanic Kingdoms, the clergy continued to be under Roman law as their personal law, in France using the Brevariumi, and in Italy portions of the legislation of Justinian. This law of the person for the clergy became the Canon Law. See H. O. Taylor, The Classical Heritage of the Middle Ages, 61.

the moral guidance and intellectual training of its members. Not infrequently the parish priests were only too ill-equipped to furnish either spiritual assistance or educational training. Ready-made penitentials were devised to assist them in dealing with the moral offenders among their flock. Two of these, of a somewhat crude and elementary character, are attributed to Theodore of Tarsus and the Venerable Bede.[1]

*Education*

In the same way the Church fostered the growth of schools, and, later, the development of a folk-literature. Secular schools disappeared during the sixth century. In their place the Church put monastic schools. The Council of Vaison was held in the Province of Arles in A.D. 529. It issued instructions "that presbyters in their parishes shall bring up and instruct young readers in their homes."[2] The second Council of Toledo at a still earlier date had laid down measures for those who were dedicated by their parents to the clerical office: "As soon as they have been tonsured or have been given to the care of appointed persons, they ought to be educated by some one set over them, in the church building, or in the presence of the Bishop."[3] The Synod of Orleans, 799, thus exhorted: "Let the priests in villages and towns hold schools, in order that all the children entrusted to them can receive the first notion of letters. Let them take no money for their lessons." We know that the cultural movement was particularly strong in the North. The Church sent masters and teachers from Kent to assist King Sigebert of the East Angles (631-7) in the school which he set up for the young.

Bede says of Theodore and his friend Hadrian:

"And forasmuch as both of them were, as has been said, well read in sacred and secular literature, they gathered·a crowd of scholars and there daily flowed from them rivers of knowledge to water the hearts of their hearers; and together with the books of the holy Scriptures they also taught them the arts of ecclesiastical poetry, astronomy, and arithmetic. A testimony of which is that there are still living at this day some of their scholars who are as well versed in the Greek and Latin tongues as in their own, in which they were born. Never were there happier times since the English came to Britain; for their kings were brave men and good Christians and were a terror to all barbarous nations, and the minds of all men were bent upon the joys of the heavenly kingdom of which they had just heard. And all who desired instruction in sacred reading had masters at hand to teach them. From that time also they began in all the churches of the English to learn sacred music which till then had only been known in Kent."[4]

Ireland became the University of Europe in the seventh century. From the British Isles the literary movement spread to

1. Ayer, A Source Book for Ancient Church History, 627-30.
2. Ayer, A Source Book for Ancient Church History, 648.
3. Ayer, A Source Book for Ancient Church History, 649.
4. Bede, Hist. Ec., IV, 2.

the Continent and yielded the Carolingian Renaissance. This vitalizing stream of influence was the gift of the Church. For not a few of the Northern Peoples the translation of the Bible was the beginning of a national literature. Notable examples of a similar impulse are to be found in the Anglo-Saxon poem, the *"Genesis,"* the *"Heliand"* by an anonymous Saxon poet, and Otfried of Strassburg's *"Christ."*[1] Indeed the whole work of the Church was educative to the New Peoples, whether directly in the school or indirectly through hospitals, cloisters, chapels or cathedrals. "Love in the hospital, work in the cloister—these were the educational powers," says Uhlhorn.[2] And with these, among the races of the North, the Church brought into being a new civilization, which it was to dominate for a full thousand years, and to which it was to transfer its conceptions of charity, its social service institutions, with fresh emphasis upon the thought of merit, and an unhealthy development towards the ecclesiastical and institutional. Men gave no longer with the purpose of helping, but to store up merit to obtain release from purgatory. As a consequence poverty was not uprooted but fostered. Neither lavish donations nor ample foundations nor endowed institutions could overcome the prevailing distress nor supply the personal touch of service which had obtained when charity was wholly congregational.

*Position of Woman*

Wherever the Christian influence extended it increased the respect for woman and made her place in the family more secure. By the seventh century wills bequeathing property among the German tribes began to show the influence of the Christian missions. A further result was some near approach to partnership in property between husband and wife and something like equality of rights. There is little doubt that the growing veneration for Mary intensified respect for woman. The idea of purchase in marriage disappeared and woman was protected by the encouragement of the custom of dower. We shall see that the Capitularies of Charlemagne are strong for the indissolubility of marriage.

No preceding Age was so notable as this for great mothers, nor so conspicuous for social achievement on the part of women. "Heavens! What women these Christians have!" broke forth Libanius, hearing the story of the pure and noble life of Anthusa, mother of John Chrysostom. And the gentle African mother of St. Augustine, Monica, will ever remain enshrined in the affection of the Christian Church for that she loved much. Her cry to her greater son was—"That I might see thee a Catholic Christian before I die!"

## (c) THE CHARACTER OF SOCIAL ACHIEVEMENTS

*World-Conquest and World-Flight*

During the previous period social service had been rendered in the world by a Church persecuted by the world. The Church had now secured its definite place in the world. It could perform its social

1. von Dobschutz, The Influence of the Bible on Civilization, 65.
2. Uhlhorn, Christian Charity in the Ancient Church, 395.

service, not only with its own inherent resources, but also with the material wealth of the State. At once two opposite impulses began to manifest themselves. One of these we may designate the impulse of world-conquest. This showed itself in the organizing of a powerful, closely integrated, hierarchical Church, and in a mission of aggressive evangelism for carrying the Gospel to the Heathen. The other impulse we may designate world-flight. This showed itself in the retiring of the ascetic from the world of men and affairs. All the social service of the period revolved between these two poles, world-conquest and world-flight. The Church passed from the struggle against Arianism to a practical struggle between asceticism and the great social needs of humanity.

*Unity of the Church*

Christianity was no longer a simple fellowship. It was membership in a great organization that was dominated by, and came to dominate, the State itself. Emperors sought to impose unity, and Theodosius legislated uniformity of belief. But it was ethical teaching and social service that were really promoting the oneness of the Church. It was Ambrose teaching in the Basilica of Milan, or Augustine preaching to the rude fishermen of Hippo Regius, or Chrysostom laboring, now in Antioch, then in Constantinople, and finally in the bitterness of an excruciating exile, if by any means he might make the Church pure and unspotted—these and not Constantine and Theodosius, who made the Christian Church a factor in these centuries. These great preachers made their pulpits for the first time in the world's history tremendous agents for righteousness. The preacher was striving to arouse to social service.

*Service Better Than Theory*

Social service was in practice a compromise between the Imperial Church and the monastic brotherhood. The Church accepted many of the views of the cloister. The monastery labored in the interests of Church extension. The monasteries threw themselves into the work of missions, and missions saved the monasteries. This was a social function that Benedict never contemplated, but that was, nevertheless, their salvation. Monks fled from the world, only to make the monasteries new centres of charity and service in the world. They spread the Gospel of the Nazarene, saved learning, emphasized the dignity of labor, and made religion a matter of living for every day of the year. But even then, religion with the monks never put service in the first place. Their ideal was contemplation. In actual practice the aim of their propaganda was not for larger views of service, not for the correct view of the Incarnate One, so much as for the correct date of Easter, and the proper tonsure. It was ritual rather than orthodoxy that mattered. So at least they thought. But they served better than they thought. And not the least of their services was that through them the Christian Church handed on the torch from Rome to the North.

*For Merit*

Social service became less a matter of spiritual enthusiasm than of conscious seeking of merit or the deliberate policy of an organized Church. Owing to the care of the poor in institutions, the deacons who previously had visited the needy in their homes, tended to fall into the background. The view of oblations as a thank-offering receded;[1] the offering of alms became meritorious. Gifts were not prompted solely by love for the poor, but to obtain the intercession of a martyr for the giver or his dead friend. Benevolence was inculcated not so much with a view to the social service rendered to the helped as for the purpose of emancipating the helper from the clogging influence of the earthly. Many found private property to be a sin, an unrighteous Mammon, by which it was good for their soul's welfare to make friends. Only a Vigilantius here and there had a sober appreciation of earthly goods and possessions. This view the Jeromes of the day never failed to attack.

*Institutionalized Service*

Social service lost much of its personal character. It became a department of the work of the Church, under the direct supervision of the Bishop.[2] His increased responsibilities and jurisdiction prevented personal attention. Social service became institutionalized, with buildings nad equipment and special workers.[3] And alms-giving became a "good work," like fasting and prayer. Uhlhorn[4] quotes a story told by Palladius concerning two brothers, both rich, who resolved to lead an ascetic life. These two brothers illustrate the two distinct tendencies of ascetic social service in this period. The one gave all his money at once to the poor, the churches, and monasteries, learned a trade and lived as a monk. The other built a monastery with his money. In this with his companions he received the poor, attended to the sick, provided for the aged and fed the poor. The monks were contending together as to which had done better when St. Pamleo decided: "They are both equal, for the one has fulfilled the saying of our Lord: 'Sell all that thou hast, and give to the poor'; the other is like the Lord, who says: 'I came not to be ministered unto, but to minister.'" The ascetic and institutional tendencies of the time are herein clearly represented.

*No Scientific Study*

In the previous period we saw that the Church made no scientific study of the causes of poverty, nor did it deal with them. It was no age of "surveys." There was simply the spirit of brotherly love alive in the Congregation. But the political situation and the new tasks had driven the Church to take action as a Church through

1. Even their destination changed about 500. Formerly designed for the poor, they now became a perquisite of the clergy.
2. Const. Apost., II, 26, 31.
3. For the relation of deacons to this work see Const. Apost., II, 44 and Uhlhorn, Christian Charity in the Ancient Church, 161-4, 177: "The services of deacons and deaconesses furnished him (the Bishop) on the one hand with information of all the distress existing in the Church, and on the other gave him the means of affording to every one who was sick or poor, just the assistance his circumstances required."
4. Christian Charity in the Ancient Church, 336-7.

the Bishop. It was official, community service that the Church was rendering. The Church acted for the community. Property left in wills to the poor went to the Church as their legal representative.

Again, in this period, the Church had no theory about poverty, beyond the immediate opportunity to help, and the merit that was being stored up beyond the grave. The introduction of the thought of merit operated to detach service from "charity" in the sense of love, and even from the aim of social good. The Church could scarcely stigmatize involuntary poverty as an evil or even a misfortune when in monasticism it proclaimed voluntary poverty a blessing, and when it deemed even involuntary poverty an opportunity for alms-giving. The social thinking of the Church lagged behind its social service. The great Preachers and Churchmen exhorted to, rather than counselled about, charity. The plan of the Church was a plan of relief, not a plan of prevention, although for the first time laws against mendicancy began to appear.[1]  The Church had no programme of social progress or social amelioration for it accepted it as no less the plan of Providence than the lot of humanity to have the poor with it always. The Church was not lacking in sympathy with the unfortunate. It had not conceived of a policy of social reform. The Church did not possess the instincts of the scientific spirit. It is highly characteristic of the times that it should build hospitals, but fail to develop the science of medicine. In the beginning of this period the Church had only emerged from the status of a persecuted church. Its great social achievement is that during this transition time it had well-nigh captured for itself the leadership of aggressive social endeavor in the civilized world.

QUESTIONS FOR DISCUSSION

1. What social services did the adoption of Christianity as the State religion enable the Church to render?

2. What social services did the Barbarian Invasions enable the Church to render?

3. Did the seven General Councils which fixed the fundamental dogmas of the Church render a social service by settling the orthodox faith, or did they cramp the development of free thought?

4. This period sees the rise of the Roman Papacy. Estimate the social service rendered by the Church in its establishment.

5. Was the Church better suited and equipped for social service when enjoying the favor of the Emperor as in this period or when suffering persecution as in the former period?

6. "The Church of the West fought for images and emblems because the autocrats of the East sought in their abolition to impose a spiritual tyranny on the Church." Was this Christian social service?

7. (a) Make a list of the various social services rendered by the Church during this period.

(b) Is the Church as free to-day as in the period studied in this chapter to meet in General Council to frame a dogma to be adopted by believers for all time to come under pain of anathema? If not, why?

8. In promoting celibacy and asceticism the Church tended to decrease the dignity of the marriage bond. Was this a social service? What attitude does the modern Church take in this matter?

1. Cod. Just. lib., II, 25.

9. For the first time we see indiscriminate charity united with something like ample means. What is the danger from this?

10. Does such organization as introduced by Gregory the Great tend to rob Charity of the personal touch? If so, is this an advantage?

11. Is there the same need for monasticism to-day as in the period under review? What services did monasticism render?

12. "It is highly characteristic of the times that they should build hospitals, but fail to develop the science of medicine." What is meant?

13. The replacing of papyrus rolls by the parchment book, or codex, is due to the need which the Christian Church felt for a more convenient form of circulation. Thus mankind was given the shape of its books. Is this a social service rendered to civilization by the Christian Church?

### BOOKS FOR ADVANCED STUDY

C. L. Brace, *Gesti Christi, a History of Humane Progress under Christianity.* J. C. Ayer, *A Source Book for Ancient Church History.* H. O. Taylor, *The Classical Heritage of the Middle Ages.* W. E. H. Lecky, *History of European Morals from Augustus to Charlemagne.* Moeller, *History of the Christian Church.* Milman, *History of Latin Christianity.* E. F. Henderson, *Historical Documents of the Middle Ages.* MacClear, *History of Christian Missions in the Middle Ages.* D. S. Margoliouth, *Mohammed and the Rise of Islam.* A. Harnack, *History of Dogma.* S. Dill, *Roman Society in the last Century of the Western Empire.* T. R. Glover, *Life and Letters in 4th Century.* Hodgkin, *Italy and her Invaders.* Bury, *History of the Later Roman Empire.* Francis Herbert Stead, *The Story of Social Christianity.*

CHAPTER V

# IN THE MIDDLE AGES

(a) THE CHURCH IN THE MIDDLE AGES

The Struggle of Forces. Charlemagne and the Carolingian
Renaissance. Disintegration. Mediaeval Life and Institutions. Cluny
and Hildebrand. Empire versus Papacy. The Crusades. The Church
Supreme. The New Spirit. Religion in Common Life. Religion in the
World. The New Light. Mysticism.

(b) SOCIAL ACHIEVEMENTS IN THE MIDDLE AGES

Instruction. Types of Service Rendered. Teaching of the Middle
Ages. Feudalism. Position of Woman. Poor Relief. Failure of
Monasticism. Hospitals. Service of the Gilds. What had the Church
Achieved? The Coming of the Friars. Practical Christian Effort. St.
Francis of Assisi. Social Service of the Friars. The Crusades.
Political Results. Economic and Social Results. Influence on the
Papacy. Mediaeval Culture, Life and Manners. Art. Architecture.
Literary and Scientific Movement. The University: Scholasticism.
Influence on Law. Jurisprudence. Travelling. The Gilds. Economic
Thought. The Church the Chief Instrument of Social Service. Improve-
ment of Morals. The Church a Dispenser of Magic and a Civilizing
Agency.

(c) THE CHARACTER OF THE ACHIEVEMENT

Religious Obligation of Self-denial and Service. Alms-giving
Indiscriminate. Ashley's Statement. Influence of Feudal Ideal. Canon
Law. St. Bernard. St. Francis. St. Thomas. Interpreters.

## (a) THE CHURCH IN THE MIDDLE AGES, TO THE FIFTEENTH CENTURY

*The Struggle of Forces*

The Middle Ages is not a time of stagnation between two
periods of active growth. Superficial observers have regarded this
period as a morass athwart the highroad of human progress. It is
rather like unto the smoother waters between the Falls of Niagara
and the Whirlpool. Beneath the surface are the struggle and strife
of many forces, each contending for the mastery—the vital force of
new Peoples, the cultural and civilizing power and forms of the old
—Mediterranean World, and the Christian Faith, which, having been
handed on from the South to the North, retained in a Teuton world
no little of its Roman mould and character and control. This Faith
could never feel completely at home in the northern latitudes until it
found more adequate expression according to the native and more
congenial spirit of German individualism.

78

## Charlemagne and the Carolingian Renaissance

The period is inaugurated by the colossal enterprises of Charlemagne. That great constructive genius sought to bring all the German people into one great Christian Empire. To that end he waged war with Saxon, Bavarian, Avar, Lombard. To that end he revised the national code in more Christian sense[1] and infused a new vigor into the internal administration of the North. Through him the Christian Church influenced the civil legislation of the Middle Ages. He laid a firmer basis for the connection of Church and State. He set bounds to the insubordination of monasteries and regulated the secular clergy. He made the payment of tithes compulsory in Western Europe and the support of clergy a legal obligation. He enjoined hospitality to strangers and travellers, and ordered his judges to give equal justice to all. The significance of Charlemagne is that he gathered up all the best, which was none too much, that still survived of the old Mediterranean civilization and refined and purified and invigorated it with the spirit and power of Christianity and the native force of the new Europeans. He then turned it as a mighty weapon against the menace of Islam in Spain, and the still untamed barbarity of Teutonism that pressed onward from the East. Mankind received from the Carolingian Renaissance the impulse that was to carry it forward far into the Middle Ages. There was a revival of theological science that caught up a strand of Augustinian theology in a discussion of Predestination. But in practice the Mass was the pivotal factor in the life of the Christian Church. And the Church with its mysteries was becoming more and more the centre of all life, just as the Church edifice itself on the market place or the village square became the visible local centre of every petty parish or little community.[2]

## Disintegration

The Frankish Kingdom reached its highest pitch under Charlemagne. In the century that followed there was a sharp decline. The disruption of the Empire yielded on the one hand the beginnings of the political outlines of Western Europe, on the other hand those feudal relations that colored and controlled the Middle Ages. The disruption was due to the incapacity of rulers, the decay of roads, the scarcity of money, the exhaustion of the Empire attributable to war. But it was none the less an expression of native Teuton individualism, the characteristic centrifugal tendency of the Northern Tribes. The disintegration was hastened by the new invasions of Danes and other Northmen, Slavs, Magyars, Saracens from abroad, and, at home, by the growing power and independence of great landed proprietors.

1. Some of his Capitularies are manifestly patterned after the Bible, e.g., that of A.D. 789. See C. L. Brace, Gesta Christi, Ch. XIII, Charlemagne's Capitularies. These laws of Charlemagne, like the Anglo-Saxon, breathe the Christian spirit more evidently than the codes of other German or Celtic tribes. The freeing of bondmen, and laws against cruelty and impurity are accompanied by religious reasons. King Alfred introduces his code with the X Commandments and with other laws from the Bible. The German Collections, Schwabenspiegel, Sachsenspiegel, have prefaces which represent the national law as an emanation of the law of God as contained in the O.T. and N.T.

2. von Dobschütz, The Influence of the Bible on Civilization, p. 71, says: "Mediaeval civilization had various foundations, but the Bible was one of them, and the most important one. That is what we find wherever we try to analyse mediaeval culture."

*Mediaeval Life and Institutions*

The Middle Ages had a meaningful and throbbing life of its own. On the economic side there is the appearance of bankers, grocers, fairs, craft gilds, gild merchants, and the Hanseatic League. In political life we see the rise of the commune, the bestowal of town charters and customs, the growth of the national state, of the Parliament in England, of the Republics in Northern Italy, of the Estates General in France. Intellectual activity was fostered by monastic and cathedral schools, and, in turn, gave birth to the movement that yielded the Universities. In social and legal relations, and coloring all other phases of life, is Feudalism, the most influential of mediaeval institutions and ideas. This institution the Church dominated. But, in the end, the Church was compelled to struggle against Feudalism in its own organized life. At length the Church became centralized, and the hierarchy supreme. But the spirit of social service was not allowed to die. It found expression in a striking development of the monastic and mendicant orders.

*Cluny and Hildebrand*

The tenth Century witnessed the most abysmal degradation into which the Papacy ever sank. But in that very period there arose from the Abbey of Cluny a reform of discipline and of monastic life that fought against the feudalization of the Church. Centralization went hand in hand with change of morals. From Cluny came the Reformation under Hildebrand. That aggressive spirit did battle with simony, enforced celibacy on the clergy, and engaged in the Investiture Contest. Hildebrand strengthened the Church so that it was able to support the struggle with the Empire for more than two centuries.

*Empire vs. Papacy; the Crusades*

It was highly unfortunate that the struggle for supremacy between the secular and spiritual embodiment of Christendom, which Western Europe was called upon to support during the zenith of the Papacy, from Gregory VII to Innocent III, and from Innocent III to Boniface VIII, should have coincided with an equally intense and a no less protracted contest between Christendom and Islam. There was great waste of life and of power in both directions. And the Crusades were only one phase of the struggle with Infidelity. War, Tribunals, Councils, all were employed against the unbeliever by the militant Papacy which regarded itself as sole Trustee both of a World-Religion and a World-Monarchy.

*The Church Supreme*

All the battles of Christendom, whether against the Christian Emperor or the Infidel, were waged to establish the supremacy of the spiritual, over the civil power, or the superiority of Christianity over Islam, not by any kind of moral suasion or by an appeal to reason but by the cogent arguments of force, by the arbitrament of the sword. Canossa and the Crusades and the battles of Hunyadi Janos had this in common that they exhibited little of the spiritual superiority of

Christianity and its leaders. The Church must at all costs be supreme It was to be an all-comprehensive, permanent, sovereign power according to the Bull *Unam Sanctam* issued by Boniface VIII in 1302. It was altogether necessary for salvation for every human being to be subject to the Roman Pontiff. All Western Europe was a single religious association. The Church was in reality a State with highly developed organization of officials, laws, courts, prisons, taxes. An imposing hierarchy, the daily and stupendous miracle of the mass, an elaborate sacramental system that reached ("indirectly," says Thomas Aquinas) to Purgatory, made the Church the indispensable instrument of salvation. The magnificent contribution made to humanity in a day when the Church, in spite of a clergy too frequently corrupt and too seldom cultured, in spite of simony, absenteeism, pluralities, neglect of preaching, sale of sacraments and moral disorders, alone of all the institutions of the land sought for the moral uplift of mankind, restrained violence, maintained culture and ministered solace to the sinful and the poor—this left the Church by far the most powerful factor in the common life of Western Europe.

### The New Spirit

Just as the Church became victorious in its struggle with the temporal power a new enemy arose, but this time from within. This was the awakened consciousness of men. The Church had kept aflame the torch of truth, but the sons of the new light turned its rays upon the Church itself and became unsparing critics. Men began anew to question. Abelard's *Sic et Non* advocated a frequent and persistent questioning as the master-key of knowledge. There were those who hesitated not to assail the sacred art of the teaching of the Fathers. It was easy to brand investigation as irreverence but the spirit of enquiry, once aroused, would not down. The Church only too often thrust the searcher after truth forth from its portals, thinking thus to do God service. It was, perhaps, too much to expect that it should do otherwise. For these eager souls doubted its ceremonies, its masses, its holy water, its relics, all that it held most dear and found most useful. They even questioned whether the Church was indeed, as it claimed, the very institute and instrument of salvation. So arose the heresies, largely anti-sacerdotal and revolutionary. The ascetic Cathares preached morality and renunciation and opposed alike the corruption of the clergy and the rites of the Church. Others strove to emphasize a more positive evangelical ideal. Pierre de Bruys, Henry of Lausanne, Tanchelm, Arnold of Brescia, Eon de l'Etoile all were agitators that greatly alarmed and disturbed the Church and anticipated the attacks of Wycliffe, Huss and Luther. For there was not merely an increasing disposition to enquire and to question, and a growing knowledge of the world. The growing knowledge of the Bible itself inspired many of these anti-ecclesiastical movements.[1]

1. von Dobschütz, The Influence of the Bible on Civilization, Ch. V.

*Religion in Common Life*

There was a considerable element of simple devotion and popular religion, the teaching of the Creed, the Lord's Prayer, the Ten Commandments. A Folk's Mass Book explained the meaning of the service and the ritual. There were Primers for the private devotion of the laity. And the Preaching Orders brought home to the people the ideals of common and helpful service. But it was perhaps not in the sphere of individual lives that the Christian Church made itself most felt, but in the common life, in the realm of mediaeval culture, life and manners. This we shall examine later in our estimate of the social service rendered by the mediaeval Church.

*Religion in the World*

The Middle Ages aimed at universality. This is seen alike in the aspirations of the Emperor and the pretensions of the Pope. Religion must be a world religion, not in a sense of world missions but world rule. This is the secret of the Church's despotism in the Middle Ages. In the field of thought the passion for universality meant the attempt to harmonize accepted beliefs, the dominance of the Schoolmen, and, till Humanism revealed to men what treasures still lay unmined in classical literature, Aristotle remained undisputed master of those who know. In fact the Stagirite was added to the number of the Saints. Scholasticism kept the human spirit in bondage to theology and logic. Nevertheless the Waldenses and Albigenses indicated that neither evangelism nor heresy were out of the range of possibility. The Mendicants, both Franciscans and Dominicans, and above all St. Francis himself, as Brother Leo depicts him in the *Mirror of Perfection*, are evidence that poverty and charity could still gain for themselves devotees. The religious life of Europe did not go by default. The dominant art of the Middle Ages, Architecture, expressed the yearnings of a heart in touch with the heavenly. Even war was Christianized in Chivalry. For the Knight must be a Christian, obey and defend the Church, respect all forms of weakness, and fight the heathen ceaselessly.

*The New Light*

"During the Middle Ages," says Symonds, "man had lived enveloped in a cowl. He had not seen the beauty of the world, or had seen it only to cross himself and turn aside, to tell his beads and pray. Like St. Bernard travelling along the shores of Lake Leman and noticing neither the azure of the waters nor the luxuriance of the vines, nor the radiance of the mountains with their robe of sun and snow, but bending a thought-burdened forehead over the neck of his mule; even like this monk, humanity had passed, a careful pilgrim, intent on the terrors of sin, death and judgment, along the highways of the world, and had scarcely noticed that they were sightworthy, or that life is a blessing. Beauty is a snare, pleasure a sin, the world a fleeting show, men fallen and lost, death the only certainty; ignorance is acceptable to God as a proof of faith and submission; abstinence and mortification are the only safe rules of life; these were the fixed ideas of the ascetic mediaeval Church." In that time good men lived ecclesiastically, wise men thought theologically, and bad men sinned heretically. But through Peter Abelard had come the radiance of the thirteenth century and the rise of the Universities. To this must be added the growth of the Third Estate, the writing of books in the vernacular, the loss by the clergy of their monopoly of learning, the study of law—in a word, the exaltation of the laity and the emergence of the sense of popular freedom. The Renaissance and the Reformation came as great emancipating experiences for the mind and souls of men.

### Mysticism

In this environment the dominant element in the history of piety was mysticism. The theological interest of the Church was to be found in Scholasticism, the fusion of the New Testament and the Fathers with the logic of Aristotle. But mysticism was the interpretation of Christianity in the way of life. The "vita beata" was the life of contemplation. It was only the mystic of the type of St. Francis of Assisi who met the claims of the community and made a social contribution. But the life of a mystic is not a thing to be communicated. The transport is his own. In the nature of the case little emphasis could be placed on external works, on fastings, vigils, social service. It was only the mystic like Master Henry Eckhart who saw that there must be not contemplation without working—"If a man were in ecstasy like St. Paul and knew of a poor man who had need of a little pottage, it were better that he should leave his ecstasy and minister to the needy." Mysticism was significant for the Mystics themselves, and for the whole future of the Church. These men were the pure in heart—they saw God. In emphasizing the accessibility to God, the immediacy of approach, they prepared the way for the Protestant Revolt. The work of Doctor Staupitz in the conversion of Martin Luther was powerfully reinforced by the Mystics, John Tauler, and the author of *German Theology.*"

## (b) SOCIAL ACHIEVEMENTS IN THE MIDDLE AGES

### Instruction

The greatest social service rendered by the Church in the Middle Ages was the instruction of the Northern Peoples in the lessons of social order and the principles of the Catholic Faith. The Church kept the Tribes under tutelage for nearly a millennium till they were welded into Nations. It inspired the Franks to withstand the inroads of Islam in the West and the Magyars those in the East and aroused the Faithful of many lands to carry war against the Crescent into the regions of the Holy Land. In every parish stood the Church, the centre of community life, the instrument of salvation, moulding and influencing every phase of thought and action. Nor was the Church content to confine its activities to merely local arenas. It contended for the highest place and the most dominant position. But it was not at Canossa, the scene of its most spectacular triumph, that we can behold the greatness of the social ministry of the mediaeval

Church. Rather we must turn to that multiple service rendered often in quiet places and with very humble persons.

*Types of Service Rendered*

The Church continued to attach a sacred significance to marriage and to purify family life by insisting on its stability. It protected and exalted woman in her own station and in her property rights. It protected the stranger, the "far-comer," the shipwrecked, and the homeless. Into all mediaeval codes it infused religious sanctions and moral regulations. It developed chivalry and its respect for woman, its greater humanity in war, and its new ideals of courtesy. In an era of constant war the Church made its influence felt in the interests of control. It curbed the barbaric passion for blood-revenge. It put legal satisfactions in the place of feuds. It preached the "Peace of God" and introduced arbitrations into disputes. It opposed the wager of battle and ordeal as means to secure evidence. It resisted the system of torture, at least until it itself incorporated this practice in the Inquisition.[1] It gave an impulse to education, founding schools, encouraging study, copying the classics. It secured the gradual diminution, or cessation, of serfdom and slavery, through acts of emancipation, through inculcating a more humane attitude, and through its influence on legislation. It fostered countless institutions of human compassion and charity.

The Church both operated through, and fought against, Feudalism. It carried on its gracious work of poor relief although it found fresh rivals in the field of philanthropy. It encouraged alms-giving by added emphasis on the merit that was thereby gained. It pervaded the Craft and Trade Gilds that were the symbol of the new municipal life. It gave the world a new type of social worker in the Friar, a new pattern for outdoor ministry in St. Francis, and a new model of Kingship in St. Louis. It sought to give an ethical impulse to economic thought and to color all mediaeval culture, life and manners. It produced an art that was religious and an architecture that aimed to express the divine. It brought Aristotle into the company of "those who know," giving him a sanction well-nigh apostolic.

In addition to these weighty contributions to human welfare the Church performed, in spite of many clerical abuses and many defects of life and narrowness of thought, that great spiritual mission that has always been entrusted to it, to feed the flock of God.

*Teaching of the Middle Ages*

We have an authentic record of the teaching of the Mediaeval Church in the tenth Canon of the Provincial Synod of Lambeth, 1281:

"We ordain that every priest who presides over the people do four times a year, that is, once in each quarter of the year, on

---

1. In the sixth century the Clergy were prohibited from witnessing the agonies connected with the system of torture to secure evidence. In 1125 Bishop Hildebert wrote: "To torment criminals, or to extort confession by torture, is not a part of the discipline of the Church." It was in the thirteenth century that the Church began to be tainted with a spirit of cruel bigotry. The Inquisition fully accepted torture and secret investigation. If the Church resorted to it, it was the Christian spirit in the Church that ultimately insisted upon its removal.

one or more festival days, either by himself or by another, expound to the people in popular language without any fanciful subtlety the 14 Articles of Faith, 10 Commandments of the Lord, 2 Evangelical Precepts of Charity, 7 Works of Mercy, 7 Deadly Sins with their progeny, 7 Principal Virtues, 7 Sacraments of Grace."

The Evangelical Precepts were—
1. The Love of God.
2. The Love of our Neighbor.

The seven Works of Mercy were—[1]
1. To feed the Hungry.
2. To give drink to the Thirsty.
3. To entertain the Stranger.[2]
4. To clothe the Naked.
5. To visit the Sick.
6. To comfort those in prison.
7. To bury the Dead.

Mediaeval charity and relief dealt with persons in distress. It did not seek to understand or to remove the underlying reasons for the existing distress. And, moreover, according to the teaching then in vogue charity operated to the advantage of the giver and doer. It was not designed primarily for the good of the recipient.

*Feudalism*

There was for generations in Europe a contest to determine which system of government should dominate the New Peoples, that of the Roman Empire or of the German Tribe. The answer was Feudalism, that set of social and legal relationships that bridged the period between the Roman Empire and the earlier monarchies of the barbarians on the one hand, and the national kingdoms of the fifteenth century on the other hand. This type of society, based on local custom, was wellnigh universal by the tenth century. It is not our purpose to examine the origins of Feudalism, but rather to indicate that the engagements between the lord and vassal and all the other feudal customs, obligations and incidents were the characteristic form of social service in the Middle Ages and were regulated by the sanction of the Church.

As the feudal system was a system of local government with an independent economy of the Manor, socially and economically, each local district was self-sufficient. The land was for all, the demesne for the lord, the fiefs for his vassals. An agreement of protection on the one hand and of service on the other obtained as between the feudal lord and his vassals. With the lord of the manor providing and caring for all in the community, the social service of the Church was in a large measure rendered unnecessary so far as that community was concerned. Feudal obligations, however, were not fulfilled unless the lord was able to enforce them. In the sphere

---

1. St. Thomas Aquinas quotes these as good works involving definite advantages for the hereafter. In this way social service becomes linked with the system of Indulgences.
2. Monasteries and parsonage houses provided entertainment and hospitality for travellers, for man and horse—E. L. Cutts, Parish Priests and Their People, 159.

of "rights" the influence of the Church operated to soften and to modify.[1] War became the occupation of the restless aristocracy. Tourneys and jousts were only play wars to fill out the tiresome periods between real wars. In this time of organized anarchy the Church interposed to regulate the constant strife. In the form of a pledge of peace the Church sought to restrain the martial ardor of the fierce barons. The phraseology has been preserved: "I, W——, Archbishop of Puy, in the name of the Holy Trinity, to all who expect supreme pity. . . . . As we know that without peace no one shall see the Lord; we order the faithful . . . . that no one shall make an attack on a Church, that no one shall plunder houses, cattle, chickens, etc., from peasants . . that no one shall attack merchants or plunder them. . . . . If any one do not keep this peace let him be excommunicated, anathematized and driven from the Church." The Clergy even sought to form Peace Associations and Brotherhoods of the Lamb of God. From the twelfth century the Church fostered Courts of Arbitration.[2] In this latter effort the Church had the co-operation of the free cities of mediaeval Europe. It was not a small contribution to foster the Truce of God.[3] It thereby succeeded in prohibiting all hostilities from Thursday until Monday of each week, and during the period of Passion Week and Easter, and also, upon the numerous fast days. In times of war it protected the cart and grain and cattle of the farmer.

When the Crusades opened, Church leaders diverted the war-like spirit of the great nobles against the Crescent and gave a longed-for peace to the folk of Europe. And in Knighthood, or Chivalry, the Church sought to christianize the profession of arms. The knight was the Christian soldier with clearly defined duties—

1. To his liege lord.
2. To his lady love.
3. To the Church. He must not only be a Christian and defend the Church on all occasions, but he must fight the infidel and never yield to the enemy.
4. He must be ready to sacrifice life for honor, for justice, for country, for God.
5. He must respect all forms of weakness and give ungrudgingly to the needy and helpless.[4]
6. He must not be tainted with heresy or treason or falsehood.

King Arthur's court furnishes us with noble types of the ideal knight. Such an one was Lancelot, who on his death was thus addressed by a sorrowing companion—"Thou wert the courtliest knight that ever bare shield, and thou wert the truest friend to thy lover that ever bestrode horse, and thou wert the truest lover of a sinful man (i.e. among sinful men) that ever loved woman, and thou wert the kindest man that ever struck with sword, and thou wert the

---

1. So the Church attacked the right of the feudal lord over the hand of his ward.
2. C. L. Brace, Gesta Christi, 154 seq.
3. This was proclaimed by no less than 30 Councils in different parts of Europe.
4. Feudal obligations and knightly duties included the care of the poor. Lay rulers and other lay persons outside the Church were coming to have social service to render. The secularization of charity, clearly manifest in the Reformation, was already beginning.

goodliest person that ever came among the press of knights, and thou wert the meekest man, and the greatest that ever ate in hall among ladies, and thou wert the sternest knight to thy mortal foe that ever put spear in breast." Wolfram van Eschenbach has given us in Parsifal the story of a knight in search of the Holy Grail, the sacred chalice which had held the blood of Christ. Only the pure in heart, in thought, word and deed, might see this. Parsifal had failed on one occasion to speak a word of kindly sympathy to a suffering man. To wipe out the stain of this failure he was forced to undergo a long atonement. But in the end through pity, humility and faith in God he found the Grail. He is the type of much that was best in the Middle Ages. Many were looking for the Grail, and in its quest they rendered many a deed of kindly service. The knight was a courtly man as well as a Christian soldier. He was dubbed a knight only after long preparation as page and squire. Though the knighthood was conferred by an older knight the Church had its part in the ceremony. The initiation of the knight was essentially religious. In Chivalry we see the social service rendered by the Church to restrain the brute force and violence of a feudal age, the creation of a society with ideals in the midst of a time of constant war.

*Position of Woman*

In the same way the Church succeeded gradually in removing the German prejudice "that bodily strength was a condition of civil capacity." This had operated to the disadvantage of the sex unable to bear arms. Women came to receive an equal part with men in the succession of property. In marriage they retained the administration of their property. An era that produced St. Catherine of Siena and St. Joan of Arc could no longer despise women.

*Poor Relief*

The relief of the poor devolved upon the Church as in every other age. We have seen how this work before the time of Constantine was regarded as a congregational duty, and how, after the alliance of the Church and State, institutions were established to care for the poor and needy and infirm. From the papacy of Gregory the Great, one-fourth of the Church revenues was devoted to the maintenance of the poor. The same proportion was observed after the tithe became compulsory in the eighth century. In England a third of the tithe went to "God's poor and needy men in thraldom."

In the readjustment that took place under Charlemagne the duty of caring for the poor was definitely assigned to the parish priests. A fourth or a third of the tithes was assigned to this purpose. And an endeavor was made to organize the work of charity and poor relief on parochial lines.

This parochial system broke down in the confusion of the times and poor relief, so far as carried on, was the work of monasteries, hospitals, crafts and fraternities, and, as ever, of individuals. There was a considerable variety of benevolent agencies and institutions without any definite policy of co-operation, and with no adequate superintendents or inspection of the recipients. By the end of the

Middle Ages little poor relief came from the tithes. What there was of parochial assistance was given from what was known as the Church stock or store, and was managed by the wardens. Sometimes this took the form of live stock. Sometimes funds were raised by Church Ales at Whitsuntide. These were festivities in the Church House or Church Tavern, where ale brewed from gifts of corn was sold, and the proceeds devoted to poor relief.

*Failure of the Monasteries*

The Monasteries, which in previous ages had done so much for charity, now, particularly in England, were tending to foster the growth of a professional beggar class. As Fuller puts it, "the Abbeys did but maintain the poor which they made." Ratzinger contends that the monasteries had not been effective in diminishing pauperism. The love of the monks for the poor had grown cold. They had yielded to idleness and luxury. Whatever there had been of careful investigation was given over, and charity took on the form of indiscriminate almsgiving at the convent gate. "Monasteries, hospitals, etc., were without what is the first requisite for an orderly relief of the poor—unity, concentration, organization. Each hospital, each convent, gave alms not only to the people of the district, but also to all strangers who chose to apply, without having any power of control over them."[1]

*Hospitals*

The hospitals of the Middle Ages cared not only for the sick but also for the aged, the enfeebled and impoverished. They were under the charge of wardens. Priests were assigned them for the performance of divine offices. Of foundations of this type there were in England at the Reformation no less than 460. Many of these hospitals came to be regarded as lucrative sources of income by their clerical administrators. Owing to various abuses many hospitals in the fourteenth and fifteenth centuries came under the direction of the municipal and other civil authorities. But throughout the Middle Ages they were associated with the Church or some Order. Especially from the eleventh century they were numerous.[2] After the Conquest English Leper Hospitals began to be founded. The Knights Hospitallers were an Order who cared for the sick in hospitals. They were religious in character and observed the Augustinian Rule. In addition to the care of the sick and the infirm they received travellers and aided in the relief of the local poor.[3] The Master or Warden of the Hospital was assisted by Canons and Chaplains who were responsible for the masses and other religious services. For it was never forgotten that this was a branch of the social service rendered by the Church. The Master of the Hospital was usually a

1. George Ratzinger, Geschichte der kirchlichen Armenpflege, quoted W. J. Ashley, Introduction to English Economic History and Theory, 313.
2. According to C. S. Loch there were four at Canterbury -- two endowed by Lanfranc, 1084, one for poor, infirm, lame and blind men and women, and one outside the town for lepers. Later hospitals were established there for leprous sisters and leprous monks. Hospitals had a variety of sources of income-- rents, produce of land, tithes, collections, begging fees.
3. E. L. Cutts, Parish Priests and Their People, 505.

cleric. Inmates on admission had to promise to participate in prayer, and to bequeath property to the Hospital.

*Service of the Gilds*

Most of the religious gilds and fraternities and other craft associations gave occasional aid to those of their members that had fallen into poverty. They furnished lodgings for the destitute, and, later, provided hospitals and almshouses.

There was much private almsgiving, especially on the part of great prelates and nobles. Ashley quotes Stowe: "I myself in that declining time of charity have oft seen at the Lord Cromwell's gate in London more than two hundred persons served twice every day with bread, meat, and drink sufficient; for he observed that ancient and charitable custom, as all prelates, noblemen, or men of honor and worship, his predecessors, had done before him."[1]

*What had the Church Achieved?*

After nigh twelve centuries of leavening activity in the world what had the Church achieved? It had formulated a fairly compact body of Christian doctrine and had anathematized all deviation therefrom as heresy. It had organized an ecclesiastical system culminating in the Pope. It had found in monasticism its highest interpretation in the way of life. Its devotees had carried its message to every country in Western Europe. In terrific encounters with Islam Christianity had proved that it would not, and need not, brook any rivals between the Pyrenees and the Hellespont. It had opened up a career to all ranks and classes of the people, not excluding even serfs.[2] But with all this great record of achievement there was something lacking. The very fact of success brought failure. When the Church had conquered the Roman Empire the victory lay less with the victors than with the conquered. The spirit of the Empire overcame the Church. In fact, the very organization of the Empire was grafted on to the Church. It was little wonder that the things of Caesar divided the allegiance of the faithful with the things of God. Nothing indicates this better than monasticism. The monk had performed signal service in Western Europe. He had removed the stigma from hand labor. He was a pioneer in agriculture. He preserved ancient manuscripts. His doors opened to receive the way-faring and the sick.[3] The Rule of St. Benedict aimed to develop in the monk, and often actually did develop, a type, faultless in humility and obedience. But monasticism was contemplative and introspective. It did not emphasize the ideal of service. Nor did the Cluniac revival awaken the Church at large to a sense of its true mission, though it did yield a more thorough organization in the time of Hildebrand.

1. W. J. Ashley, An Introduction to English Economic History and Theory, 329.
2. E. L. Cutts, Parish Priests and Their People, 129.
3. In England the parish priest was required to entertain strangers and to support a room for them. He must also devote a third of the tithe to the poor. But each monastery had an almonry where the almoner relieved travellers, palmers, chaplains, leprous, mendicants and the sick. He visited the old, infirm, lame, blind. The old clothes of the monks, the leavings of meals, maundy gifts, he dispensed to widows, orphans and other needy.

*The Coming of the Friars*

We have seen the social service rendered in an earlier period by the monks of Western Europe. But in the course of time the Benedictine monasteries lost much of their primitive character and ideals. They began to wane. They became in some cases resorts of luxurious indolence, in others hotbeds of vice. New Orders arose to correct and curb the distempers of monastic life—the Order of St. Cluny[1] and the Cistercian and Carthusian Orders. At an early period, also, was established the Order of St. Augustine destined to play an important rôle in the progress of the Reformation movement, but already unique in that it was composed chiefly of ecclesiastics. In 1094 Robert of Arbrissil founded the Order of Fontevraud to care for fallen women and to raise them to a new life of holiness.[2] The association of the Trinitarians and that called De Mercede had the distinct mission of redeeming from slavery those who had fallen into the hands of the infidel.

But the most important development of the Middle Ages was the growth of the Military and Mendicant Orders. The former included the Knights of the Hospital, the Knights Templar, and the Teutonic Order. They all owed their origin to the burst of crusading zeal which marked the eleventh and twelfth centuries. For nearly two centuries these military Orders formed the most renowned portion of the Christian armies. They established an enviable reputation for intrepid daring. Of the three vows of poverty, chastity and obedience they regarded only the third. With the increase in power and wealth they fell into disrepute and disappeared about the time of the Reformation. The two Mendicant Orders, the Franciscans and the Dominicans, or the Grey and Black Friars, arose with the development of town life and the revival of a money economy. Their ideals were Mendicancy and Preaching. St. Francis and St. Dominic invented a new type of clergymen, the begging brother or Mendicant Friar (Latin, *frater*). He was to do exactly those things, and render those services, which the parish priests were failing to accomplish—to lead a life of self-sacrifice and active social service, to defend the faith against all manners of heresy, and to evangelize the fold at large with a more vital sense of spiritual worship.

*Practical Christian Effort*

What the world needed was to learn that the religious life could be lived as well outside as within monastic walls, and could find expression not less in Christian action than in doctrinal formula. This contribution was made by the Friars. And of these not the least was St. Francis of Assisi, "little brother Francis," a sort of mediaeval amalgam of John Wesley and William Booth. His programme was practical Christian effort. He stood afar off from the intellectual bickerings of Nominalist and Realist alike. "A man has

1. The foundation of this Order was a reflection of the social, economic and political reorganization in France after the disintegration of the Empire of Charlemagne.
2. R. C. Trench, Mediaeval Church History, 432.

no more knowledge than he works, and he is a wise man only in the degree in which he loves God and his neighbor," said St. Francis.

## St. Francis of Assisi

St. Francis revived the whole mediaeval conception of charity. The teachings of St. Augustine, St. Benedict, and St. Bernard fell into the background, and practical social service in humility and poverty took their place.[1] Though the sight of lepers was disgusting to St. Francis he lived among them and served them. His was the chivalry of service. His Rule was the Rule of simple goodness, kindness and consolation. One day he was walking near the Church of St. Damian and entered to pray. As he prayed the Crucified addressed him—"Francis, seest thou not that My House is being destroyed? Go, therefore, and repair Me it." "Gladly will I do it, O Lord," replied the prostrate worshipper. Straightway he sold his horse and all the goods he was carrying. When the priest, astonished that any one should be so mad as to give everything he possessed to the Church, refused to accept, Francis flung his money into the Church through a window. His father began to persecute him. His friends cried out against him as a madman. They flung the mud of the streets and stones at him. But nothing daunted Francis asked alms for St. Damian. As the days passed, the fuller meaning of the Master's injunction surged into his soul—"Repair My House! Build My Church." His work in life was to be the repairing of the Father's House, the Master's Church.

The three chief authorities for the life of St. Francis are the Mirror of Perfection, the Little Flowers, and the Legend of the Three Companions. One must not read them with a microscope. They will repay those who have imagination enough and sympathy enough to remember that the thirteenth is not the twentieth century. Their value is altogether lost to him who jeers when St. Francis preaches to the birds and makes the swallows hold their peace. It is a different world from ours, a world of dreams and miracles. And one must no more smile when Brother Juniper plays seesaw to abase himself than doubt when St. Francis converts the fierce wolf of Agobio. St. Francis attracted a group of friends about him. His character and deeds of mercy awakened admiration till in the end the cities and villages of Umbria rang their bells as he approached.

We are happy in having preserved to us a meeting of St. Francis with Innocent III, who was, if not the most remarkable individual of the Middle Ages, at least the greatest of all popes, and, in his day, the political arbiter of Western Europe. Before the meeting the Pope dreamed that he had seen in a vision the Church of St. John Lateran about to fall. A certain Religious, small of stature, and lowly, held it up by setting his own back thereunder. When St. Francis appeared the Pope recognized him as the Religious of his dreams, and approved his Rule. They went, St. Francis and

---

1. Those who took on poverty to serve, as opposed to the poor in general, were *pauperes Christi*, "Christ's poor." They adopted "evangelical poverty"

his companions, to the miserable, the helpless and the despairing. They were convinced that the Gospel ought, could, and therefore must, be preached to the poor. "To the poor, by the poor," says Canon Jessopp. "Those masses, those dreadful masses, crawling, sweltering in the foul hovels, in many a southern town, with never a roof to cover them, huddling in groups under the dry arch, alive with vermin; gibbering *cretins* with the ghastly wens; lepers by the hundred, too shocking for mothers to gaze at, and therefore driven forth to curse and howl in the lazar-house outside the walls, there stretching out their bony hands to clutch the frightened almsgiver's dole, or, failing that, to pick up shreds of offal from the heaps of garbage—to these St. Francis came. More wonderful still, to these outcasts came those other twelve, so utterly had their leader's sublime self-surrender communicated itself to his converts. 'We are come,' they said, 'to live among you and be your servants, and wash your sores, and make your lot less hard than it is. We only want to do as Christ bids us do. We are beggars, too, and we have not where to lay our heads. Christ sent us to you. Yes, Christ, the crucified, whose we are, and whose you are. Be not wroth with us, we will help you if we can.' " In other ages many have helped the poor, but St. Francis, to keep them, lived even as the poor themselves lived, in poverty.

This was not abstract religious meditation. This was real Christian service. The Legend of St. Francis states (xv)—"They were zealous each day in prayer and in working with their hands, that they might altogether put away from them all slothfulness that warreth against the soul. They would rise at midnight in their zeal and pray most devoutly with measureless weeping and sighing. They cherished one another with a right inward love, and served each other and nourished him, even as a mother doth her only and well beloved son. Such a charity did burn within them that it seemed easy unto them to yield their bodies unto death, not for the love of Christ alone, but also for the salvation of the souls, nay, even of the bodies of the brethren."

*Social Service of the Friars*

St. Francis died at Assisi on October 4th, 1226. He did not aim to make scholars, yet in England the Franciscans became the most learned body in Europe, and of the English Franciscans the greatest were Alexander Hales, Roger Bacon, Duns Scotus and William of Ockham. Though not himself a Franciscan, Robert Grossetesste, afterwards Bishop of Lincoln, was their first Lector at Oxford. The Franciscans had taken the vow of poverty. It was impossible for them to possess books and scientific instruments. Roger Bacon could obtain parchment and ink only by the special permission of the Pope. Their care for the poor led them to study sickness and disease. They devoted themselves to a study of medicine. This led them to pay attention to physical studies at which they greatly distinguished themselves. They gave an impulse to Bible study at the mediaeval Universities. But it was not learned work that constituted their crowning glory. If many were great scholars, more were great preachers who spoke with spiritual earnestness and simplicity. The Franciscans were notable for their plain language, good stories, their bubbling humor, and, withal, their seriousness of purpose. It was the habit of the Friars to dwell in common houses at great centres like Oxford. And it was this system that led to the adoption of Colleges in Oxford. Their work of practical social service and deeds of mercy, their cure of souls, their popular preaching, their religious poetry—all these made them an agency than which none was more active for good in the Middle Ages.

## The Crusades

That series of conflicts with the Crescent, known as the Crusades, made a spectacular display of the might of the Christian Church, but dissipated its power. In the eighth century there had already been a clash between Christianity and Islam, between East and West, between Europe and Asia. Western Christianity, now consolidated, took Feudalism into its service and returned to conquer the East. Waged primarily to secure the safety of pilgrims to the Holy Places, these wars were designed to set up Christian rule in the Holy Land. In the Truce of God the Church restrained the warlike ardor of its members, but in the Crusades the Church inspired the military passions of Western Europe to what was regarded as a holy warfare. It is not within our purpose to sketch the melancholy story of the Crusades, but we must appreciate the contribution which the Church through them made to the life of Western Europe.

## Political Results

The political results were enormous. They drove the turbulent elements to the Levant and enabled the growing nations to establish the reign of law in their absence. They held the Turk back for at least two centuries.[1] They contributed tremendously to the unification and consolidation of more than one state by putting the authority of the feudal barons into the hands of a national monarch.

## Economic and Social Results

The Crusades were no less significant on their economic and social side. They gave an impulse to Mediterranean commerce and introduced many articles like sugar and cotton to the common use of the West; and silks, spices, camphor, musk, pearls and ivory, and other Easter products became objects of trade between India and Europe. They developed craftsmanship, heraldry, chivalry. They hastened the freedom of the cities and the emancipation of the serfs. They united all Europe in a war for an idea and greatly stimulated the intellectual life of the West. "The Crusader," says Hall,[2] "brought back from the East new science, new art, and many

1. It must not be forgotten that the Eastern Church stemmed the tide of Mohammedanism for many centuries and enabled the Western Church to achieve its task of culture and mission enterprise. Nor must it be forgotten that the battle with the Turks took place also on a more northerly sector and was waged by the Magyars.
2. T. C. Hall, History of Ethics within Organized Christianity, 367.

new inspirations, but also new vices and new doubts. . . . . The Crusades did, in fact, break the power of Mahometan invasion and stayed the onward rush of Eastern culture."

*Influence on the Papacy*

They fostered the power of the Pope. If a prince went on Crusade he acknowledged the Pope; if he remained at home he was anathematized.[1] They fostered the idea, that was to prove so destructive to liberty of thought, that a religious war was especially pleasing to God. They contributed to a larger horizon of thought that was to lead in the future to a revolt against papal authority. They displaced social relations and increased the importance of secular and commercial, as against religious, interest, although, for the time being, the armed service for Christ seemed to elevate the spiritual over the temporal power. They gave an impulse to Indulgences which were to undermine the power of the Pope in the fifteenth century, and to national feeling which almost overthrew the Papacy itself in the sixteenth century.

*Mediaeval Culture, Life and Manners*

The Christian Church made its contribution of social service in the field of mediaeval culture, life and manners. It made its influence felt in the intellectual life, in the art of the time, the view of history and of the world,[2] the books that were written, the universities founded, and the cathedrals that were built. But it was belles-lettres that first developed in the vernacular. History and sermons persisted in Latin. In this regard the Church was a conservative force. In the realm of mediaeval Natural Science exact observation was made subservient to the necessity of pointing a moral or of illustrating the truths of Scripture. A Bestiary of the twelfth century, after describing the edifying habits of beasts and birds in its study of zoology, thus speaks of the pelican—

> "The pelican is a bird of such fashion as is the crane, and it is found in Egypt. . . . . Its nature is such that when it comes to its little ones, and they are large and beautiful, it wishes to fondle them, and to cover them with its wings. But the little ones are fierce; they seize him to peck him, and wish to devour him and pick out his two eyes. Then he takes them and pecks them, and slays them with torment, and thereupon leaves them—leaves them lying dead. On the third day he returns, and is grieved to find them dead, and makes sore lamentations when he sees his little ones dead; with his beak he strikes his body so that the blood gushes forth; the blood goes dropping down and falls upon his birdlings: the blood has such virtue that by it they come to life. . . . .
>
> This bird signifies the son of Mary, and we are the young birds in fashion of men. We are so raised and restored from death by the precious blood which God shed for us, as the

---

1. Compare the experience of Frederick II.
2. von Dobschutz, The Influence of the Bible on Civilization, Ch. IV. Note the influence of the Bible and of St. Augustine's "City of God."

birdlings are which were three days dead. Now hear by science what that signifies—why the birdlings peck at the father's eye, and why the father is angry when he kills them thus: he who denies truth will put out the eye of God, and God will take vengeance upon that people. Have in remembrance that this is the meaning."[2]

*Art*

There were ideal and dramatic elements in the Christian story, so that it is not to be wondered at that the Christian Faith should have made a distinct contribution to Art. Every quality of beauty and strength, every deed of sacrifice and service, that could appeal to poet, painter, or builder, for imaginative creation, was there in the life of the Founder from the Cradle to the Cross, from the Crucifixion to Ascension. The distinctive gifts of the Middle Ages were the Madonna and the Pointed Gothic Cathedral. The holy Madonna was depicted as the highest type of womanhood, of surpassing sweetness and divine purity, with love and joy ineffable as the Mother of our Lord and the most exquisite sorrow with the sword-pierced heart. "At the sight of the Virgin," declared Savonarola, "at the sight of her great beauty, all men remained stupefied; but such was the sanctity that shone in her that she never inspired an evil thought; every one felt himself inspired with respect for her." The Sistine Madonna at Dresden is the best expression of the more than earthly beauty of her divine motherhood.

The chief centre of Art from the Carolingian period till the twelfth century was Germany, and here the Gothic influence dominated. The Church encouraged religious Art. Particularly in the North this found its highest expression in the great Churches and Cathedrals. All the other arts contributed to the master art of Architecture to give worthy expression to the religious and church life of the times.

Books were written by monks. The monks were responsible for the illuminations, for painting (miniature) in manuscripts and on vellum which encouraged virtue by depicting the anticipated joys of heaven and warned against sin by the spirited portrayal of the devil and hell. A Synod of Arras, 1205, decreed that what the illiterate could not behold in the Scripture, this they should contemplate in pictorial art. In France religious art was beautified in the twelfth century by the use of painting on glass. A curé in Troyes painted three windows of a church "to serve as catechism and instruction to the people." Vasari stated that painters "traced saints on the walls and on the altars, in order that by this means men, to the great despite of the demons, might be better and more devout."

It was in Florence that Giotto (1267-1337, "the father of Christian Art," introduced the natural treatment of sacred subjects. According to Vasari he was no less remarkable as a Christian than as a painter. In the Church of Santa Croce in Florence we have the finest expression of his art. He dominated the Florentine school just as

Simone Martini (1283-1344) dominated the Siena School. But it is the religious motive that inspired all. It was the Church or Convent with its altar-pieces and frescoes that gave scope and place for the employment of their art. Many painters never took up their pencils without first having recourse to prayer. A member of the school of Bologna never commenced painting without a severe fast the evening before and without partaking of the sacraments during the same day, that his imagination might be purified. Whenever Fra Angelico of Fiesole painted a crucifixion the tears streamed down his cheeks. The epitaph of such a saintly artist exhibits the spirit of the age—"To me be it no glory that I was as a second Apelles; but that all my gains I laid at thy feet, O Jesus!"

And sculpture was also inspired by the Faith. It was in carving groups for choirs or for baptisteries or sacred subjects for Churches that Ghiberti and Donatello and Della Robbia and Michelangelo expressed their splendid genius.

*Architecture*

The second great contribution of Christianity to Art in the Middle Ages was the Pointed Gothic Cathedral as a temple of worship and aspiration. The previous styles in Architecture had the horizontal as their chief line; but in Gothic this became vertical. Though it developed from previous types it seemed to come as a new gift to the world of art. Freeman says: "As the style developed there came, too, a marvellous lightness. As the stately piles were lifted to heaven they seem to have partiallly lost their earthly nature, to have become spiritualized and hallowed for their sacred purposes. The spirit of Gothic Architecture is in the truest sense the spirit of the Middle Ages, the spirit of faith and wholehearted striving after God."[1] "Everything in it should be aspiring," declares Brace.[2] "The thoughts of the worshipper should be called upwards to the infinite and everlasting. The great aerial spaces within, the mystery of arch beyond arch, and arcade over arcade, the broad sweeps of richly-colored light and deep shadows, the immense height of the interior, the continual upward tendency of every portion of the building—from the foundation and flying buttress and external pinnacle through the arches and groins meeting in the elevated nave, to the succession above of galleries, clerestories, arches, broaches, cusps, pinnacles, crockets, and roof, till the top of the dizzy spire was reached by the eye—all gave the mind of the spectator an impression of the boundless and the eternal." Such a creation is the Cathedral at Cologne. We had often seen it before the War. But as we entered it when we were with the Army of Occupation, side by side entered Canadian and German—in the presence of those immense stretches there were no earthly fueds, there was only worship of God.

Such creations as the Gothic Cathedral were made possible only by the reverence and painstaking work of master builders. Fraternities of masons and other builders were inspired with a religious enthusiasm unequalled at any other period of the world's history. For admission to even the lowest trade a workman's moral

1. Freeman, History of Architecture.     2. Brace, Gesta Christi, 489.

conduct and honor must be stainless, he must have served a regular apprenticeship. If he was not good and honest he was not permitted to possess tools. Masons and builders in the Middle Ages have been called a "lay church," working "not for profit, but for the salvation of their souls." These devout laborers "went from one country to another as artists to express their love of beauty and their adoration of Christ in temples which should be houses of worship and symbols of majesty and harmony for all succeeding ages." They wrought with the utmost conscientiousness each minute and unseen part. They were building not for man but for God to see. In renewing Sainte Chapelle, which had been erected in Paris in 1202, workmen found the most exquisitely carved stone flowers on the pinnacles of the roof. There they were for well-nigh seven hundred years unseen by a single human eye. But the old workman had had his reward. He had done honest and reverent work for the love of God, and not for human hire. In the spirit of devotion he had given it to the Eternal. It was thus that the Cathedrals were built, without haste, in reverence, by workmen that needed not to be ashamed.

*Literary and Scientific Movement*

Charlemagne had made himself the centre of a literary and scientific movement. There had gathered around him a group of writers and thinkers who profoundly influenced their own, and bade fair to influence subsequent, times. Charlemagne's work as an educationist showed itself in two directions—the annotation of the Scriptures and the establishment of schools. But the coming of the new barbarians, the break-up of the Empire and the disorder of the unruly feudal lords all conspired to throw the world back into barbarism. Under Otto the Great and his scholarly brother, Bruno, there was a marked revival of interest in learning in Germany during the tenth century. Then came the days of the travail of the spirit till Peter Abelard (1079-1142) by his great gifts aroused an unprecedented enthusiasm for learning. Soon the teachers and students became so numerous that they organized themselves into corporations and gilds from which in turn sprang the Universities. Abelard established a school of divinity in Paris in which he had 5,000 pupils. In this were trained a Pope, 19 Cardinals, and more than 50 Bishops.

*The University*

The University was the child of the Church. The University Statutes compelled clericality of dress. The Rector had to be a cleric. Kings and Popes granted privileges to the Students, the former to keep them in their domains, the latter to keep them more directly under the authority of the Church.

*Scholasticism*

The influence of the Church upon learning is shown in Scholasticism. The Schoolmen were full of admiration for the logic of Aristotle whom they knew in bad Latin translations from the Arabic. They accepted all the doctrines of the Church, and employed the processes of Aristotle to arrive at their interpretations. "It is not necessary to understand first in order to believe," said Guitmond, Bishop of Aversa, "but first to believe in order to understand afterward." The great Schoolmen were the Swabian Albertus Magnus and the Italian St. Thomas Aquinas. It was a friar, Roger Bacon, 1214-1294, "Doctor Admirabilis," who would burn all the books of Aristotle. He became the Father of Modern Experimental Science through his research in physics and chemistry. He insisted upon a reformation in the sciences by a careful study of nature.

*Influence on Law*

All the Saxon and Norman laws were influenced by the Church. King Alfred introduced his code with the Ten Commandments. King Canute's laws have the tone of a sermon. In King Ethelred's dooms the religious impulse is particularly marked. These laws protected the working classes in the matter of Sunday labor. They regulated conduct in the matter of shipwrecks, false swearing and feuds. They always introduced a more humane and Christian influence, restraining passion and barbarism, curbing personal revenge, and encouraging judicial integrity and private righteousness. One effect of the Faith among the Northern Peoples was to repress feuds by encouraging fines. In the introduction of his laws King Alfred attributed to Christianity the ordaining of *bot,* or money fines, to repress feuds. The New Peoples, when christianized, drew up codes with monetary penalties. Fines rather than fighting, the determinaton of evidence by witnesses rather than by duel—this was the policy encouraged by the Church. Then fines proved inadequate. Evil doers had to be repressed even at the sacrifice of life. Says Brace: "The fines which were once a safeguard of order now became a composition with guilt. Capital punishment here was an offspring of the spirit of true humanity. Thus one of the great movements in human progress, the substitution of law and legal penalty for private revenge, was especially aided on the continent of Europe by Christianity."[1]

*Jurisprudence*

The jurisprudence of the Middle Ages rested on a religious conception—the thought of God as Judge. Compurgation or Wager of Law, the Judgments of God such as Wager of Battle and the Ordeal were employed to ascertain the will of the allseeing and all-knowing God. The burden of proof rested on the negative side. The Law was a quaint combination of Teutonism and Christianity. The Church played a notable part in these trials. It surrounded them with ceremonies to make them impressive. Each party affirmed the justice of his cause and confirmed it by a solemn oath on the Gospels or on a relic of approved sanctity. The Wager of Battle came to be strenuously opposed by the Church. In the latter half of the twelfth century Peter Cantor argued that a champion undertaking the combat relied either on his superior strength and skill, which is manifest injustice, or on the justice of his cause which is presumption, or on a

---

1. Gesta Christi, 141.

special miracle which is a devilish tempting of God. In the Ordeals there was a reliance upon the interposition of superhuman agency in the Ordeals of Boiling Water, Red Hot Iron, the Cross, the Eucharist, Relics. For centuries such matters as the ownership of a farm could be settled in Europe by a duel. From the middle of the twelfth century ecclesiastical legislation sought to bring about changes. Council after Council boldly declared against trials by battle. A Canon was published prohibiting Christian burial to those who fell in such combats. Those who engaged in these contests were also held incapable of being witnesses or of succeeding to property. At the same time the Church possessed and developed an ecclesiastical legal procedure of its own, having large recourse to excommunication and the interdict to enforce its will.

## Travelling

The Church at all times exhibited the most lively interest in the traveller. When the disintegration of Charlemagne's empire had brought chaos into the body politic there set in the decay of that road system of Western Europe that had been the glory of Roman engineers. The Roman Church, finding that the support of public highways became an excuse for the levy of innumerable tolls rather than a matter of constant local concern, tried to supply the part played by the Roman imperial road system. The dangers of transit have always prompted the prayers of the Church. The Church voluntarily submitted to the "trinoda necessitas," which comprised the maintenance of bridges. The Lateran Council, 1179, forbade the enslaving or despoiling of the shipwrecked. And the Church encouraged for the sake of its pilgrims the erection of bridges and the care of highways.[1] The Pope was Pontifex Maximus, in fact as well as in name, Chief Bridge-Builder. There were always a large group of wandering ecclesiastics or religious wayfarers—Friars, Pardoners, Pilgrims, Crusaders. The three greatest writers of the last half of the fourteenth century all wrote of human life under the figure of a pilgrimage—William Langland, John Wycliffe and Geoffrey Chaucer.

## The Gilds

The Gilds of the Middle Ages were of two types—the Gild Merchant and the Craft-Gild. They were formed to embody a trading monopoly or to prevent anyone from practising a trade who had not been duly admitted to the corporation. They regulated industry, and preserved order. But, as well, they served as beneficiary societies and were social and religious organizations. They cared for the sick and the imprisoned. They buried the dead, gave dowries to poor girls and rendered other social services. They constituted a system of lay charity and social service apart from the Church, but not out of touch with it.

The gild merchant of Lynn Regis is mentioned as early as 1205 in a charter granted by King John. It had a large membership. It possessed a gild hall which still exists. In 1389 it supported

---

1. R. C. Trench, Mediaeval Church History, 433.

thirteen chaplains "daily and yearly to pray as well for the king, his ancestors, and for the peace and welfare of his kingdom, as for the souls of all aldermen, brethren, and benefactors of the said gild; also for the souls of all the faithful deceased." Six of these chaplains officiated in the Church of St. Margaret, four in the Chapel of St. Nicholas, and three in the Chapel of St. James, all in Lynn. In addition to its religious activity, the gild contributed largely by money and by administration to the charities, educational work and public improvements of the city.[1] An Ordinance of the Gild Merchant of Southampton states—

"And when a gildsman dies, all those who are of the gild and are in the city shall attend the service of the dead, and gildsmen shall bear the body and bring it to the place of burial. And whoever will not do this shall pay according to his oath, two pence, to be given to the poor. And those of the ward where the dead man shall be ought to find a man to watch over the body the night that the dead shall lie in his house. And as long as the service of the dead shall last, that is to say the vigil and the mass, there ought to burn four candles of the gild, each candle of two pounds weight or more, until the body is buried. And these four candles shall remain in the keeping of the steward of the gild."[2]

An Ordinance of the Gild Merchant of the Holy Trinity of Lynn Regis states—

"If any of the brethren shall fall into poverty or misery, all the brethren are to assist him by common consent out of the chattels of the house of fraternity, or by their proper own."[3]

An Ordinance of the White-Tawyers states—

"Also, if by chance any one of the said trade shall fall into poverty, whether through old age or because he cannot labor or work, and have nothing with which to keep himself he shall have every week from the said box 7d. for his support, if he be a man of good repute. And after his decease, if he have a wife, a woman of good repute, she shall have weekly for her support 7d. from the said box, so long as she shall behave herself weel and keep single."[4]

The Craft Gilds were also connected with the production of religious dramas, called "Mystery plays," because produced by the "Misteries" or Craft Gilds. These Mysteries dealt with the historic portions of the Old and New Testaments. The Miracle Plays dealt with the Lives of Saints. The Moralities were plays in which the Virtues and Vices were personified. "Out of these naïve little representations of the birth of Christ or his passion and resurrection," says Von Dobschütz,[5] "sprang gorgeous miracle-plays which sometimes lasted four days and brought the whole story from the creation to the last judgment before the bewildered eyes of the spectators.

1. The town as well as the Church was engaging in charity and social service.
2. Translations and Reprints from Original Sources of European History, II, 1, 13.
3. Ibid., 17.                                    4 Ibid., 23.
4. The Influence of the Bible on Civilization, 84.

Nothing could make the Biblical history so familiar to the people as these plays, in which hundreds took part as performers, and thousands attended as onlookers. There was but little art. They had no scenery; the actors simply moved about in the open space. But it was highly realistic. We are told that they nearly killed the man who was acting Judas Iscariot. It was also amusing. Mediaeval piety did not refrain from putting in just before the crucifixion a sarcastic dialogue between the blacksmith who had to provide the nails, and his wife, ending in a scuffle between them. People liked to see this. It was on account of these undignified scenes, which kept increasing, that the plays were abolished by secular and ecclesiastical authorities in the sixteenth and seventeenth centuries, when through humanism and the Reformation taste and piety had been refined."

*Economic Thought*

The influence of the Church was strongly felt in mediaeval economic theory. The "Pretium Justum," or just price, was the conception dominant in the Middle Ages. It was considered out-rageous to sell a thing for more than this rate. In the same way the Church forbade the payment of interest on money. Interest was regarded as wicked, and money as a dead and sterile thing. Church Councils ordered that impenitent usurers should be denied burial and have their wills annulled. In this way money lending devolved upon the Jews. And this accounts in part for the treatment of this unhappy people. The fanatical attacks upon them began at the time of the Crusades, and arose from the wild desire to avenge the blood of Christ. They were accused of falsifying the Bible and adding curses against the Christians. The more enlightened of the clergy, including Innocent III, tried to shield them without success. In this dark blot upon mediaeval civilization both economic and religious considerations operated. But the teaching of the Church was respon-sible for both. The Jews could not join the Gilds, which were Christian. They came to be more and more shut within a particular quarter of the city, called Jewry. From the thirteenth century, when they began to wear a peculiar badge or cap, they were terribly maltreated.

*The Church the Chief Instrument of Social Service*

In the Middle Ages the Church was the chief instrument of social service. There was no strong central government to carry out vigorous policies of poor relief. And the local authorities left this task in the more efficient and sympathetic hands of the ecclesiastical organization. Charity was parochial. The Church devoted to this work one-third of the tithe, and the proceeds of certain collections taken in the Church itself.[1] The Church carried out its kindly mission in a more or less spasmodic and impulsive manner. Institu-tions to house the destitute and sisters of mercy were numerous in every town.[2] There was no attempt to co-ordinate what was done by monasteries, friars, parishes, nor to survey the whole field of need.

1. Distributions of food were made at Church festivals, at funerals and marriages.
2. T. M. Lindsay, History of the Reformation, I, 142.

The poor were helped without question by each separate agent, without regard to the assistance given by others. This could scarcely be otherwise when almsgiving was practised not for the good of the recipient but for the eternal salvation of the giver. St. Bernard, indeed, took another view. He regarded charity as for the glory of God and the advantage of the needy. But Thomas Aquinas would give the whole human race a contingent right in the property of each individual. The individual must not appropriate anything to himself. Others have claims on what is ours. The extent of almsgiving is to be determined by the need of the recipient, and by the wealth of the bestower.

*Improvement of Morals*

Towards the end of the Middle Ages there were not wanting within the Church men who, in spite of persecution by the Church itself, sought to render social service in the way of reformation and an improvement of morals. Such a man was Girolamo Savonarola, the Florentine Preacher and Dominican Prior of San Marco. Called to leadership in the city he began to correct the morals of the Florentines. He undertook to recall priests and citizens to the practice of Gospel precepts. He was eminently practical in his sermons and carried on a work of moral reform from his pulpit. He lashed the vices of the time. He instituted a crusade against gambling, denounced luxury, made provision for the relief of the necessities of the poor, not so much by encouraging a promiscuous almsgiving as by providing employment for the needy and out of work. He manifested a rare political wisdom and resisted the Pope. He organized a children's militia to collect alms for the poor, to seek out in a house-to-house visitation "vanities" for the "bonfire of vanities," and to reprove ostentatious modes of dress. Lucas tells us that his bonfires were a consuming fire for the destruction of "lascivious pictures, immoral books, masks, mirrors, false hair, cosmetics, cards, dice, daggers, all the apparatus of licentious gallantry, of extravagant play, of vindictive passion." In these fires many a precious work of art is also said to have perished. In not many did the passion for moral reform burn with so much ardour as in the case of Savonarola, nor was the method employed by the constituted authorities to repress so striking or so cruel. Yet in the souls of many an individual was glowing an enthusiasm for reform and service, all the more remarkable because the Church itself was growing lax and indifferent.

*The Church a Dispenser of Magic and a Civilizing Agency*

The Christian Church was the chief civilizing agency of the Middle Ages. It watched over and ordered a man's life from the cradle to the grave. It undertook to prescribe proper conduct and right thinking at every step. By its sacraments it related to the divine every important phase of the individual's career. The sacraments were the great agents of the Church. The Church believed that their repetition for the individual inculcated in him the truths that they symbolized, that they linked him to the unseen and mysterious. In fact the supernatural was the proper realm of the Church. Everything related to it partook of this supernatural character. In this way relics could achieve benefits of the most extraordinary nature without the wish or intention of the person on whom they were wrought. "On the translation of the relics of St. Martin of Tours in 887," says Medley, "two important beggars who lived comfortably on the profits of their infirmities determined to quit the district of Tours before the procession carrying the relics arrived, for fear lest they should be involuntarily healed. Their fears were well grounded; the relics reached the soil of Touraine before they quitted it, and they found themselves healed and their occupation gone."[1] The Church in the Middle Ages was thus a great dispenser of magic as well as a civilizing agency. It could rescue one from the clutches of demons in this world no less than from the jaws of hell in the world to come. To appreciate fully the social service rendered by the Church in the Middle Ages this consideration must never be lost sight of. It was this multiple position of the Church, however, as a civilizing agency, as a governing power, as a dispenser of magic, no less than as a christianizing influence, that gave the Church, and particularly the Papacy, its great power. The Papacy was unable to bear the strain of this great load of responsibility placed upon it. It yielded to corruption and despotism. And corruption and despotism brought the revolt of the Protestant Reformation.

## (c) THE CHARACTER OF THE SOCIAL ACHIEVEMENT

*Religious Obligation of Self-Denial and Service*

Social service was conceived of as conferring merit upon the individual. Almsgiving and charity were sure passports to the life eternal. They were religious obligations. Consequently the institutions that engaged in direct social service were religious in character —monasteries, hospitals, chantries, gilds, and, of course, the parish church. The prevalent view of religion emphasized self-denial. St. Francis, giving his all to the poor and to the Church, is typical of the teaching of the times. As institutions such as monasteries did not permit private ownership, all possessions, apart from what was necessary to support the common life of the institution, were available, in theory at least, for God's poor. So arose hospitals, schools, lending-houses and other institutions to help the needy. An almoner dispensed the monastery's bounty. Others ministered to the sick, visiting and bestowing relief or advancing loans usually without interest.

*Almsgiving Indiscriminate*

In the courts of kings and bishops the office of almoner became a fixed institution. Even as early as the time of King Oswald in England there had been such a man. Bede tells of him the following story :—

"When raised to that height of dominion, he always continued humble, affable, and generous to the poor and strangers. In short, it is reported, that when he was once

1. Traill and Mann, Social England, II, 766.

sitting at dinner, on the holy day of Easter, with the aforesaid bishop, and a silver dish full of dainties before him, and they were just ready to bless the bread, the servant whom he had appointed to relieve the poor, came in on a sudden, and told the king that a great multitude of needy persons from all parts were sitting in the streets begging some alms of the king; he immediately ordered the meat set before him to be carried to the poor, and the dish to be cut in pieces, and divided among them. At which sight, the bishop who sat by him, much taken with such an act of piety, laid hold of his right hand, and said, "May this hand never perish." Which fell out according to his prayer, for his arm and hand, being cut off from his body, when he was slain in battle, remain entire and uncorrupted to this day, and are kept in a silver case, as revered relics, in St. Peter's Church in the royal city."[1]

In the same way bishops were the patrons of the poor. Stephen Langton made the appointment of an almoner obligatory for all bishops. That advantage was taken of the episcopal generosity is evidenced from the circumstances that one Bishop of Ely gave warm meat and drink daily to 200 persons.[2] Death was made the occasion of large doles. A Council of the ninth century decreed that a tenth of the possessions of the Bishop should pass to the poor at his decease. "Funerals," says Dimont, "became the happy hunting ground of professional mendicants." The same writer quotes the circumstances that John of Gaunt ordered that his body should not be buried for forty days, and that fifty marks should be distributed on each of those days and five hundred on the last day. This habit of making large gifts to charity at death sprang from the conception that social service brought merit and advantage to the giver without respect to the character of him who received. This fundamental weakness undermined the whole social activity of the Middle Ages. It created poverty by feeding it indiscriminately. It encouraged impulsive, heedless, giving. Charity abounded. But it failed materially to alleviate or remove distress.

*Ashley's Statement*

Ashley has summed up the character of poor relief in the Middle Ages: "No attempt was made by the State as a whole, or by any secular public authority, to relieve distress. The work was left entirely to the Church, and to the action of religious motives upon the minds of individuals. If it had ever been attempted to organize charity in a systematic way, making the parish priest "the relieving-officer" for his parish, and the tithes the fund whence aid was to be furnished, that attempt had altogether broken down. Well-nigh all the assistance that was given to the poor was in the form of alms-giving; almsgiving by magnates, ecclesiastical and lay, by monasteries, by hospitals, by gilds, by private persons; and almsgiving that was in the vast majority of cases practically indiscriminate,

1. Bede, Ecclesiastical History, III, VI.
2. C. T. Dimont, Encyclopaedia of Religion and Ethics, sub. Charity.

whatever it may have been in theory. No attempt was made by any public authority, secular or ecclesiastical, to take a comprehensive view of the situation, and to co-ordinate the various agencies. The reckless distribution of doles cannot have failed to exercise a pauperizing influence in many localities, by rendering it easy for those who did not care to work to live without."

*Influence of Feudal Ideal*

The key-note of the Middle Ages, its life and activities, is to be found in the Feudal System. The universe itself is only a magnified feudal system. Duties and services are feudal obligations. Religious and social service is rendered to a Divine Feudal Over-Lord. It is rendered in the heart of the social order or disorder of the day—a feudal environment. There is always the nice adjustment of reward to service. This holds true in the sphere of religion. The works of supererogation achieved by our Master actually "constrain God" to reward the doer of good deeds, for there is merit to spare. The doer of social service has a lever to move even the Divine. And yet Albertus Magnus had a greater thought. He rooted service in love. He would abominate the very thought of loving God for reward. He taught that we ought to keep the commandments not from fear of punishment, but to purify our minds.[1] Innocent III placed almsgiving before even fasting, not for its social significance, but because of its saving power for the individual soul. But he would have it done in love and in purity of life and conduct. For almsgiving in sin does not help us at all. The end is the soul's own felicity and it must be done in obedience to rule.[2]

Hall emphasizes, what others have pointed out, that the almsgiving of the Middle Ages corrupted both the givers and the receivers. The ever-present power of the confessional and the teaching of the books of penitence served only to place ethical and religious relations on a footing of bargaining between God and man, or on a feudal basis. In this feudal relation God was represented by the priests. He had given power to them to perform the miracle of the mass, to hear confessions, to wipe away in baptism the inherited guilt. They were the personal dispensers of the divine grace to man. The Church had its bells, its relics, its consecrated burial grounds, its daily miracles. Even the humblest faithful could fend off evil by the sign of the cross. God had become a Feudal Lord, and Christ and his saints workers in a supernatural magic. This was the compelling motive—a mysterious contact with the unseen. The Schoolman did not live in the world of facts and of reality, but in one of logic and discussion. And all the time there was a world there that needed to be reformed. They accepted the social conditions of the time, war, serfdom and all. They reminded the faithful that the duty of the soul was submission to authority, and particularly the spiritual authority of Rome. Social service was for the profit of the soul of him who rendered it. It was not the product of a divine

1. Hall, History of Ethics within Organized Christianity, 313.
2. Ibid., 354.

compassion. Such was the teaching of the Middle Ages. Such was not the practice of St. Francis, and of those who caught his spirit. With him all service was prompted by love and sympathy.

*Canon Law*

And finally in this period, when the will of the feudal lord was law in his domain, and the Manor was a unit of jurisdiction with its Manor Court Rolls, its bailiff's accounts and Compotus Rolls, the Church rendered a service through its Canon Law. This stood as a law above the whim and caprice of local judgments, and even in civil matters reminded the mediaeval world of the ideal of social justice.

*St Bernard, St. Francis, St. Thomas: Interpreters*

There were three distinct attempts in the Middle Ages to vitalize and to interpret social service among men. St. Bernard sought to give life to monastic establishments, and power to the Crusading movement. He would have institutional and co-operative effort function more fully in the way of service. St. Francis trusted to personal activity in humility and poverty, to a life of helpfulness lived outside monastery or hospital, among the people themselves. It is St. Thomas Aquinas who is responsible for developing the ecclesiastical theory of service. He classified and analyzed the phases and problems of almsgiving and charity and made social service morbid and self-conscious. There is little doubt that much of the spontaneous impulse and eager enthusiasm of compassion dropped away. Service became introspective, without thought of its social aim and function. Its power for good was largely impaired as it became linked with the Church's system of Indulgences and the thought of barter for benefits in the world to come.

QUESTIONS FOR DISCUSSION

1. Were the Crusades a social service rendered by the Church?

2. In Mysticism did the Church render a social service?

3. How did the social services of the Friars differ from those of the Monks?

4. What social service did the mediaeval Church render in the field of culture and learning?

5. What social service did the mediaeval Church render in the field of art and architecture?

6. What social service did the mediaeval Church render in the field of law?

7. What social service did the mediaeval Church render in the field of Gild organization?

8. What motives prompted almsgiving and charity in the Middle Ages?

9. In the long struggle between the Empire and the Papacy in the Middle Ages, did the Church render a social service? If so, what?

10. There were three attempts in the Middle Ages to vitalize and to interpret social service among men, by St. Bernard, by St. Francis, by St. Thomas. State the work and views of each.

11. "The Church only too often thrust the searcher after truth forth from its portals, thinking thus to do God service." Was there social service rendered here? By whom?

12. What social service did the Church render for women, for the poor, for the slave, and in the matter of war during the Middle Ages?

BOOKS FOR ADVANCED STUDY

E. L. Cutts, *Parish Priests and Their People.* C. L. Brace, *Gesta Christi, a History of Humane Progress.* E. F. Henderson, *Historical Documents of the Middle Ages.* W. J. Ashley, *Introduction to English Economic History and Theory.* T. C. Hall, *History of Ethics within Organized Christianity.* Freeman, *History of Architecture.* University of Pennsylvania, *Translations and Reprints from the Original Sources of European History.* Hastings' Encyclopaedia of Religion and Ethics, sub. *Charity.* Traill and Mann, *Social England,* ii. Bryce, *Holy Roman Empire.* R. L. Poole, *Illustrations of Mediaeval Thought.* Rashdall, *History of Universities in the Middle Ages.* Mills, *History of Chivalry.* Vincent, *Age of Hildebrand.* G. W. Cox, *The Crusades.* Townsend, *The Great Schoolmen of the Middle Ages.* A. Jessopp, *The Coming of the Friars.* Inge, *Christian Mysticism.* Trench, *Lectures on Mediaeval Church History.* *The German Theology.* Francis Herbert Stead, *The Story of Social Christianity.*

CHAPTER VI

# IN THE TRANSITION CENTURIES—UNDER THE RENAISSANCE, THE REFORMATION AND TO THE INDUSTRIAL REVOLUTION

(a)  THE CHURCH IN THE TRANSITION CENTURIES

The End of the Tutelage of 1,000 Years. The Renaissance. Significance of the New Impulse. The Meaning of the Reformation. Social and Political Environment of the Reformation.; A Deepened Spiritual Life. The Struggle Between the Reformation aṅd the Counter-Reformation. England. The Netherlands. France. Germany. Results of the Reformation. In Great Britain Religious Toleration Becomes Political Necessity. In France Royal Resistance to Papal Jurisdiction. Movements in Roman Catholic Church in France. Religious Life in England in Eighteenth Century. Pietism. New Spirit of Investigation. The Enlightenment.

(b)  NEW CONCEPTIONS AND METHODS

Decline in Practical Service. Removal of Old Motive. Services Rendered. Protestantism and Progress. Christian Missions. England. On the Continent. Awakening of England. Insignificant Missionary Achievements of Early Protestantism. Social Views of the Reformers. Aggressive Policy of Roman Catholic Missions. Zwingli at Zürich. Calvin at Geneva Suppression of Monasteries in England. Under Edward VI. Under Mary. Under Elizabeth. A New England. Knox in Scotland. Development of Social Conscience in Reformed Churches. Wars of the Seventeenth Century. Struggle for Civil Liberty and Religious Toleration. Contribution of Radical Sects and the New World. The New World. Changing Social and Economic Conditions. Industrial Revolution. Revival. New Social Humanitarianism. John Wesley.

(c)  CHARACTER OF SOCIAL ACHIEVEMENT

New Teaching, But Diminished Social Activity. Insignificant Achievements, But Foundations are Laid. Laissez-faire Unable to Solve Social Problems.

## (a) THE CHURCH IN THE TRANSITION CENTURIES

*The End of the Tutelage of One Thousand Years*

The Christian faith came to the Northern Nations by way of the Roman world. For a full thousand years the Germanic peoples had been under the tutelage of the Roman Church. The time was come for these to express their religious life after their own genius. And that genius was pronouncedly individualistic. The particularism of the North could never be aught but restless under the Church that regarded itself as the divine instrument of salvation as trustee for the souls of all men.

## The Renaissance

The Renaissance was a larger movement than a "rebirth of learning." It was the transition from the old to the new culture. It stood in the same relation to thought that the Industrial Revolution did to work, or the Reformation to religious life. It was the *laissez-faire* of the intellect. Along with the restrictions of trade gilds and the pretensions of Pope and Emperor must go Scholasticism and the hampering influence of Aristotle. The Renaissance was the flower of the Mediterranean spirit. The din of feudal arms had interfered with the free thinking of the Middle Ages. A freedom as great as ever was enjoyed by Hellene in an environment as peaceful as the arms of Rome had been able to establish was now to be the possession of Italian and German who for more than a millennium had been learning from Christianity the lesson of the worth of a man. Such, at least, was the dream. The turmoil of the Reformation went far to shatter that dream.

## Significance of the New Impulse

Never before had the world witnessed so universal an impulse to free-thinking. Every phase of life was quickened. The movement stirred Italy for two centuries. It crossed the Alps to Germany and England, and during a period of two generations stimulated the intellectual life and literary activities of these peoples. The Renaissance and the Reformation, the French and the Industrial, Revolutions are parts of one movement, according as that movement affected the sphere of culture, church life, national politics and the industry of men. It was the reaction against the mediaeval. The Renaissance and the Reformation, the French and the Industrial, discovery of the treasures of classical learning, its recovery of manuscripts from the sack of Constantinople, its displacement of Aristotle by the Humanists. But, as well, it included the death-blow to the conventional in art, the application of investigation and experiment in the realm of science, the telescope, the compass, gunpowder, the discovery of America, the rise of National States, the revolt against ecclesiastical authority, the recovery of the text of the Roman Law and the revival of Civil, as opposed to Canon, Law as a subject for students. In a word the Renaissance was the growth of the secular spirit. It was the appreciation of this earthly life with its achievements and point of view.

Founded more than has been realized upon the efforts of previous centuries, the Renaissance was, as Symonds has called it, the liberation of the reason from a dungeon. No longer were men to be shut up to a limited theological interest. The printing press gave an impulse to thinking as wide as human interests themselves. In the North the Renaissance is seen at its best in the work of Johann Reuchlin, Desiderius Erasmus, and Ulrich von Hutten. But everywhere it "revealed to men the wealth of their own minds, the dignity of human thought, the value of human speculation, the importance of human life regarded as a thing apart from religious rules and dogma."

*The Meaning of the Reformation*

The Reformation was, as has been stated, a typical German movement. The eighth century had witnessed one religious contest between Rome and Germany. On that occasion Rome had won. St. Boniface and his associates had from great centres like Erfurt given Roman Christianity to the German people. The sixteenth century witnessed another contest. Martin Luther, another monk of Erfurt, led a movement, chiefly against Rome, which gave the world the native, German interpretation of Christianity. But this movement must not be thought of as exclusively religious. It was religious, but it was social and political as well, just as in England it was political, but social and religious as well. Everywhere it was a struggle waged in behalf of the individual, both the individual person and the individual nation, against the mediaeval, the Roman and the Imperial. The Renaissance taught that a man has the right to think for himself. The French Revolution and the American Revolution and the earlier growth of national states all showed that men had the right to protest against social systems that oppressed, and that states might regulate themselves. So too the Reformation made it for ever clear that a soul might discard the Church system of audit and account in matters spiritual, and seek out the way to heaven, the Pope and the College of Cardinals to the contrary notwithstanding.

It was fitting that such a religious protest should arise in the religious experience of a single soul. As Harnack has stated, "Luther was the Reformation." The principles were involved in his life. Every man was to be his own priest and enjoy direct access to God. So insistence was laid upon the natural, upon faith, upon the Bible, upon the Church as simply a company of God's people. Luther took up the work of Paul and Augustine on one side, and, on the other, that of Wycliffe and Huss. He went back to the Ancient Catholic Church rather than to the New Testament Church to forge his weapons to fight Rome.

*Social and Political Environment of the Reformation*

There were social and political, as well as religious and ecclesiastical, circumstances that conditioned the Reformation. In England since the time of John Ball, Jack Straw and Wat Tyler, there had been a century and a half of social revolt and unrest. And Germany especially was the scene of social discontent with bitter class hatred and the peasants restless. In Switzerland the peasants had risen and defeated Charles the Bold. In France and England progress had been made towards national consciousness, but in both cases through resistance to the Pope himself.

*A Deepened Spiritual Life*

It is not our purpose to sketch the history of the Reformation either on the Continent or in the British Isles. In both, causes lay deeper than occasion. Great numbers left the fold of the Roman Church. The result was a deepened spiritual life both in the Protestant Churches and in the Church which they forsook. Reform came within the Roman Church as well as without. The movements associated with the rise of the Society of Jesus succeeded in bringing the defection practically to a standstill. But they also yielded a Catholic reaction in a Counter-Reformation that suppressed whatever features were regarded as akin to the Lutheran Revolt. In the Council of Trent the Roman Catholic Church codified its principles, and codified them in the mediaeval sense. The Church was to remain a Papal and reactionary Church, a sacramental institution with scholastic teaching, but with a stricter discipline, a reform of morals, a better training for its clergy, a larger use of the Inquisition, a more aggressive missionary propaganda, and a more careful use of the confessional.

*The Struggle Between the Reformation and Counter-Reformation—England*

Inevitably the Reformation and the Counter-Reformation came almost immediately to close grips. In England the reigns of Mary and Elizabeth bore the brunt of this contest. Under Mary this manifested itself in a general religious reaction, the Spanish marriage, a return to Roman obedience, the Marian persecutions. But her repressive policy was a failure and only the death of Mary herself prevented an outbreak. Under Elizabeth there were the efforts of Parsons and Campion, the influence of Mary Queen of Scots, the relentless attitude of the Pope, and the attack of Spain. The Jesuits were persecuted. The execution of Mary destroyed all hopes of a Roman Catholic Queen, as the defeat of the Armada blasted all hopes of a Roman Catholic Kingdom. There set in on the basis of Puritanism an Ultra-Reformation which in turn produced an Anglican reaction.

*The Netherlands*

In the Netherlands Philip II determined to extirpate Protestantism from his dominions. He would be champion of the Pope and the Jesuits. When the Inquisition was established an open break occurred, and Philip despatched the Duke of Alva to eradicate heresy and to restore Spanish authority. The tyranny brought about a rising of the Nation. William of Nassau, Prince of Orange, who espoused Protestantism, became the leader of resistance and laid the foundation of the Dutch Republic.

*France*

In France during the sixteenth century a long series of bloody civil wars between Protestants and Roman Catholics culminated in the Edict of Nantes, which provided a general amnesty and a guarantee against Protestant persecution, and in the Edict of the Grace of Nimes which made of French Calvinism a political power as a state within the State.

*Germany*

But Germany, which had brought the Protestant Revolt to Europe, was destined to feel the heaviest brunt of the burden of the

Religious Wars. The hostilities of the Protestant Union and the Catholic League led to the Thirty Years' War with all its terrible results. There was a fearful destruction of life and property. Thousands of villages were wiped out. Augsburg saw its population reduced from 80,000 to 16,000; Bohemia from 2,000,000 to 800,000. Germany and Austria lost from one-half to two-thirds of their people. All life was unspeakably barbarized by suffering and privations. Finally the Treaty of Westphalia recognized both Calvinism and Lutheranism as equal in rights to Roman Catholicism. The Reformation was for ever established in Europe, but at a cost that staggered humanity. The question will never be settled whether it had not been wiser to proceed by the slower educational methods of Erasmus than by the relentless, unyielding warfare of the Wittenbergers. At any rate the dream of German nationality was postponed for centuries through the religious hatred that the struggle engendered.

*Results of Reformation*

The main result of the Reformation movement was that religion was made more scriptural, more rational, more personal, more spiritual, and more national than it had ever been. With the rejection of papal authority and the sacrifice of the Mass went also for a large part of Christendom the worship of the Virgin and of the saints, the adoration of images, the exclusive priesthood, indulgences, purgatory, compulsory celibacy, the confessional, prayers for the dead, and other features of religious worship that had prevailed in Western Europe for centuries. New national Churches had grown up in nearly every country in North-western Europe.

*In Great Britain Religious Toleration Becomes Political Necessity*

Civil struggles over religious and political issues were not confined to the Continent. Under the Stuarts England witnessed a development of despotism in both Church and State that led rapidly to the downfall of episcopacy and the monarchy and the triumph of Puritanism under the Commonwealth and Protectorate. But Puritanism also was to taste the bitterness of failure. With the Restoration in politics came a restoration in religion, an era of retaliation that precipitated a struggle for religious toleration. From the downfall of James II toleration became a recognized condition of government in England. For William and Mary had let it be known before coming to England that, in their opinion, "no Christian ought to be persecuted for his conscience or be ill-used because he differs from the public and established religion." The Bill of Rights was framed on the principle that religion does not need the employment of physical force. But the Conventicle Act, the Act of Uniformity, the Test Act, and the Corporation Act were not repealed. Popery and religions that denied the Trinity were not to be indulged. Toleration on a large scale was a fact. It was a fact because it was a political necessity. The Stuarts could not make England and Scotland Episcopalian, any more than Cromwell could make them Presbyterian, by any sort of external compulsion. William and

Mary became sovereigns of an Episcopalian England and a Presbyterian Scotland. This made toleration a practical necessity. Toleration was far from entire, but it was a great advance on the "killing times" and the era of mutual persecution.

Meanwhile in America a more avowed, and a no less constructive work for religious liberty and civil democracy had been achieved by the so-called "Sects" of the Church. Freedom of conscience had been written into the political constitutions of the New World by the Pilgrim Fathers, by Roger Williams and his Rhode Islanders, by William Penn and his Quakers. And here, too, popular education was receiving a mighty impulse.

### Royal Resistance to Papal Jurisdiction in France

With the passing of the seventeenth century propaganda by the sword had become a thing of the past. The Reformed Churches in many of the countries of Western Europe lived under the jurisdiction of the secular rulers. On all sides was an aspiration for "freedom." Westphalia had declared that religious unity was impossible. After destroying the Anglican Establishment Cromwell had championed Independency as against Presbyterianism. In France the Crown championed the struggle against papal jurisdiction and its lawyers prepared the way for the revolt of the Jansenists against the influence of the Jesuits. Louis XIV would dominate both Church and State, and so resisted the Holy See.

### Movements in R.C. Church in France

Jansenism grew out of controversies on grace. The Jesuits had nearly driven St. Augustine out of Roman Theology. The net result of the Port Royalists, the Provincial Letters and Quesnel's Moral Reflections was that henceforth the Roman communion was rent into two parties—the Conservatives led by the Jesuits, and the Progressives, who were almost Gallican. There is no doubt that this cleavage contributed to the overthrow of the Jesuits. And the Jesuits were the most important political, if not social, force in the Roman Catholic Church. At the same time the growth of Quietism, with its ideal of the soul in perfect inaction, passive under the Divine Light, tended to belittle even the practice of charity.

### Religious Life in England in Eighteenth Century

In England during the eighteenth Century Bishop Butler, the greatest of the English clergy, bemoaned a "general decay of religion which is now observed by every one." For religious movement and interest one must go to the Wesleyans. In the Church of England itself there was wealth enough and sufficient dignity among the prelates and in high places, but the utmost degradation in the lower clergy. The mail features of the time relate themselves to controversy. The Bangorian controversy arose over the denial of the existence of a visible Church and the Church was split into two parties over subscription. The Deistical controversy was an attack upon the formal creeds, an attempt being made to prove that a religion of nature was sufficient for the needs of man. This controversy called forth Butler's Analogy of Religion and Berkeley's Dialogue of Alciphron. The lowest point of the religious life of England in the eighteenth century coincided with the latter days of the ministry of Robert Walpole. He had stood for peace. Every year without war meant prosperity for England. But the gentleman squire and his policy had been a dead weight in nearly every department of English life.

With the fall of Walpole in 1742 the era of new departures was inaugurated. There was a renaissance of religious, literary, artistic, political, and agricultural activity. Locke and Berkeley had their criticisms carried forward by David Hume. William Pitt became the leader along fresh political paths. In literature we have Dr. Johnson; in art Hogarth, Reynolds, Gainsborough, Romney; in agriculture Robert Bakewell, who introduced a new era in alternate husbandry and stock breeding. In the realm of inventions we have the Industrial Revolution with James Hargreaves and the Spinning Jenny, Richard Arkwright and Roller Spinning, Crompton and the Mule, Cartwright and the Power Loom, James Watt and the Steam Engine. And in the Church the deadness of the times was broken by the vitalizing work of the Wesleys and George Whitefield.

*Pietism*

In the Lutheran Church the seventeenth Century witnessed a reaction against cold dogma. On the basis of the writings of Jacob Boehme and Johann Arndt, Spener founded Pietism, instituting meetings for prayer and other religious exercises. At Halle, Francke founded the Orphan Home which greatly stimulated the spiritual and intellectual development of Germany. Pietism gave an impulse to the study of the Scriptures and of Church History and inspired much of the mission activity of the Herrnhutters.

*New Spirit of Investigation*

In the meantime, in the world of thought, readjustments were being made owing to the spirit of investigation that had arisen. Descartes started with doubt to search all that had passed as knowledge, to become convinced only of his own existence. He separated thought and existence, mind and matter, and raised a problem which was to disturb the minds of thinking men for many a day. To this problem Spinoza came with his answer of pantheism. Then attempts were made in turn to explain each side by the abolition of the other. In England and France the trend was towards materialism, with the thought of spirit as a sort of finer matter. In Germany the movement was towards idealism under Leibnitz, Wolf, Kant, Hegel and Fichte.

*The Enlightenment*

The last half of the eighteenth Century saw what is known as the Enlightenment, the Illumination, the Aufklärung. The great discoveries in science, the awakening in philosophy, the resolve to attain freedom in politics and in thought, a break with the immediate past only to return to primitive nature and pristine liberty—all served to make modern society. But there was nothing here that struck a deep religious note. All this, however, profoundly reacted on the Church itself in the days to come.

## (*b*) NEW CONCEPTIONS AND METHODS

With the Renaissance and Reformation social service in the Christian Church parted into two great streams. In the Roman Catholic Church, mediaeval conceptions persisted with the teaching of "merit," the thought of profit to the giver to be reaped from almsgiving, lavish giving without probing into the need of the recipient, and a false emphasis upon religious, as contrasted with secular, work. But in the Protestant Churches the old system and its narrow views were completely discredited. The new era introduced new conceptions, most of which were intimately connected with the dignity and worth of the individual man. The new impulse given to the study of the Scriptures furnished a religious basis to views of social service, the very opposite to those entertained by the Church of the Middle Ages. New principles guided social work in the Protestant Church—

1. The good of the recipient, not of the bestower, must be the prime consideration. And the assistance rendered ought to be effective.[1]

2. Only the worthy should be helped. Strict enquiry should be made into applications for aid. The unfortunate and the helpless, not the lazy or professional mendicant, should be assisted.[2]

3. Useless and excessive almsgiving should yield to aid suited to the particular need of the special individual. For as charity should not be indiscriminate, neither should it be lavish.

4. There should be a system in relief and some constant policy for social work.

5. Civil and municipal authorities, whose offices and functions were now, according to the teaching of the Reformers, no less sacred than those of the Church itself, should recognize that upon them devolved responsibility for caring for the needy. As early as 1388 ecclesiastics had been excluded in Nuremburg from the administration of a charitable fund.[3] This principle was but amplified and extended in the Protestant Church, although it laid itself open to the taunt of the Roman Catholic Church that it failed altogether in the matter of charitable activity. This was so far true that in England there was for a time a practical

---

1. Crowley, however, in 1550, after describing the tricks of beggars, says:
        "Yet cease not to give to all
            Without any regard,
        Though the beggars be wicked
            Thou shalt have thy reward."
W. J. Ashley, An Introduction to English Economic History and Theory, Pt. II, 331.
    2. The numerous Church holidays and the thought of begging as work had encouraged these.
    3. By the close of the fifteenth century the belief was becoming general that the funds set apart for the poor were not being properly administered. There was a considerable change from clerical to lay management. Bequests for poor were being placed in the hands of town councils. Lindsay, History of the Reformation, I, 144.

extinction of charity, and in many places municipal laws were passed to suppress begging. One of the most interesting and important of the civic reformations was that at Ypres.[1]

*Decline in Practical Service*

There is little doubt that, though the Renaissance and Reformation mark a fresh impulse in the theory of social service, yet there was actually a distinct decline in the practical service rendered.[2]    The reason is not far to seek.    The sources of social work were largely the great monasteries.    When the money economy had arisen in the late Middle Ages these, as being landed estates, had fallen upon evil days and become impoverished.    Others through indiscriminate almsgiving had become centres of pauperization. When they had been despoiled and dissolved, they fell, not to the new Church authorities, but either to secular princes and dignitaries or to some special foundation such as Wolsey's Colleges.    This was the case on the Continent as well as in England.    For in Zürich Zwingli also devoted monastic funds to educational purposes.    The Protestant contribution in the first instance was along the line of better organization and better supervision.    Secular guardians were appointed.    Funds were consolidated.    Poor rates were levied.    The whole community was held responsible for its charity and social service.    For its own special contributions the Church found its resources in collections, fines for swearing, legacies, the royal bounty, the poor-rate, and the parish estate.

*Removal of Old Motive*

The theory that there was no merit in good works must be held responsible for a declension of zeal in social work.    There was no corresponding motive, no personal incentive, as yet implanted that was vital enough to inspire self-abnegation.    "The function of Protestant Christianity," says J. K. Mozley, "has been to insist on the importance and uniqueness of each individual soul, to inculcate a set of theological doctrines, to diffuse a spirit of rational morality, and, here and there, to inspire certain of its adherents with a passion for social reformation."[3]    The change from Roman Catholicism to Protestantism was meaningful for social service.    Time was to be required to reveal the fact that the new Religion had also a social sense.    For the present it gladly surrendered to the State, held now in Protestant teaching to be no less divine than the Church, the responsibility of social effort.    But in the meantime there was not a little of suffering.    Protestantism had no penance inflicting alms-giving upon the disciplined.    The number of beggars was also vastly augmented.    These were in part the product of the distress of the times, the consequence of the social revolution that accompanied

1. W. J. Ashley, An Introduction to English Economic History and Theory, Pt. II, 337 ff.

2. Ibid., 306; C. T. Dimont mentions in this connection the sermons of Latimer and quotes from one, "On the Ploughers," "Charitie is waxed colde; none helpeth the scholer, nor yet the pore."

3. The Achievements of Christianity, 37.

the work of the Reformation. For the destructive work of Wolsey and Cromwell had proceeded at too precipitous a pace.

*Services Rendered*

When one seeks to survey during this period, the types of service rendered by the church itself, apart from the State, he finds little that was new or original. The primary interest had come to be Theology. Deism was too cold to have an ardent social creed—it put God too far off to have an impelling motive. *Laissez-faire* was too unconcerned with the common good; Quietism, too inactive; Protestant Scholasticism, too bent on theological distinctions. The tendency in Protestant countries was to leave the care of the poor to the State. Parliament, it is true, passed Poor Laws, but these had little of the social sympathy that the Roman Catholic Church had long given to the needy. Besides, the laws themselves inevitably had many defects, for it was a comparatively new field of legislation that was being opened up. Of course, there were, as always, individuals who gave alms, who ministered to the distressed, who had the tender heart of their Lord for all in need. And in these cases there was much of genuine sympathy displayed. For charity was no longer reckoned, at least among the Protestant Churches, as a sure passport to heaven. What seemed lacking was a moral dynamic. There was apparently a coldness, a calculation, even a callousness, about the new religion at the outset that seemed to leave all social service to the Roman Catholic Church. For this, Protestant Theology, which gave to Church and State, both equally sacred, their separate spheres and functions, must bear responsibility. Protestantism was engaged in the preaching of the Word, in making the adjustments of its own growth, in the problem of religious toleration, and occupied with waging the Religious Wars. It had little time or resources to embark upon the enterprises of social ministration and alleviation. This was, in any case, now held to be the proper duty of the State. It was the warmth of sympathy and humanitarian impulses engendered by the religious revivals of the eighteenth century that changed this attitude and stimulated to service.

What there was of social service lay in other directions. There was a revival of Christian missions, in zeal for which Roman Catholics far excelled as being eager to compensate the Papacy for its tremendous losses in the Protestant Revolt. But the Moravians also kindled a new missionary interest and set a shining example for other Protestant Churches. A new field was opened in the formulation of social theories; in the framing of Christian Community Ideals, as in More's *Utopia* and Luther's *Address to the Christian Nobility of the German Nation;* and in actual experiments in administration, as at Geneva, at Herrenhut and in Paraguay. The vigor of fresh life was manifested in the creation of democracy and in the new impulse to national life as in Scotland and in Holland. The inspiration of new thought found a scope in the larger fields of constitutional problems and the higher politics, as in the seventeenth century struggles of England for the great stakes of civil liberty and religious toleration. The changed ethical standards were reflected in the new conscience and sense of responsibility in public affairs. Daringly creative projects were successfully carried through in the planting of new colonies, where freedom of conscience was insisted upon, in America. New ideals struggled for expression in the impulse to International Law, in the changing of the social order itself, in the promotion of education;[1] and in Pictorial Art. A fresh opportunity of helpfulness was revealed, and grasped, in alleviating some of the early suffering associated with the Industrial Revolution. Old enemies under new guises were grappled with in combating the rationalism that was assailing the foundations of religion itself, and in encouraging resistance to feudal despotism. But no social achievement of the Church was more notable than its success in preparing for the new social humanitarianism whose results, far outstripping anything ever beheld in the world of service hitherto, were to render the nineteenth century notable for its contribution of practical reforms.

Nor can we overlook the relation in which the Church stood to the development of the new invention of Printing. "It was the Bible," says von Dobschütz, "which trained printers and translators and thereby made a noble contribution to modern civilization and literature."[2] It was the Bible that Gutenberg chose to be the first printed Book and on which he labored for four years. To print the Bible presses were established all over Western Europe. Though the clergy were rather opposed to this, printed copies were purchased by the Churches, and a market provided. It was in collaboration with the printer and the translator into the vernacular that the Reformer was able to make the Bible a book of the people, and thereby to mould more than one modern language. In this way the Protestant churches established the Bible as "the authority for daily life in a modern, that is, non-ascetic sense." Closely associated therewith was an impetus given to education, to provide good preachers and also a better understanding of the Word.

*Protestantism and Progress.*

In any estimate of the social service rendered by the Christian Church since the Reformation one is constantly confronted with a point of view that would represent the creation of the modern world itself and all progress as due to Protestantism. In a very challenging series of Public Lectures in the University of Berlin in the summer semester of 1910, Professor Adolf Harnack gave an admirable statement of the debt we all owe to Protestantism. Perhaps the best discussion of the whole subject is by Ernst Troeltsch in *Protestantism and Progress,* a historical study of the relation of Protestantism to the modern world.

Troeltsch follows the influence of Protestantism through the various departments of the Family, Law, the State, Economics and Society, Science and Art, and finally Religion itself. He finds that

1. W. E. Hammond, The Dilemma of Protestantism, 18.
2. The Influence of the Bible on Civilization, Ch. VI.

while Protestantism has furthered the rise of the modern world, often largely and decisively, in none of these departments, except, of course, Religion, does it appear as its actual creator:

"What it has done is simply to secure for it greater free-dom of development,—and that, moreover, in the various departments in various ways. . . . All it has done anywhere is to favor, strengthen, color and modify the course of the development. . . . The modern State, its freedom and con-stitutional form, its officialdom and military system, modern economics and social stratification, modern science and art, are everywhere, to a greater or less extent, already arising before and apart from it. They have their roots in late-mediaeval developments. . . . Protestantism, when all is said and done, only in its own domain did away with the hindrances which the Catholic system, for all its splendor, opposed, by its essential nature, to the rise of the modern world, and, above all, it gave to the mass of new, free, secular ideas, the firm foundation of a good conscience, and an impulse towards progress."[1] . . . "On the whole, the important political and economic results of Calvinism were produced against its will. Religious toleration and liberty of conscience are mainly the work of mystical Spiritualism; the formation of Churches on the basis of voluntary associa-tion, and the independence of the religious community in relation to the State, are the work of the Baptists and of the aspect of Calvinism which was allied to them; while the philological and historical understanding of Christianity and its archives is due to humanistic theology. . . . . Protes-tantism is, after all, in the first place a religious force, and only in the second or third place a civilizing force in the narrower sense. It is, therefore, not to be wondered at that its really revolutionary effects are in the main to be found only in the religious sphere."[2]

Troeltsch maintains that Protestantism renounced the all-embracing hierarchic power that had dominated civilization in the Middle Ages, and that, therefore, its relation to civilization became a much looser one. Protestantism is a religion of personal conviction and conscience. It is adapted to modern civilization, but does not possess a closely intimate connection with it as a system. The influence of Protestantism on the social structure and the formation of classes is, so far as it exists at all, mainly indirect and unconscious.

It will be interesting to indicate some of the indirect and unconscious results that, according to Troeltsch, are traceable to Protestantism. Protestantism overthrew a civilization of authority, a church-directed civilization. In its place has come a civilization with ideals independently arrived at, "the authority of which depends on their inherent and immediate capacity to produce conviction." In this civilization human opinion becomes important, and toleration

1. Troeltsch, Protestantism and Progress, Ch. VI.
2. Troeltsch, Protestantism and Progress, 175.

.necessary. Scientific thought reigns instead of ecclesiastical infalli-
bility. The interests of life become limited to the present world.

It must not be forgotten, however, that there was a development even within Protestantism. The early Protestantism of Luther
and Calvin was as much a Church civilization as was that of the
Middle Ages. It claimed to regulate State and society, science and
education, law, commerce and industry, according to the supernatural standpoint of revelation. But modern Protestantism has
handed all these concerns over to voluntary effort and personal conviction. Modern Protestantism has "in principle recognized alongside itself a completely untrammelled secular life, which it no longer
attempts to control, either directly or indirectly, through the agency
of the State."[1] Troeltsch also points out that the significance of
Lutheranism and Calvinism lies in different directions. The practical
influence of the latter has been much greater in all matters of ethics,
organization, politics and social questions.

In the history of religion, in the matter of social ethics, in
the department of science it was not the Protestant Revolt that concluded the Middle Ages. The Modern Age was not ushered in till
after the end of the great struggles for freedom in the seventeenth
and eighteenth centuries. Troeltsch indicates the significance of
the Reformation in the matter of the family relation:

> "Protestantism abolished the monastic and clerical view
> of the conjugal relation, encouraged the increase of population,
> so important for the rise of the modern State, created in its
> pastorate a new social order and a pattern of family life as
> Protestantism understood it. By abolishing the sacramental
> character of the married state, it put marriage on the basis
> of a more ethical and personal relation, made possible divorce
> and re-marriage, and thus prepared the way for a freer move-
> ment of the individual. The ideal of virginity entirely disap-
> pears from religion and ethics."[2]

Nor can Protestantism claim the credit for the humanization
of punitive justice and the abolition of trial for witchcraft. This
was the gift of the Enlightenment. Neither were the secular State,
the modern idea of the State and an independent political ethic
the creation of Protestantism. What Protestantism did was to free
the State from all and every kind of subordination to the hierarchy;
it taught men to regard civil callings as direct service of God and
not as indirect service through the intermediary of the Church. That
meant the final independence of the State.

> "Protestantism intervened in the development of the
> State in the direction of autonomy, and powerfully furthered
> it."[3] "It inspired the civil government to set before it the
> widest civilizing aims, and put into its hands the care of
> education, moral order, oversight of food supply, and spiritual
> and ethical well-being."[4]

1. Page 45.
2. Page 93.              3. 108.                    4. 109.

The upshot was that civilization was separated from the Church, and the State became the organ of civilization. Out of the struggles of the seventeenth century and later, grew the great ideas of the separation of the Church and State, toleration of different Church societies alongside of one another, the principle of Voluntaryism in the formation of these Church-bodies, liberty of conviction and opinion in all matters of politics and religion.

The economic results of Lutheranism were confined to the strengthening of the national government and to the education of a humble and patient working class. Calvinism, on the other hand, fostered the industrial capitalism of the middle class. It developed the "spirit of the calling." It inspired men to work in the world and to build up an accumulation of capital. A new asceticism of work came into being. Troeltsch says:

> "On the basis of this economic attitude arose the early capitalism of the Huguenots, of Holland, England, and America; and even to this present day in America and Scotland, as well as among the English Nonconformists, the higher capitalism is clearly seen to be closely connected with it. A similar development has taken place among the Pietistic groups, which were to a great extent allied to and influenced by Calvinism . . . and also among the Baptist communities . . . for they all, finding themselves excluded from public life, turned to economic activities."[1]

Protestantism, then, had a great but indirect influence on the family and law, on politics and economics, in its recognition of the modern independent State, the official class, and military organization. Calvinism, especially in its great international policy, approved and filled these with its spirit of heroism for the honor of God. Protestantism displayed a noble activity in the founding of schools. Its educational zeal has given to the nations a greater and more individual alertness of mind. The Protestant sects, the Anabaptists, and the later Baptists, the Quakers, the Methodists, the Pietists have tended to elevate the middle and lower classes. On their expansion into great societies they have been recognized and tolerated by the State. Their radicalism has become toned into a sober citizenship. They have played a large part in the creation of the middle classes of the towns of England and the New World.

Further, Troeltsch contends, it cannot be said that Protestantism opened up the way for the modern idea of the freedom of science, of thought, and of the press. Its contribution was to destroy previously existing Church-controlled science and to secularize educational institutions. The State was able henceforth to foster science from the point of view of its own interests. Science needed no longer to conform with the Church's point of view. Protestantism encouraged a spirit of historical criticism, especially in relation to Catholic tradition and Church history. It developed humanistic studies. It encouraged exact thinking and scholarly study. But, as stated above, the great contribution of Protestantism must be sought

1. 137. See also R. H. Tawney, Religion and the Rise of Capitalism.

in the field of Religion itself. It related religion to individual conviction. It is only in recent years, however, that this individual conviction has been related to social service.

The thesis laid down by Troeltsch is challenging. His whole treatment constitutes an acute criticism of Protestantism and of its relation to progress. But if the criticism is penetrating, it is also partial and unfair. For Protestantism, notably as set forth in the teachings of the earliest and greatest of the Reformers, does not actually withdraw from the field of social service. It recognizes the sacred mission even of the so-called secular and natural. The State, too, is divine, and an honored ally of the Church. It is at least open to question, however, whether its confidence in the State and in secular institutions was misplaced. But the Protestant world-view regards all service, which is touched by the spirit of Christ, and not merely service rendered by the organized Church, as essentially Christian. The social achievements of Protestantism are larger and more numerous than the sum total of the precise social services rendered by Protestant churches. They include the services of the State, of the School, of the Family, of every institution and agency impregnated by Christ's spirit and suffused by his love. Indirect as may be the service of Protestantism in these regards, it is none the less real and vital.

*Christian Missions*

One type of social service in this period was the extension of Christian missions. Here the Roman Catholic Church was, on the whole, more active than the Protestant. The Counter-Reformation aroused the Roman Church to recoup itself for its losses. In the new lands and among aboriginal tribes it would compensate itself for the disasters that had befallen it in Europe. The leading Reformers among the Protestants had no great enthusiasm for missions. Erasmus, it is true, in a treatise on the Art of Preaching, speaks glowingly of the call to mission work—"There are surely in these vast tracts barbarous and simple tribes who would easily be attracted to Christ if we sent men among them to sow the good seed." He details the obstacles which had prevented men from dedicating their life to this task: want of faith, fear of difficulties, hardships, death: "It is a hard work I call you to, but it is the noblest and highest of all Would that God accounted me worthy to die in such a holy work. . . . No one is fit to preach the gospel to the heathen who has not made his mind superior to riches or pleasure, aye, to life and death itself." Edward VI issued instructions to navigators that "the sowing of Christianity must be the chief interest of such as shall make any attempt at foreign discovery or else what is builded on other foundations shall never obtain happy success or continuance."

*England*

The first recorded missionary subscription in England was £100 given by Sir Walter Raleigh to introduce Christianity into Virginia. In North America John Eliot, 1604-1690, became the Apostle to the Indians. The Long Parliament issued a manifesto in favor of his work, and, to support it, the first English Missionary Society was founded in 1649. Cromwell was much impressed by this missionary activity, and had completed a scheme for the training of missionaries and the spread of missions when death interrupted his plans.

### On the Continent

The Dutch sent out missionaries to the East Indies, and their services were rewarded at a rate of so much for each convert baptized. In Germany the Pietists aroused a sense of responsibility for the heathen. Francke not only was the means of sending out Ziegenbalg, the first Protestant missionary to work in India, but he inspired with his ardor Count Zinzendorf, who, in turn, kindled with missionary zeal the Moravians. In the first two decades of the missionary activity of the Moravians they accomplished more for the cause than the whole of Protestantism had succeeded in achieving for two centuries. Among their early missionaries none was more notable than John Beck, who labored in Greenland.

### Awakening of England

The first Protestant missionaries in India were Lutherans, Danes, Germans, Swedes, not English. In England, however, in 1698, Dr. Bray succeeded in establishing the Society for the Promotion of Christian Knowledge, and in 1701, the Society for the Propagation of the Gospel in Foreign Parts. It was, however, the Evangelical Revival that at last aroused the missionary zeal of England.[1]

### Insignificant Missionary Achievements of Early Protestantism

Protestantism cannot boast of its missionary achievements during the first centuries of its life. It needed Carey to blaze new paths and to arouse the conscience of the Churches. As late as 1796 the General Assembly of the Church of Scotland declared that "to spread abroad the knowledge of the Gospel amongst barbarous and heathen nations seems to be highly preposterous. . . . Whilst there remains at home a single individual without the means of religious knowledge, to propagate it abroad would be improper and absurd."

### Aggressive Policy of Roman Catholic Missions

In the meantime the Roman Catholic mission had been much more aggressive. The Council of Trent definitely challenged the faithful to plant the cross in the new lands. Missionaries pushed forward with discoverers and traders, and not infrequently themselves led the way. Dominican friars worked among the natives in the Spanish dominions. The Jesuits set up a paternal but benevolent rule in Paraguay. François Xavier was the greatest of their heroic missionaries. He labored in the Far East. Nobili toiled in India, Ricci in China. The methods of these pioneer missionaries left much to be desired. In one month Xavier baptized 10,000 converts. Political motives, love of power, commercial interests, were mingled

1. Mrs. Creighton, Missions.

with a real missionary enthusiasm. There was too great a willingness to accommodate their message to the ideas and beliefs of the people who were to be converted. But there was scarce a land of first rate importance in either North America or Asia where the Roman Catholic missionaries did not toil with self-sacrifice and devotion for the Cross. The supremacy of the Roman Church and the authority of the Pope were proclaimed on a scale that went far to compensate for loss of influence through the Protestant Revolt. The *Jesuit Relations* are a mine of information that reveal a notable story of the romance of Roman Catholic missions in what is now Eastern Canada.

*Social Views of the Reformers*

The views of the Reformers on social and economic questions were grounded on a religious basis. Luther's were expressed in many of his writings, but chiefly in his Sermon on Good Works, his Address to the Christian Nobility of the German Nation respecting the Reformation of the Christian Estate, and his Treatise concerning Christian Liberty.[1] He discussed the relation of the temporal to the spiritual power. He stated—"A cobbler, a smith, a peasant, every man, has the office and function of his calling, and yet all alike are consecrated priests and bishops, and every man should by his office or function be useful and beneficial to the rest."[2] Luther expressed views on the following matters that he would have considered by the Councils—the exploitation of the lands of Christendom by ecclesiastics, the paying of annates to the Pope, commendams, reservations, the office of Datarius at Rome, pilgrimages, celibacy, annual festivals, processions, masses for the dead, indulgences, the need of reform in the Universities, usury, the great banking house of the Fuggers, the public brothels, church wakes and other matters. Of saints' days, he wrote—

> "There are some foolish prelates that think they have done a good deed, if they establish a festival to St. Otilia or St. Barbara, and the like, each in his own blind fashion, whilst he would be doing a much better work to turn a saint's day into a working day, in honor of a saint."

Of poor relief and charity he declared:

> "It is one of the most urgent necessities to abolish all begging in Christendom. No one should go about begging among Christians. . . . Each town should support its own poor and should not allow strange beggars to come in, whatever they may call themselves, pilgrims, or mendicant monks. Every town could feed its own poor; and if it were too small, the people in the neighboring villages should be called upon to contribute. As it is, they have to support many knaves and vagabonds under the name of beggars. If they did what I

---

1. "Luther's Economic ideal," says Troeltsch, Protestantism and Progress, 130, "is conceived wholly from the point of view of agriculture and handicrafts, and he takes for granted the Canon-law prohibition of interest."
2. Address to the Nobility, The First Wall.

propose, they would at least know who were really poor or not. There should also be an overseer or guardian who should know all the poor, and should inform the town council, or the priest, of their requirements; or some other provision might be made. There is no occupation, in my opinion, in which there is so much knavery and cheating as among beggars; which could easily be done away with. This general, unrestricted begging is, besides, injurious for the common people. I estimate that of the five or six orders of mendicant monks each one visits every place more than six or seven times in the year; then there are the common beggars, emissaries, and pilgrims; in this way I calculate every city has a blackmail levied on it about sixty times a year, not counting rates and taxes paid to the civil government and the useless robberies of the Roman See; so that it is to my mind one of the greatest of God's miracles how we manage to live and support ourselves. . . . It is enough to provide decently for the poor, that they may not die of cold and hunger. It is not right that one should work that another may be idle, and live ill that another may live well, as is now the perverse abuse."[1]

And Luther struck a heavy blow at the mediaeval teaching about merit and good works—

"From all this it is easy to understand why faith has such great powers, and why no good works, nor even all good works put together, can compare with it, since no work can cleave to the Word of God or be in the soul. . . . If you were nothing but good works from the soles of your feet to the crown of your head, you would not be worshipping God, nor fulfilling the First Commandment."[2]

Luther's emphasized freedom, but it must not be thought that he failed to realize or stress the principles of service. He enunciated his position in two propositions in "Concerning Christian Liberty"—

1. A Christian man is the most free lord of all, and subject to none.
2. A Christian man is the most dutiful servant of all, and subject to every one.

### Zwingli at Zürich

In Zürich Zwingli was a social reformer as well as a religious leader. Practical reforms followed in the train of his teaching. A large portion of the revenues of the Cathedral was devoted to the purposes of education. Monasteries were abolished. The festivals were limited in number. Civil and ecclesiastical regulations were established in regard to the poor. A school and theological seminary were founded out of church property. The civil authority set up a

---

1. Address to the Nobility, 4, 21. Linday, History of the Reformation, I, 143, says "Some towns began to make regulations against promiscuous begging by able-bodied persons, provided work for them, seized their children, and taught them trades—all of which sensible things were against the spirit of the mediaeval church."
2. Concerning Christian Liberty.

marriage court. And Zwingli aimed at the social and political, as well as the moral and spiritual, regeneration of his native land. Unfortunately this Swiss movement became involved in the political situation.

## Calvin at Geneva

No more notable illustration of social service rendered by a Reformer can be found than in the case of John Calvin at Geneva. Besides teaching Theology to the Reformed Churches of Western Europe Calvin created a "City of God" in Geneva and tested the foundations and principles of modern democracy. He constituted a community on the basis of a confession of faith, a system of elementary education, and a sweeping programme of social reform. He insisted on Sabbath observance, strict ecclesiastical discipline, and close supervision of recreation. He abolished popular festivals, theatres, card-playing and dancing, and regulated even the food and clothing of the inhabitants. He gave the world one of the most remarkable examples of a theocracy under the forms of ecclesiastical republicanism.[1]   "But," says Calvin, "although I am nothing I know that I have suppressed 3,000 tumults in Geneva."[2]   He founded a University. He created a Church and a system of Theology. And Lindsay points out that he did three things for Geneva, all of which went far beyond its walls—"He gave its people a trained and tested ministry, its homes an educated people who could give a reason for their faith, and to the whole city an heroic soul which enabled the little town to stand forth as the Citadel and City of Refuge for the oppressed Protestants of Europe."[3]

Williston Walker says of Calvin:

> "Calvin's influence extended far beyond Geneva. Thanks to his *Institutes,* his pattern of church government in Geneva, his academy, his commentaries, and his constant correspondence, he moulded the thought and inspired the ideals of the Protestantism of France, the Netherlands, Scotland, and the English Puritans. His influence penetrated Poland and Hungary, and before his death Calvinism was taking root in southwestern Germany itself. Men thought his thoughts after him. His was the only system that the Reformation produced that could organize itself in the face of governmental hostility, as in France and England. It trained strong men, confident in their election to be fellow workers with God in the accomplishment of his will, courageous to do battle, insistent on character, and confident that God has given in the Scriptures the guide of all right human conduct and proper worship. The spiritual disciples of Calvin, in the most varied lands, bore one common stamp. This was Calvin's work."[4]

And Fisher says of Calvinism in relation to civil liberty:

1. Benjamin Kidd, Western Civilization, 321.
2. H. Y. Reyburn, John Calvin, His Life, Letters and Work, 316.
3. T. M. Lindsay, History of the Reformation, II, 131.
4. A History of the Christian Church, 400.

"Calvin vindicated the right of the Church to perform its own functions without the interference of the State. The Church thus became the nursery of liberty. Wherever Calvinism spread—in England, Scotland, Holland, or France —men learned to defend their rights against the tyranny of civil rulers. Moreover, the separation of Church from State was the first step in the development of religious freedom. After that step was taken, the State would gradually cease to lend its power to the Church as the executioner of its laws. In the Calvinistic system, laymen took a responsible part in the selection of the clergy and in the management of the affairs of the Church. The privilege of governing themselves, which they enjoyed in the Christian society, they would soon claim in the commonwealth. Nor was the pervading principle of Calvin's theology—the idea of the sovereignty of God—without an influence in the same direction. In comparison with that Almighty Ruler upon whose will the lives and fortunes of men depended, all earthly potentates sank into insignificance. At the same time the dignity of the individual was enhanced by the consciousness that he was chosen of God. Uplifted by such ideas and by the aspirations which they created, the people were able to humble the might of kings."[1]

There is, however, one startling fact to consider. Calvinism once bade fair to conquer much of Western civilization. It was driven by an external authority, the Will of God, which was as relentless and rigid as anything ever conceived of in Roman Catholicism. And Calvinism did make its contribution. But one cannot close his eyes to the failure of Calvinism. Inroads were made by Arminianism in Holland and England. Bishop Butler's *Analogy* helped to restrict the sway of Calvinism. The Wesleyan movement entered the contest. But it was probably the supposed cruelty of Calvinistic eschatology that contributed most to the decadence of Calvinism. Fisher draws attention to the decline of Calvinism:

"The reduction of the area of Calvinism, and its partial disintegration in communities where it had long been established, is a fact which challenges attention. If we go back to the dawn of the seventeenth century, we find that the Reformed or Calvinistic creed, to say nothing of its prevalence in Bohemia, Hungary, and other regions of less note, was dominant in Switzerland, the Palatinate, Holland, the Protestant Church of France, of Scotland, and in England, where, to the end of the reign of Elizabeth, the theological influence of Calvin was a controlling power."[2]

But, as we have indicated, Calvinism made a contribution which greatly helped to shape the Modern World.

*Suppression of Monasteries in England*

In England the Reformation meant the emancipation of the Church from the control of Rome and a reform of ritual and doctrine,

1. G. P. Fisher, History of the Christian Church, 329.
2. G. P. Fisher, History of Christian Doctrine, 549.

but it meant more. The doctrine of royal supremacy involved in the first instance a right of royal visitation. This led to the suppression of the monasteries, which profoundly disturbed the social life of England. Monks and nuns wandered forth to beg. The populace joined in the spoliation. A new nobility arose on the spoils. The lands passed into the hands of private owners. And the dissolution produced three insurrections, one each in Lincolnshire and Cumberland, and the Pilgrimage of Grace. There were suppressed in all 644 monasteries, 90 colleges, 2,374 chantries or free chapels, and 110 hospitals.

### Under Edward VI

The reign of Edward VI saw a reformation in public worship and education. As charitable activity tended to decrease, owing to the suppression of the monastic agents who had devoted themselves to this work, Edward's Injunctions ordered the placing of an alms-chest near the high-altar. The incumbent was to remind his flock that, as they had formerly bestowed much substance "otherwise than God commanded, upon pardons, pilgrimages, trentals, decking of images, offering of candles" and other "blind devotions," they should now be more ready to help the poor and needy. In the First Book of Homilies the sixth Sermon is by Bonner. It enforced the practice of Charity. During this same time an agrarian revolution had been disturbing England. The mediaeval Church and the mediaeval agricultural system broke up at the same time. Peasants did not distinguish between economic and ecclesiastical causes, between inclosures and the abolition of the Latin Mass. So great did the ferment become that a rising took place in the Eastern Counties under Ket, and another broke out in Devonshire. As a consequence Somerset was overthrown. At the same time, from whatever cause, occurred a deterioration of morals which the Reformers constantly deplored. And the clergy, insufficiently provided for, were brought face to face with a new poverty.

### Under Mary

In Mary's reign a series of revolts was precipitated by the marriage treaty with Philip. These were partly religious, partly national. They broke out in Devonshire, the Western Marshes, the Midlands and Kent. Only the last was formidable, but the Queen's personal courage saved the day. The Marian persecutions lie between the Spanish marriage and the Queen's death. There were burned at the stake 5 bishops, 21 clergy, 8 gentlemen, 84 artisans, 100 husbandmen and laborers, 55 women and 4 children. And many were forced to flee from England. This persecution made a return to Rome forever unthinkable.

### Under Elizabeth

In Elizabeth's reign came the final severance from Rome, and the growth of Puritanism within the Anglican Church—the two events that were to determine the religious life of England for many years. The settlement was based on national independence. It allowed a wide freedom of opinion. Elizabeth set herself against the Puritan movement. This movement strove ever for political liberty, but sought to fasten on the community a social tyranny often exceedingly irksome. The Puritans looked askance at sports, the arts, the theatre, indeed, all that had made "merrie Englande."

## A New England

The same Tudor era that saw the church reformed saw also the social system transformed. The village copartnership of the Middle Ages gave place to a new type of farming that left the agricultural laborer in dire need. No less than four Poor Laws were required in this reign to regulate his condition. And with the increase of poor-law relief the charities and social service of the parish church decreased in amount. A new commerce sprang up. The religious wars on the Continent crippled the rivals of England. A reform of currency led to a revival of trade. A national literature was produced. The spirit of adventure led to overseas discoveries and explorations. Protestant refugees from Flanders and other continental lands stimulated industry. Modern England was born and social problems of a modern character began to emerge. But it should be noted that the very development of self-consciousness on the part of the State, its aggressiveness in every direction, made the Church's position in many ways more difficult, and, in particular, tended to oust the Church itself from the old forms of social service.

## Knox in Scotland

In Scotland the Reformation had tremendous social significance. But no feature of the Reformers' activity was of greater importance than the establishment of the Parish Schools, which for centuries determined the life of the nation. In Knox, moreover, the religious and the political were intimately related. He gave to Scotland not only its Church but many of its political convictions, independent, sane, and reverent. For in asserting the responsibility of private judgment Knox gave the mind of his people a challenge to which they nobly responded. In the Reformation the Scottish nation was created. This was the service that the Church rendered in that crisis—it created a unity of feeling, sentiment and belief.

## Development of Social Conscience in Reformed Churches

There can be little doubt that the social conscience was more highly developed in the Reformed Churches than in the Established Churches of the Lutheran and Anglican type. The cause is evident. There was a greater integration of congregational life and a more eager desire to build up their Church life according to the tenets and practice of the New Testament Church. They endeavored to train a Christian fellowship engaged in active social service. They were sensitive to the claims of the poor in their midst and zealous in all works of charity. But, as observed above, the State itself was assuming an aggressive attitude, and making the Church's task difficult.

*Wars of Seventeenth Century*

Then came on the Continent the Religious Wars and in England the Puritan Revolution. Scotland did not escape the trial of its faith, for the Stuarts would have Bishops, even if Tulchan Bishops. In all this the religious and the political issues were closely intertwined.

*Struggle for Civil Liberty and Religious Toleration*

The solution that was achieved in England was seen in religion in a gradual extension of freedom of thought and action. In politics was established the principle that the function of the government was to interpret, and give effect to, the mind of the nation and not to dictate a policy however admirable. Both King and Army came under the control of Parliament, and toleration became the working rule of the constitutional life of Britain. There were many byproducts of the religious and political struggles of the Century—the translation of the Bible, the founding of New England by the Pilgrim Fathers, the attainment of religious freedom in the New World, the bitter Puritan attack on sports, Sabbatarianism, the execution of Laud, Strafford and the King, the pamphleteering of John Milton, the disappearance of Bishops for two decades from English Church life, the Westminster Assembly with its Catechisms and Confession, the rise of the Quakers and the Independents, the Civil War, the Commonwealth, the Protectorate and the Restoration. With the Restoration came the impulse and the opportunity to defy all Puritan ideas of morality. The recovery of freedom was celebrated by an orgy of vicious living and writing. The remaining years of the century in England were devoted to the struggle for religious toleration. The literature of controversy was largely concerned with the question of "comprehension." Locke became a great exponent of toleration. As a part of the same contest came the abolition of the censorship of the Press in 1695. Another result of the century-long struggle was the union of England and Scotland on the basis of a common commerce and separate religions. This Union typifies the modern era—toleration in religion and the new commercial spirit.

*Contribution of Radical Sects and New World*

In this Study it is essential not to confuse the "rights of man" and democracy. The English Revolution of 1688 led to the recognition of the rights of the individual, but without democracy, that was not to come till the nineteenth century. On the other hand the New England States had democracy without liberty of conscience. The Independency movement of the seventeenth century in England, especially stimulated by the earlier Anabaptist and othr radical movements, implanted Puritan religious principles in the North American Colonies. Liberty of conscience obtained first in Rhode Island under the influence of Roger Williams. These Puritan principles, says Troeltsch,

> "not content with the old practical character of English liberties, regarded the freedom of the person, and especially of religious conviction, as a right conferred absolutely by God

and Nature, which is essentially inviolable by any State. It was only in virtue of being thus put on a religious basis that these demands became absolute, and consequently admitted of, and required, a theoretic legal exposition. It was thus that they first passed into Constitutional Law as a fundamental doctrine, finding their way from the North American State-constitutions into the French, and thence into almost all modern constitutions. What the purely practical English Law, utilitarian and sceptical toleration, and abstract literary theorizing, had either not felt to be necessary, or not succeeded in securing, was now secured by the energy of a principle based on religious conviction."[1] . . . "The parent of the 'rights of man' was, therefore, not actual Church Protestantism, but the Sectarianism and Spiritualism which it hated and drove forth into the New World."[2]

*The New World*

The Church rendered a distinct and definite service across the Seas in the new Colonies planted in America. In New France the Roman Catholic Church dominated the whole life. In the English-speaking settlements to the South the influence of religion, and notably of Puritanism, was no less marked. Von Dobschütz has given illustrations:

"When, in June, 1639, all the free planters of the colony of New Haven assembled together in a general meeting to consult about settling civil government according to God, the first question laid before them by John Davenport was: 'Whether the Scriptures do hold forth a perfect rule for the direction and government of all men in all duties which they are to perform to God and men, as well in the government of families and commonwealth as in matters of the Church.' This was assented unto by all, no man dissenting, as was expressed by holding up of hands. The second question was whether all do hold themselves bound by that (plantation) covenant that 'in all public offices, etc., we would all of us be ordered by those rules which the Scripture holds forth to us.' This was answered in the same way. Therefore it was voted unanimously, 'that the Word of God shall be the only rule to be attended unto in ordering the affairs of government in this plantation.' Before they went on to select officials from their number, the chapter on the institution of the seventy elders (Ex. 18) was read, together with Deut. 1: 13 and 17: 15 and 1 Cor. 6: 1-7, and one of the planters declared that he had felt scruples about it, but that these had been removed by reading Deut. 17: 15 at morning prayers. When a difference arose between two members of the colony they referred it to arbitration, in accordance with 1 Cor. 6: 1-7." . . . When questions and scruples arose between New Haven and Massachusetts about the justice of an offensive war, New Haven referred to

1. E. Troeltsch, Protestantism and Progress, 119-20.
2. E. Troeltsch, Protestantism and Progress, 122.

the story of Jehoshaphat, king of Judah. . . . In the laws
framed by the colonists themselves the Bible was constantly
appealed to. . . . The Civil government took it as its own
duty to make sure that the resolutions of the synod were really
in accordance with the Scripture and only then to give their
approbation. It was the secular power which felt bound to
the Word of God and to superintend its strict observance. But,
in fact, state and church were not to be distinguished in this
period of New England history. . . . In 1647 the General
Court passed a law ordering that each township containing
over fifty households should appoint a schoolmaster, and if
there were more than a hundred families, a grammar-school
was to be supported. This care for education was inspired by
the desire of securing a true interpretation of the Bible, as is
proved by the following statement of motives: "It being the
chief project of that old deluder Satan to keep men from the
knowledge of the Scriptures, as in former times by keeping
them in an unknown tongue, so in these latter times by persuad-
ing from the use of tongues, that so at least the true sense and
meaning of the original might be clouded by false glosses of
saint-seeming deceivers; that learning may not be buried in
the grave of our fathers in the church and commonwealth,
therefore ordered, etc. . . . The Bible was the fundamental
source of all knowledge. Harvard College was founded to be
a training-school for ministers, who should know the truth
and its source."[1]

*Changing Social and Economic Conditions*

In estimating the social service rendered by the Church, then,
it is necessary to recall that in the transition centuries under review
civilization itself spread to every part of the globe. There was also
a larger output of the various productive agencies with a corresponding increase in wealth, luxury, comfort. The Industrial Revolution transformed the whole character of work, and science made
increasingly important contributions to the agencies of production.
The revolution of work that began about the middle of the eighteenth
century consisted in the substitution of machine labor and such
motive forces as steam and electricity for manual labor. The
Revocation of the Edict of Nantes had brought to England refugee
Huguenots, whose coming led to an improvement in skill. William
III had adapted English institutions to commercial purposes and
organized England financially. The founding of the Bank of Eng-
land, the reform of Finance, the combination of the East India
Companies in 1698, the purification of the currency all prepared
England for the Industrial Revolution. And the peace policy of
Walpole gave her a chance to gather and develop wealth.

*Industrial Revolution*

Before the Industrial Revolution began, less than 200 years
ago, no tall chimney vomiting clouds of smoke reared its dirty mass

1. The Influence of the Bible on Civilization, Ch. VII.

aloft as a minaret of an industrial faith. No large factories with windows all ablaze with light, no din of machinery, no blast furnaces, no odors of chemical works, no large industrial capitalist class, few large towns, comparatively few wage earners were in existence. Industry was carried on in much the same way as it had been from the beginning of time, in domestic workshops. Old Crassus of Rome, could he have spoken English, would not have felt out of place on the streets of London in the year of grace, 1740. Industry was carried on in family workshops or cottage factories. There lived together the family and the apprentices. The weaver received the equivalent of his own product. He controlled his own labor. He had no vote. He had no voice in politics. He never had to go on strikes, nor was he liable to be locked out.

Then came the great revolution in work, that changed the whole trend of life, and altered the conditions under which social service of any character had to be rendered. England ceased to be mainly agricultural. Big towns and large factories sprang up on all sides. A division of labor followed, that tremendously increased the output and developed trade, but restricted the activity of the laborer to some single stage in a process. The acute problem of the Labor Class with its animosities towards the new mercantile and industrial capitalists, the growth of Trade Unions, the necessity of regulating the work of women and children in the factories, the legislation to provide sanitation in factories and the fencing of dangerous machinery, the rise of democracy—these are some of the effects of the great change that transformed the whole environment for social service.

Anyone who has read of the return of Silas Marner, after thirty years' absence, to his native place, Lantern Yard, this time with Eppie, will have been impressed with the profundity and some of the pathos of the change—

> "It's gone, child," he said, at last, in strong agitation, "Lantern Yard's gone. It must ha' been here, because here's the house with the o'erhanging window—I know that—it's just the same; but they've made this new opening; and see that big factory. It's all gone—chapel and all."

This wonderful readjustment of society, manifest in a myriad ways, with its tale of woe and suffering, its record of triumphs and conquests, is the result of the inventive era of industry. Arkwright, Kay and Watt were but the vanguard of a great host of inventive geniuses and productive workers that have transformed the life of the common man. A Fabian essayist has written—"From the inventions of these men came the machine industry with its innumerable secondary results—the Factory system and the upspringing of the Northern and Midland industrial towns, and the evangelization of the waste places of the earth by the sale of grey shirtings." The Industrial Revolution meant an attempt to rationalize the material world. So far from reaching a conclusion in the eighteenth century it is even yet at its height in our own day.

*Revival*

The middle of the eighteenth century was the lowest point in the religious life of modern times. With the revival of the Wesleys came a new moral enthusiasm which communicated itself to more than one part of the Church. This found worthy expression in new ideals of social service. There was a revival of kindness, a new passion of helpfulness, and new attempts to remedy the ignorance, the physical suffering, and the social degradation of the outcast and the poor.[1] This new human sympathy is the glory of the declining years of the eighteenth century. Jonas Hanway sought to put an end to infant mortality. Raikes of Gloucester established Sunday Schools,[2] which were the beginnings of popular education. Hannah More espoused the cause of the agricultural laborer. Penitentiaries and lying-in-hospitals were founded. In this atmosphere of genuine feeling for the afflicted and needy were trained Wilberforce, Clarkson and John Howard.

*New Social Humanitarianism*

The Transition Period, from the Renaissance and the Reformation to the Industrial Revolution, began with a new sense of individualism. It ended with the beginnings of a new social humanitarianism.

*John Wesley*

The sense of the need and significance of individual salvation and the rise of the new social humanitarianism coalesce in John Wesley. To begin with there was a pronounced Puritan strain in him. He had an overpowering experience of Divine love. At Oxford the Holy Club that gathered around him and his brother Charles not only showed a high regard for Holy Communion, and a great and methodical zeal for spiritual living, but—and this was the new note— they exhibited a rare passion for prisoners and a most tender solicitude for God's outcast children. It needed the evangelical conversion in Aldersgate Street, however, to fire his heart with the love that poured out his whole life in service for the Kingdom.

Wesley found the organization of the Church of England too rigid to overtake the work that lay at hand in England. Augustine Birrell has told us of his career as a preacher: "John Wesley contested the whole Kingdom in the cause of Christ during a campaign which lasted forty years. He did it for the most part on horseback. He paid more turnpikes than any man who ever bestrode a beast." His field preaching was in itself a new type of social service. He responded to the claims of America by consecrating Coke as a bishop and dispatching presbyters for the work. He had one test of social service. Bishop Butler, author of *The Analogy,* declared that Wesley had no right to preach in his diocese. Wesley simply rejoined: "I can do most good here, so here I stay." That was the new day that

---

1. This had been manifest even in the seventeenth century, particularly in the establishment of Foundling and other hospitals in England and France. In this work St. Vincent de Paul played a notable part.
2. These grew out of the "charity school" founded "to teach poor children the alphabet and the principles of religion."

was being ushered in, the day of "doing most good." And to that task Wesley consecrated every energy. Dr. Johnson complained that Wesley was too busy for conversation—"John Wesley's conversation is good, but he is never at leisure. He is always obliged to go at a certain hour. This is very disagreeable to a man who loves to fold his legs, and have out his talk as I do."

Brash has given us this happy picture of Wesley's social influence:

"This man, of five feet three inches, of weight eight stone ten, 'an eye the brightest and most piercing that can be conceived,' with his finely chiselled face which came to view again in that of the Iron Duke, loved men and women not for what they were but for what they might be: he loved colliers, drunkards, cock-fighters, prisoners, because he saw in them the children of the One Father. He gave first his love to God, and that exalted his love for men—that is why it never grew cold. He commands the eighteenth century on the religious side as much as Johnson on the literary. Lecky has told us that Wesley saved England from a revolution, but we must remember that he brought about another revolution which has done more to break down social barriers than men realize—for he taught men and women the essential oneness of us all, that One is our Father and we are all brethren. His doctrine of faith stripped off the superficial disguises of life and revealed the divine possibilities of all men. Wesley was always ahead of his century; he was a great forerunner with regard to social reform; he lived on as little as possible, and gave the rest away. Hampson says, 'Perhaps the most liberal man in England was Mr. Wesley. His liberality to the poor knew no bounds.' He gave the people cheap literature, founded schools and orphanages, wrote numerous pamphlets on public questions, and his last letter was one in which he encouraged Wilberforce in his great fight against slavery—that traffic which he termed 'that execrable villainy, which is the scandal of England, of religion, and of human nature.' This 'brand plunked from the burning' broke up the frost of the eighteenth century by the glow of his flaming message. He formed a society which has become a world-wide Church; he brought inspiration to all the Churches, and his message still rings down the years—'The best of all is God is with us!' "

John Richard Green has pointed out that the Methodists themselves were the least result of the Methodist revival, that in the nation at large appeared a new moral enthusiasm. There arose a high resolve "which has never ceased from that day to this, to remedy the guilt, the ignorance, the physical suffering, the social degradation of the profligate and the poor." This philanthropic impulse fostered popular education, helped the agricultural laborer, and inspired the work of prison reform. Green sums up the social influence of the movement: "A passionate impulse of human sympathy with the wronged and afflicted raised hospitals, endowed charities, built churches, sent missionaries to the heathen, supported Burke in his plea for the Hindoo, and Clarkson and Wilberforce in their crusade against the iniquity of the slave trade."

## (c) CHARACTER OF THE SOCIAL ACHIEVEMENT

*New Teaching, but Diminished Social Activity*

The Reformation introduced better principles but inferior achievement into the social work of the Christian Church. In insisted on investigation, and that was gain. It laid emphasis on the benefit to the recipient rather than advantage to the giver.[1]  But its whole emphasis on the individual undermined the thought of social responsibility. And Luther's new thought of the sacredness of the natural and the civil made it possible for the Church to devolve upon the State social responsibilities it had carried for more than a thousand years. The Church tended to commit the temporal welfare of the people to the civil power which, unlike Roman Catholicism, it regarded not as an alien but a friendly, even a divine, ally. It reacted against the mediaeval theory that begging invested beggars with a religious character,[2] that charity was a special command of Christ, and, therefore, to be under the immediate supervision of churchly authorities. Church life became democratic before the social responsibilities of democracy were grasped by the people. The Reformation destroyed in the monasteries the older means of charitable activity before it was able to replace them with other effective agents for caring for the poor. But the poor in many countries became revolutionary, the new churches were burdened by controversies and the difficulties of pioneering a new movement, and the civil authorities did not immediately address themselves with effective sympathy to the task of poor relief. And the world learned yet again what St. Francis had felt in the Middle Ages that there can be much teaching of doctrine side by side with a low standard of social activity.

*Insignificant Achievements, but Foundations are Laid*

There followed hard upon the Reformation and the Counter-Reformation the austerities of Puritanism, the deadness of Lutheranism, the problems of Church and State involved in the Puritan Revolt and Restoration and the Religious Wars. Apart from the new freedom from ecclesiastical authority, and whatever of missionary enterprise is associated with this period, we have little, at any rate within the Protestant Churches, that is vital and fresh, except in the larger problems of political significance. The Deism and materialism that followed the reaction proved a dead weight upon the Church's activities for many years. It needed the Evangelical Revival in England, and the rise of Pietism and the Enlightenment on the Continent to awaken a new life with sufficient warmth to produce a sense of philanthropic obligation and social responsibility.

1. In Jeremy Taylor's Holy Living we have, says Dimont, "the more balanced consideration which includes both sides."
2. The Mendicant Orders were based upon the thought. For an account of "cheese hunters" and other beggars, see Lindsay, History of the Reformation, I, 142.

The Reformation made religion individualistic, but individualistic as over against the mechanical instrument of salvation that the Church had become. The influence of Pietism and the Wesleyan Revival made religion personal. There grew out of this personal experience an impulse towards active social service which was sometimes not largely represented in the original movements, especially in Pietism. The secret of this social expression of the new religious experience lay in the content that was given to congregational fellowship and in the new ideals of liberty and humanity that were finding place everywhere in the middle of the eighteenth century.

The new world interest that arose out of the discoveries of Captain Cook, the new religious fervor that was engendered by the great Revival, the fresh blows at despotism in thought and government that came from the Enlightenment and the American and French Revolutions, the new problems of social and economic life that the Industrial Revolution produced, the repeated preaching of the doctrine of the Rights of Man and the new Gospel of Liberty, Equality and Fraternity with all its democratic implications—all these created a new need and a new opportunity for social service in, and through, the Christian Church. But it was in the next period that the service was to be rendered, and then, more than ever had been the case before, not by the Church alone, but by lay forces which in most instances owed no little of their inspiration to the Church.

*Laissez-faire Unable to Solve Social Problems*

In the transition from the Middle Ages social service ceased to be exclusively ecclesiastical. It became secular as well. For charity and poor relief became municipal and civil policies. In the same way, in the transition from the Enlightenment to the Modern Age this double direction received a further impulse. The social service movement within the Church we shall have occasion to trace. The social movement outside the Church in its development took on many forms but received its most pronounced expression as an agitation in Socialism. But both within and without the Church it was to become manifest that Laissez-faire could never solve the problems of the world. The gospel of inaction as preached in the eighteenth century became bankrupt. Just because man is man he can and ought to transform his environment. It was just this work that the humanitarian movement took in hand.

### QUESTIONS FOR DISCUSSION

1. In the Renaissance the world witnessed an impulse to free thinking. Should it be the social service of the Church to stimulate free thinking or to guide and control the thought of its members? State the proper function of the Church in this respect.

2. Among Protestants truth has its binding force based primarily on inner personal conviction, not on submission to authority as such. Did Protestantism render a service or disservice in effecting this revolution?

3. "Protestantism has tended to limit the interests of life more to the present life." Discuss.

4. Is the emphasis which Protestantism has laid upon the Bible a social service?

5. Did Protestantism create democracy? Did it introduce freedom of conscience? Did it render a social service in abolishing Purgatory? Did it perform a social service in doing away with a single-moulded Church civilization, based on a Creed, embracing the whole of Society?

6. "The genius of Catholicism is much more favorable to Art than is that of Protestantism. . . . Protestantism killed legend and miracle outside of the New Testament and fostered a spirit of unimaginative practicality. This is especially true of Calvinism." Discuss.

7. "Calvinism has come to terms with democracy and capitalism." Discuss.

8. "Modern Protestanism, even when it carries on the orthodox dogmatic traditions, is completely changed from the Protestantism of Lutheranism and Calvinism." In what respects? Is the change itself a social service? See Troeltsch, *Protestantism and Progress*, 44-5.

9. "A large part of the basis of the modern world, in the departments of the State, society, economics, science and art, arose quite independently of Protestantism, and has been produced quite independently of Protestantism, and has been produced partly by a simple continuance of the developments of the late Middle Ages, partly by the influence of the Renaissance, and especially by the Renaissance as modified by Protestantism, partly by the Catholic nations like Spain, Austria, Italy, and especially France, after the rise of Protestantism and independently of it. Nevertheless, the great significance of Protestantism for the arising of the modern world is incontestable." Discuss.

10. The tyranny of Spain and the Inquisition brought about a rising of the Netherlands and laid the foundations of the Dutch Republic. Is the rise, then, of the Dutch Republic a social service of the Church?

11. Would a more peaceful evolution following the educational methods of Erasmus have been a greater social service on the part of the Church than the violent and abrupt Protestant Revolt or Reformation?

12. Are the Puritan Struggles against tyranny in State and Church, Monarchy and Episcopate, a social service rendered by the Church?

13. What social service was rendered by Presbyterianism in the seventeenth century?

14. What contributions to freedom were made by the Baptists and the Quakers?

15. Why was Deism unsuited to stimulate social service? And why Quietism?

16. Did the emphasis on the "Rights of Man" stimulate to social service in the eighteenth century?

17. Was it a social service on the part of Protestantism to remove the old motive to social service that obtained in the Roman Catholic Church?

18. Was the Roman Catholic conception of social service more calculated to promote Foreign Missions than the Protestant conception? If there was something defective in the early situation or nature of Protestantism that its Foreign Mission achievement should appear so inadequate as compared with both the Roman Catholic achievement of the time and the Protestant achievement of the nineteenth and twentieth centuries, what was the defect, and how was it later removed?

19. What social service was rendered by Luther? Calvin? Zwingli? Knox? Cromwell? The Pilgrim Fathers? The Covenanters?

20. Was the suppression of the Monasteries in England a social service on the part of the Church? If so, why and how?

21. In the eighteenth Century there were: An Industrial Revolution, a Political Rebirth in the French and American Revolutions, a Religious Revival, and a New Day for Art and Agriculture—all produced by a new impulse of life. What had the Church done to create this impulse?

22. "The revolutions, at once religious, political and social, which herald the transition from the mediaeval to the modern world, were hardly less decisive for the economic character of the new civilization than for its ecclesiastical organization and religious doctrines." What economic changes has Tawney in mind?

### BOOKS FOR ADVANCED STUDY

T. M. Lindsay, *History of the Reformation,* 2 vols. Ernst Troeltsch, *Protestantism and Progress.* Ernst von Dobschütz, *The Influence of the Bible on Civilization.* Alfred Plummer, *English Church History,* 1509-1575, 1575-1649, 1649-1702. C. L. Brace, *Gesta Christi.* Traill and Mann, *Social England,* Vols. III-V. Wace and Bucheim, *Luther's Primary Works.* Kóstlin, *Martin Luther: His Life and Writings.* H. Y. Reyburn, *John Calvin.* Abraham Kuyher, *Lectures on Calvinism.* Prothero, *Statutes and Constitutional Documents,* 1558-1625. Gardiner, *Constitutional Documents of the Puritan Revolution,* 1625-1660. W. B. Selbic, *Congregationalism.* John Brown, *Puritan Preaching in England.* Scudder, *Nineteen Centuries of Missions.* Hurst, *History of Rationalism.* G. Holden Pike, *Wesley and His Preachers.* W. H. Flitchett, *Wesley and His Century.* W. B. Brash, *Methodism.* F. J. Snell, *Wesley and Methodism.* Hagenbach, *History of the Church in the Eighteenth and Nineteenth Centuries.* Warner, *Landmarks in English Industrial History.* Francis Herbert Stead, *The Story of Social Christianity.* R. H. Tawney, *Religion and the Rise of Capitalism.* James Moffatt, *The Presbyterian Churches.*

CHAPTER VII

# FROM THE FRENCH REVOLUTION TO THE GREAT WAR

(a) The Church From the French Revolution
to the Great War

France Before the Revolution. The Roman Catholic Church From the French Revolution. The Humanitarian Movement in England. The Church in the early Victorian Age. Later Developments in England. Scotland. The United States. Canada. Transition to Modern Viewpoint.

(b) Social Achievements

A survey. Auguste Comte. Factory Legislation. Social Economics. Advocacy of Reform. Contribution of Church. Popular Education. Abolition of Slave Trade and Slavery. Abolition of Serfdom. Prison Reform. Position of Woman. The Home. International Relations. Foreign Missions. The Church not Bankrupt in Service. Time Would Fail.

(c) Character of Social Achievement

## (a) THE CHURCH FROM THE FRENCH REVOLUTION TO THE GREAT WAR

*France Before the Revolution*

The French Revolution meant the eclipse of the spirit of Richelieu, Mazarin and Louis XIV and the triumph of Voltaire, Rousseau and Turgot. In a situation of economic discontent rationalism became constructive. Because Kings would not become philosophers, philosophers were forced to assume the role of kings. Within the clergy itself there was the same cleavage into the privileged and unprivileged as in the other ranks in society. The upper clergy were practically feudal lords and great landed proprietors. Many lived secular lives devoted to pleasure, and were as loose in their morals as in their beliefs. They used the Concordat of Francis I to shield themselves from Rome. The Church, in fact, had lost its hold upon both social influence and religious leadership. There was a godless Church in France before there was a godless Revolution. It was Voltaire, and not the Church, that gave himself up to reform the religious life of the nation just as Rousseau endeavored to reform its social life. It was Voltaire's desire to destroy the "old imposture founded 1,775 years ago," the Christian Church. According to his fierce indictment it had "torn France with its claws, destroyed man with its teeth, and put ten million to death by torture." He believed that freedom of thought and religious liberty would greatly contribute to human welfare and happiness.

140

*The Roman Catholic Church from the French Revolution*

The first Revolution was political. It meant the setting up of the first representative body that France ever possessed. The second Revolution was the social overthrow. This took place on August 4th, 1789. All the old feudal privileges were abolished. On that night the Old Régime passed away. The Assembly sought to reorganize the Church. It confiscated its property and made its priests salaried officials of the State. A civil constitution was given to the clergy. The third Revolution ended the monarchy, and inaugurated the Year I of French Liberty, a Year with months divided into decades and days dedicated to agricultural implements, vegetables and domestic animals. Under the Terror an anti-Christian movement set in. There are times when the thought of God with the common man, even with the seemingly irreligious man, apparently becomes superior to that of the dogmatic theologian or professional ecclesiastic of the day. At such times multitudes lose interest in the Church and its work or become hostile to them, and the humanitarian forces of the world outside the Church receive a tremendous impetus. Such a time was this. The Bishop of Paris abjured the Christian faith "which superstition had imposed upon him." Anacharsis Clootz declared himself "the personal enemy of Jesus." November, 1793, saw the establishment of the Worship of Reason, whose High Priestess, a beautiful actress, sat on the altar of Notre Dame. Then Robespierre repressed this cult to introduce the worship of the Supreme Being, no less revolutionary and no less anti-Christian in nature. During this period the Committee of Public Safety wrought hard for the common good. They abolished imprisonment for debt. They, first of all sovereign powers, abolished negro slavery. First of all European government, they outlined a system of public education which included common schools. Children were to be taught to read on the basis of the Declaration of the Rights of Man and the Constitution of 1793. After the Terror, however, the observance of the Catholic faith was again sanctioned. Atheism, apart from the reforms already mentioned failed to prove itself constructive in the affairs of man. Then came Napoleon, for whom religion yielded no scruples. He forced the Pope to extremities and concluded with him the Concordat. However humiliating for the Papal See, it was the herald of a Catholic Restoration. The Concordat made the Roman Catholic Church a department of the Napoleonic Empire. "I regard religion," Napoleon said in 1806, "not as the mystery of the Incarnation but as the secret of social order." The Revolution, according to a witty Frenchman, had gone to mass.

When the Restoration came it was a subordinate and impoverished Church that was re-established. The supremacy of the Pope became once more the fundamental doctrine of the Church in the matter of organization. The Roman Catholic world was definitely centralized in Rome. It is directly to Rome, then, that we must ascribe responsibility for such matters as the condemnation of Bible Societies and the attack on Free Masons. Liberty has met there a consistent opponent, whether in religion itself or in the press. Pius

IX became the most outspoken exponent of reaction in the Roman Church. After promulgating the dogma of the Immaculate Conception of the Virgin, he undertook to prepare an exhaustive exposition of the rôle of the Church in modern society. According to the Encyclical *"Quanta Cura"* Catholic civilization, prosperous in the Middle Ages, has been enfeebled by Lutheranism, Jansenism, Voltaireism, and Socialism. Society, built up in a heterodox spirit, needs nothing so much as to be reconstructed on the basis of legitimate authority. The fundamental error is "Naturalism," namely, the idea that human society can be constituted and governed without supernatural religion. It was the *"Syllabus,"* however, that set forth what the Roman Church regarded as the eighty principal errors of our times. It condemned the supporters of religious liberty, lay citizenship, lay marriage, and lay schools. The Syllabus concludes by condemning this proposition :—"The Pope can be and ought to be reconciled and keep pace with progress, liberalism, and modern civilization." The Roman Catholic Church, therefore, has expressed its definite preference for the Middle Ages. The Vatican Council hailed the Pope infallible. The reaction was complete. The Church was ready to turn its energies to the conflicts with lay governments that filled the years to the Separation of Church and State in France. During the nineteenth century the Roman Church lost all material power. But for this loss it more than compensated itself through the effective concentration of all Church authority in the person of the Pope. Thanks to Mussolini, however, the Papacy in 1929 reestablished a temporal sway in the Vatican City.

### The Humanitarian Movement in England

In England the evangelical movement which had moulded English religious life in the latter years of the eighteenth century succeeded in arousing men in the early nineteenth century to study social and religious problems. The laity, particularly the laity closely associated with church ideals, was stimulated to undertake definite philanthropic activities. Thus Wilberforce aroused the conscience of England and achieved the abolition of the slave traffic, Hannah More lent her powerful aid to social movements, and Mrs. Fry and John Howard became pioneers in the cause of prison reform.

### The Church in the Early Victorian Age

Much concern was felt for the future of the Church at the era of the Reform Bills. Dr. Arnold declared in 1832—"The Church, as it now stands, no human power can save." Roman Catholics were no longer debarred from either House of Parliament. Coleridge brought the spirit of the biblical-critical movement from Germany. In the poets was found an enthusiasm for humanity and liberty. Milman published his history of the Jews, in which Gladstone detected the beginnings of a new rationalism. The theories of the geologists disturbed men. Creeds were restudied. The emancipation of Roman Catholics roused in many the fear that the people might become Romanists. In opposition to the liberal and utilitarian theological point of view the Oxford Movement began. Men were to be taught Church principles—catholicity, the continuity of history, the spiritual basis of order. The final upshot was the Tractarian Movement and the Catholic Revival. Newman went over to Rome and took many with him. Wiseman and Manning brought new life to a Church that had been virtually proscribed for three centuries. Within the Anglican Church itself was a rebirth of what are called "Catholic" principles and points of view.

But, what is more important still for our present purpose, throughout England Religion came back to the people. Once more the poor had the Gospel preached unto them. On all sides and in all churches was evidence of renewed parochial activity. The masses of the folk became the object of more solicitous care on the part of religious workers. For, as one writer has put it, "the revival also restored that half of the Christian religion which was lost sight of in the days of Calvinistic individualism,—the duty to our neighbor." Men like Frederick Denison Maurice became interested in national education and in the condition of the poorer classes. Many allied themselves with the Christian Socialists. In this movement Charles Kingsley for a time found a place, writing *Yeast* and *Alton Locke,* by reason of his interest in the working classes. Maurice and Kingsley preached with a new emphasis the doctrine of social duty. At the same time Lord Shaftesbury carried on the social work which Wilberforce had begun in the abolition of the slavery of the negro abroad. Shaftesbury secured reforms in the poor law, in the treatment of lunatics, and in the condition of factory operatives. Of the enterprises that the new revival produced and inspired, not all, be it noted, were directly the work of the Church as such, but they were, nevertheless, indirectly the achievement of the Church, for the leaders confessedly derived their inspiration directly from the message of the Church and the spirit of Christ. Another result of the controversies of the nineteenth century was the growth of the Broad Church. This school welcomed biblical criticism and favored comprehension. Mark Pattison, Benjamin Jowett and Frederick Temple had no fear for the democratic movements of the day, and were not averse to engaging in philanthropy on an "unsectarian" footing.

*Later Developments in England*

After 1865 there took place in England a remarkable development of the Roman Catholic Church, a ritualistic movement in the Church of England with more elaborate use of vestments and ornaments, an impulse to scholarship, and the steady growth of non-conformist churches. Much in the way of exclusive privilege for the Church of England has been shared. Sister churches in the British Isles have been disestablished. But both at home and abroad has taken place a great increase of religious influence and philanthropic activity. In the Great War the Church did much to hearten and sustain the nation. It ministered to the wounded and dying and bereaved. It learned a larger brotherhood in the discharge of a splendid service. Out of this grew the Lambeth Conference with its deliverance on Union.

## Scotland

For more than 100 years, 1733-1843, the Church of Scotland was ruled in turn by Moderates and Evangelicals. Then in the early nineteenth century came the Row Controversy that lost for the Church of Scotland Macleod Campbell and, later, Edward Irving; the Voluntary Controversy that raised the question of the Establishment; and the Ten Years' Conflict which terminated in the Disruption. Chalmers led forth the Free Church, resolved to sacrifice all State protection and support, but determined to be free. The Free Church was to learn, however, in the Judgment of 1904, and by another sacrifice, that there was a thraldom to documents as well as to the State establishment, and that the final guarantee for freedom is, in the words of Principal Rainy,—"that Church will be free that dares to be free." There has been, however, another side to the history of the Church in Scotland. If there has been an era of separations and disruptions, there has been no less a splendid succession of unions that reached its culmination in 1929 in the marriage of the United Free and Established Churches, a marriage which goes a long way to make the Church in Scotland free, national and United. In the Scottish Churches the battle of free and reverent criticism has been fought and won, though at the sacrifice of the most brilliant of Scottish sons. And a new sense of responsibility and opportunity has yielded unimagined results in missionary enterprise at home and abroad, and in social amelioration and philanthropic effort of the highest value.

## The United States

In the United States the eighteenth century witnessed a movement analogous to the rise of Methodism in England or the growth of Pietism in Germany. This was called the Great Awakening. It laid great emphasis on "conversion" as the normal method of entering the Kingdom of God. The American Revolution called for a complete reorganization of Church life and work, particularly in those churches that had retained an intimate connection with the Mother Country. The troubles of the times led to a great religious depression, from which the revival of the last decade of the eighteenth century aroused the nation. The interest stimulated in this and subsequent revivals continued to the Civil War. To this inspiration may be traced the rapid spread of the Sunday School movement, the larger use of the prayer-meeting, and the inauguration of an aggressive policy in the matter of foreign missions.

Perhaps the outstanding achievement of the nineteenth century was the overtaking of the colossal home mission work of the Church. During that period civilization spread from the Atlantic seaboard to the Pacific. In this great march westward the Church kept pace, and not seldom outstripped, other national forces and organizations. This religious activity was accompanied on the part of the Church by efforts for social righteousness. Duelling, intemperance, slavery, all engaged the attention of the Church. The Civil War for a time caused bitter separations and divisions, but time has brought some reunions. Immigration from Ireland and from Southern Germany, and more recently from Italy and Eastern Europe, largely promoted the growth of the Roman Catholic Church. This Church has covered the land with convents, hospitals, and institutions of higher learning. Other features of the past half-century in the church life of the United States have been the greater emphasis laid upon an educated ministry, the larger part played in church work by women, the growth of biblical criticism, the decline of denominational rivalries, the spirit of co-operation particularly in the matter of foreign missions, and the increasing conviction that the Churches should give social expression to the Gospel in their day. The whole socializing of Christianity has kept step with a broadening theological development. Walker states:[1]

"Not a rescue by individual salvation only, but the establishment of a reign of righteousness among men, has become
increasingly the ideal. Christian outlook, without ceasing to
be other-worldly, has become this-worldly also. Emphasis
is placed on service in preventive and reformatory effort.
The duty of the Church to share in civic betterment is
emphasized. A great enlargement has come in the conception of the Church's mission. Adjustment has been awkward
and has been but partially accomplished, since the organization of the churches has been adapted to the older and more
limited vision. To find organs for the work of the new has
not been easy. This difficulty has led to a large relinquish-
ment to secular organizations, manned, indeed, chiefly by
members of the churches and infused with the spirit of
Christian helpfulness, of much social service with which the
Church should have a more direct relation. The sense of
obligation in the churches is undeniably rapidly augmenting."

In two fields this conception of the work of the Church has had opportunity to find expression,—in the foreign field, and in the support which the churches gave the nation when the United States entered the War. A no less difficult field of social service has been furnished in the great cities.

## Canada

Church work in Canada dates from the beginning of the French régime, and for the Roman Catholic Church in Quebec it has been uninterrupted since that day. The work of Protestant churches lies almost wholly in the period now under consideration. For a considerable period the churches maintained close affiliations with parent churches in the British Isles, and even in some cases with those in the United States. Finally a tendency to unite for the building up of indigenous churches asserted itself. The Presbyterian Church alone

1. History of the Christian Church, 587.

witnessed seven different unions. The Methodist Church emerged from a series of similar unions. In 1925 these two churches with the Congregational churches united to form The United Church of Canada. Although the churches of Canada have not been backward in foreign missions, and have been keenly aggressive in social service, yet the outstanding accomplishment to their credit is that they have grappled successfully with an enormous home mission problem. The sudden irruption of a diverse population that scattered itself over half the continent presented a challenge that the churches have boldly accepted, and that will call for their best effort for many days to come.

*Transition to Modern Religious Viewpoint*

This period coincides with the transition to the modern religious viewpoint. A greater difference in fundamental thought exists between the eighteenth and twentieth centuries than was caused by the Protestant Reformation. A new treatment of the problems of history and literature has emerged. The scientific method has altered the emphasis in the discussion of revelation and inspiration. Men now lay greater store by the inner and spiritual than by the external and authoritative. Discoveries have given a new view of nature and of man's relation to, or part in, that nature. All this has caused much heart-burning in the church, and has called for restatement of belief. A completely different theory of knowledge has revolutionized the thought of revelation. Historical criticism has insisted on a new standard of evidence and given a different value to much that was old. The whole range of social studies, that had not yet emerged in the eighteenth century and the attempts to reconstruct theology in the light of the new point of view have disturbed many in the Church rather than the Church itself. That the new movements had a contribution to make to the life and work of the Church may be gathered from this one consideration, that never since Apostolic times has the Church given itself more ardently than in recent years to what it conceives to be its social mission in the life of men. In order to escape from bickering and controversies men have turned from the outer to the inner, from the formal to the spiritual, and, therefore, to the social.

(*b*) SOCIAL ACHIEVEMENTS FROM THE FRENCH
REVOLUTION TO THE GREAT WAR

*A Survey*

We have traced the story of Social Service within the Christian Church from the days of the Founder of the Faith. In every age we have seen a conscious endeavor to express in terms of helpful ministry the obligations of brotherhood and love. In the early period of the Pagan Empire the service rendered was congregational in scope and inspiration. The alliance with the State enlarged the area, perfected the organization, but dampened the enthusiasm of the Church's social service. The spirit of the world entered in the moment of ecclesiastical triumph. Then the Church undertook a double responsibility,—to minister to the needy in the Empire and to evangelize the Northern Tribes. It stemmed the barbarism of the Teutons, refined their crudities, checked their warlike propensities, corrected their narrow individualism as best it could, and tutored them against the day of the Reformation. Unfortunately much of the social service of the Middle Ages was rendered for the sake of the bestower of alms, for merit to Church members, not for the good of the recipient. In fact the reproach has been levelled against the times that the ideal which the Age strove to attain was a rich Church among a multitude of poor. It was not only inevitable, it was advantageous, to have the poor with them always.

It was Lutheranism which bore the brunt of the early struggle against Rome. It had far less of the spirit of social service than Calvinism which "fused religious faith with the demand for political liberty and social justice." The task of service became the consolidation of the national states, above all in England, Scotland and the Netherlands. But there was something lacking of intensive service. Then came the Evangelical Revival of the eighteenth century with its new warmth and passion and tremendous social implications. The ardor of that movement provided the enthusiasm for the social achievements of the subsequent century: the movements against slavery, the agitation for prison reform, the measures for poor relief. Thence was derived no little of the inspiration which led to the wider sympathy which yielded the Emancipation and Reform Bills, the Repeal of the Corn Laws, the growth of Trade Unions, and labor and factory legislation. The nineteenth century produced a succession of social prophets in Maurice and Kingsley, Ruskin and Carlyle; a new birth of missions, Home and Foreign; the rise of interdenominational or extradenominational service institutions like the Salvation Army and the Young Men's and Women's Christian Associations; Charity Organization Societies; the establishment of Social Settlements and other institutional church movements; temperance agitations; fights against alcoholism; redemptive work; Bible Societies, and many similar forms of activity.

As one reviews the history of the Church since the Reformation, particularly that of the Protestant Churches, even during the nineteenth century, the impression is received that the Church has not directly itself engaged in a large amount of social service. This is an altogether wrong impression. The special census report of the United States in 1903 gave one-third of the benevolent institutions of .that country,—hospitals, nurseries, homes,—as connected with the Church. Even in the case of public institutions a very large bulk of the support comes from members of the Church. It is no small achievement to have inspired, even indirectly, citizens and the State as well, to embark upon social reform, and then, when the first efforts of state legislation, particularly in the matter of poor relief, tended in the direction of mere repression, to have awakened a wider sympathy and a more generous sense of responsibility. No one will deny that the Church has only too often failed in being a wise almoner, but it has kept fragrant and fresh sympathy for the poor and love to men, which are the root and spring of all social endeavor. It is true that in the nineteenth century the Church seldom stood sponsor for great measures or sustained crusades of social and moral reform, and that in the second quarter of that century it was the economic writers of England that sought to reform poor laws, and active philanthropists that fought to protect women and children in mines and factories. But these very men owed much to the Church. Their accomplishments must surely be reckoned as the indirect, if not the immediate, achievements of the Christian Church.

The Church was far from being neutral on all these matters. It would be difficult, for instance, to overestimate the influence of a Churchman like Thomas Chalmers. As minister of the Tron parish, Glasgow, he tried to remedy the ignorance and vice of his parish. His experiments in parochial organization have suggested many of the modern methods of dealing with the dependent classes, and are forerunners of charity organization societies and settlement work. In Edinburgh he devoted much time to abolish pauperism. He found the public relief of the poor bad and degrading. He met the need by voluntary organization. But there were only too few men of the Chalmers type in the Church, and the Church of the Victorian age had neither the social programme nor the social passion of the present.

In attempting work for the betterment of the poor in Gateshead and the East End of London, William Booth found himself hampered by the methods and attitude of the regular Churches. It was not his desire at first to found a new religious body or sect. He wished rather to supplement the work of the larger bodies. But he found himself constrained to organize first the Christian Mission and then the Salvation Army, and to add his very valuable social work to his spiritual aims. Speaking of the relation between these spheres of activity, the Salvation Army Year Book (1913) said: "In the beginning it was to save souls from Hell that the General started his campaign, and ere long both he and his workers saw that many souls could not be saved unless their temporal needs were also regarded. . . . The Social Work is the daughter of the Spiritual,— the beautiful offspring of a worthy mother."

It remains true, however, that until very recent decades it would be difficult to mention many specific social crusades inaugurated by the organized Churches themselves.

### Auguste Comte

The significance for growing Humanitarianism of the French philosopher, August Comte, founder of Positivism, must not be overlooked. His Positive Philosophy became known in England through the translation of Harriet Martineau. Comte believed that both the human race and the individual passed through three intellectual stages. In the *theological* stage, supernatural causes are assigned to all phenomena; in the *metaphysical*, the gods are displaced by abstract forces; in the *positive*, the mind applies itself to observation and classification, and seeks to understand the universe in terms of laws. When Civilization reaches the positive stage, science is born, and, last of all to emerge as the final and inclusive science, comes Sociology. But Comte himself, through an experience of love, found awakened in his own life spiritual and religious cravings. This led to his invention of the Worship of Humanity. He himself became the high priest of this new Religion. He encouraged his followers to worship the great benefactors and heroes of the race. Comte, then, was the founder of a cult and the father of Sociology. His insistence upon the careful, scientific study of Society, his feeling for Humanity gave an impulse to Humanitarianism which found concrete expression in improved Factory legislation and in other projects for social betterment.

*Factory Legislation*

The Church as such has taken no part in promoting Trades Unions or in securing Factory Legislation. But when one contemplates the funeral benefits, the strike benefits, the unemployed benefits, the sick and accident benefits, the superannuation benefits of the most prominent Trades Unions one feels the throb and pulse of a brotherhood that is akin to the spirit, nay that is the spirit, that is Christian. And, whether rightly or wrongly, one has the impression that much of this is possible only because of centuries of effort and teaching on the part of the Church. When purposes and aims are so akin, however, it would have been agreeable to have found more intimate intercourse and assistance and more open mutual appreciation. In any case it remains true that Trade Unionism is more divorced from the Church in some countries than in others, perhaps of all countries most closely allied in Great Britain.

A consideration of Factory Legislation is instructive. This began with the protection of a small class of pauper apprentices in textile mills in England. It has been extended to embrace every manual worker in every manufacturing industry. It has resulted in the regulation of hours of labor, sanitation, age for beginning work, protection against accidents, meal-times, holidays, methods and rules of remuneration. The advance was made slowly at first. Spencer Walpole has declared that it took twenty-five years of legislation to restrict a child of nine years to a sixty-nine hours week, and that only in cotton mills. Men like Robert Owen anticipated the cumbersome progress of Acts of Parliament in the arrangements and rules of their mills. When one seeks the effective cause for this factory legislation writers set down as most largely responsible such matters as the growing interest in social science, humanitarianism, economics, health, education. We are told that it was achieved "at first chiefly as a measure of protection by the governing classes, impelled by the agitation of working men, in later times partly by the pressure brought to bear by trades unions, partly through the increased interests taken in questions of public health, and the growing sense of solidarity in the community as a whole."[1] In no instance is it stated that the Church has directly inaugurated the crusade for this social legislation. In no case is the Church credited with any

1. Hutchins and Harrison, History of Factory Legislation, 252.

special sympathy with the poor and struggling. One has the right to ask whether more rapid progress might not have been made if the Church had shown itself less neutral. In any case it ought not to be forgotten that here as elsewhere in social reform advance is conditioned by public sympathy and the spirit of brotherly love created in the community, and here the efforts of the Church are of fundamental significance.[1] The Church till recent decades has confined its task to the intensive cultivation of what it considered its own field. Nevertheless that the effective leadership which yielded the beneficent social achievements of the past century has come from Christian men and women who have been devoted members of the Christian Church and have gladly acknowledged its inspiration and guidance is clearly seen from the work, among others, of Shaftesbury, Plimsoll, Raikes, Howard, Elizabeth Fry, Florence Nightingale, Oberlin, and the founders of the Y.M.C.A., and of the Labor and Temperance Movements.

*Social Economics*

The Industrial Revolution, with its ushering in of machinery, the application of science to industry and the upgrowth of the factory system, with the resultant increase of wealth in the hands of the few and the rise of fresh class distinctions, has since the opening of the nineteenth century changed the whole complexion of society. The Church has witnessed the competition of three main rival systems of social economics,—Capitalism, Socialism, Syndicalism, with Communism or Sovietism on the extreme Left.

Capitalism has been modified by such intervention and social reform as the Factory Acts and by occasional experiments in co-partnership. Syndicalism would vest the ownership and control of industry in the workers. Socialism would vest them in a bureaucratic central state, declaring that things socially necessary should be socially owned and controlled. There has been the widest divergence among Socialists as to the method to be employed for attaining their coveted goal. The Fabians represent the evolutionary, Marx and Engels and Lenin the revolutionary type. The Soviet experiment in what was formerly Russia has assumed an altogether anti-Christian, if not even an anti-religious character. The danger to the Church is certainly not lessened by the fact that it is aggressively propagandist and missionary far beyond the limits of the old Czarist territories.

It was in a specific economic environment that Socialism grew up. It became the philosophy of the "suffering classes." For many it assumed well nigh the validity of a religion. Its earliest exponents found in Socialism the New Christianity, a social fulfilment of the Kingdom. It voiced the strivings of the workers in factories. Like

---

1. "Whether charities are identified with any particular denomination or not, it is usually, though, of course, not uniformly the people of the Churches that support them." A. G. Warner, American Charities, 377. The same writer declares that in the gift of both personal service and money the Jews are perhaps more systematic and more liberal than either Roman Catholics or Protestants. He states: "The largest hospitals are likely to be supported by whatever denomination has the largest wealthy membership in any large city," 378.

the Chartist movement it was the voice of the propertyless and unprivileged, into whose lives in the first half of the nineteenth century Kingsley and Dickens give us meaningful glimpses.   It was a reaction against an economic arrangement, a revolt against Capitalism, a demand for a different kind of ownership, a plea for a juster order.   It was vibrant with sympathy for the oppressed, with belief in humanity, and a desire for freedom.   One needs to read William Morris to understand some phases of its ethical appeal.   It insists that the ethical is more fundamental than the economic, and the human more to be regarded than the thing.

Before the Great War, Socialism was already attaining the dimensions of a political force.   Since the Armistice it has captured the leadership of great States.

## Advocacy of Reform

Of the Socialists many of the earlier Utopians identified their theories with the ethical teaching of Jesus.   And not a few individual Christian men felt that the Church was profoundly interested in the same problems that Socialism sought to grapple with.   But in the main Churchmen and Christian Socialists have been content with the advocacy of reform.   They would pour the Christian spirit into the institutions that were in existence.   This is not Socialism.   For it is not war against Capitalism.   In the face of the present economic arrangement the Church is simply neutral.   It is interested in the ethical and religious.   The Roman Catholic Church, has, however, definitely pronounced against Socialism.   But Protestant Christianity has never allied itself with Socialism, nor yet made war against it.   Even in more recent decades, when it sought to work out the social implications of the faith, it has proceeded independently. "Socialism and Christian ethic," says S. A. Mellor, "are not essentially related either historically or intellectually."   They both have as ethical notes "altruism, brotherhood, love for one's neighbor, service of the community, sympathy with the oppressed."   But the dynamic and the motives are poles asunder.   Each, perhaps, has made a contribution to the other,—Christianity to the very existence of Socialism through the social teachings of Jesus, and Socialism, through the vigor of its propaganda, to the renewed interest which the Church has taken in social questions.

## Contribution of Church

It would be difficult to assess the contribution made by the Church in its inculcation of benevolence, unselfishness and honesty, and its insistence upon stewardship and fair dealing in trade.   It has recalled men, not always, however, with complete success, to the feeling of the injustice of permitting great masses to persist in abject poverty or the few to waste immense wealth in senseless and luxurious display. It has indirectly stimulated insurance, old age pensions, and other devices to promote the welfare of many.   It has waged warfare against intemperance, and has won notable victories for prohibition, particularly during the period of the Great War.   It has, however, failed since the War to speak with any great degree of unanimity upon the question of Prohibition. In this matter the Church in America has taken a much more pronounced attitude than the Church in Great Britain.

*Popular Education*

But in these as in all other social efforts the Church has made its most splendid contribution through the encouragement that it has unceasingly given to movements for popular education, for it has felt that an enlightened community pervaded with ideals of service was the most splendid contribution that it had within its gift. At the same time, the unhappy divisions of the Church itself and the consequent denominational rivalry have had the unfortunate result that, particularly in America, the influences of religion have been withdrawn from schools, and popular education has been almost completely secularized.

*Abolition of Slave Trade*

It was Christian teaching rather than direct Christian effort that undermined Slavery in the Middle Ages—the belief in the brotherhood of man and in the infinite worth of every human soul. The growth of municipal life and the loosening of social bonds through the Crusades both contributed to hasten the development. In many countries slavery gave place to serfdom. And serfdom was passing away before the emancipating moral power of the Christian Faith when two events transpired that turned back the tide of this beneficent movement. These were the discovery of America and the beginnings of the voyages to the Negro coasts of Africa. The provision of cheap negro labor for America revived slavery in the earth. For four centuries this abominable traffic was persisted in to work the mines and soil of the New World. Brace thus describes the slave trade:

> "But when one thinks that during four hundred years men and women and children were torn from all whom they knew, and sold on the coast of Africa to foreign traders; that they were chained between low decks so that there was not even room to rise, and thus in filth and disease and loneliness, the dead often chained to the living, made that horrible "middle passage," each morning the corpses being thrown into the sea, the living when temporarily released, plunging into the ocean as the least of sufferings, or the sick dying from heartache and home-sickness; that during all these hundreds of years the sighs and groans and prayers of these wretched creatures rose to heaven; that when they reached the New World, they were consigned to only a less degree of misery in the mines, or under the lash in the cane and rice-fields; that many millions were thus treated, and out of three and a quarter millions of negroes, according to Bancroft, thus imported to various colonies in a century by Great Britain, 250,000 were thrown into the sea on the passage—one may well feel that this is the

great crime of history, the one before which all others pale in enormity and wickedness."

It is lamentable to think that the Church stimulated this nefarious business by teaching that to convert a stolen negro would far outweigh the sin of enslaving him. It shocks the Christian conscience to remember that Las Casas recommended the first importation to relieve his beloved Indians, and that Spain concluded ten treaties authorizing the sale of 500,000 human beings "in the name of the Most Holy Trinity." We hang our heads in shame that Protestant Great Britain for a full century and a half enjoyed an unenviable pre-eminence in this nefarious trade. Lord Eldon declared in Parliament in 1807 that the slave trade "has been sanctioned by parliament, where sat jurisconsults the most wise, theologians the most enlightened, statesmen the most eminent." Even the Society for Propagating the Gospel in Foreign Lands owned slaves in the Barbadoes and did not even give them Christian instruction.

To their everlasting credit be it said of the Quakers that they protested against the slave trade in the seventeenth century: "Though the negroes are black, we cannot conceive there is more liberty to have them slaves than it is to have other white ones." And again and again through the eighteenth century they renewed their protests.[1] They were, in fact, the only religious body in America, which, as a whole, forbade the holding of slaves. In 1774 the Quakers of Pennsylvania excluded from membership all who bought, sold or kept negro slaves. In 1774 Rhode Island gave up the traffic and in 1784 abolished slavery. A belief grew up in several places that the Christian religion freed slaves. So in 1667 and again in 1705 Virginia passed a resolution declaring that the act of baptism did not emancipate.

In England the Quakers waged a similar war against the slave trade. Their petition to the House of Commons, 1783, set forth:

> "Your petitioners regret that a nation professing the Christian faith should so far counteract the principles of humanity and justice as by the cruel treatment of this oppressed race, to fill their minds with prejudice against the mild and beneficent doctrines of the Gospel."

Other religious men aroused an opposition to the trade: Baxter, Warburton, Paley, John Wesley, Whitefield.[2] They urged Christian principles to combat both slavery and the slave trade. In 1773 Wilberforce began to write against the slave trade. In 1780 Clarkson joined in the crusade: "If we oppress the stranger as I have shown, and if by a knowledge of his heart we find he is a person of the same passions and feelings as ourselves, we are certainly breaking, by the prosecution of the slave trade, that fundamental rule of Christianity which says, we shall not do that unto another which we wish should not be done to ourselves." After a long and bitter

1. For the movement against slave-trading and slave-holding among the Quakers, see *The Journal of John Woolman*, 1720-1772, in the *Harvard Classics*, Vol. I.
2. He subsequently permitted the introduction of slavery into Georgia.

struggle the slave trade was abolished in the British Empire in 1806-7. In the Congress of Vienna in 1815 the European powers undertook "to use especial efforts to abolish the traffic reproved by the laws of religion and nature."

The United States abolished the slave trade in 1807, and the great civilized Powers soon followed the example set by Great Britain and the United States, although as late as 1849 no less than 50,000 slaves are said to have been imported into Brazil alone.

*Abolition of Slavery*

Inspired by the same Christian principles was the movement for the abolition of slavery. It was religious influence and humane feelings, if not the direct action of the Christian Church, that in England sought first to ameliorate the condition of the West India slaves, and then to abolish slavery in its entirety. It cost the national exchequer no less than 20,000,000 pounds sterling to set the slaves free in 1833. But after a bitter struggle it was accomplished, and the sound heart of England gladly made the necessary sacrifice. Sweden followed in 1846; France in 1848; Denmark, Uruguay, Wallachia, and Tunis in 1849; and Portugal in 1855.

In the United States the very fabric of the Union itself was threatened before the slaves were ultimately set free as a war-measure. Those were unhappy years in 1830-1850 when more than one branch of the Christian Church proved recreant to the high message of the Christ and sought to prove the right of slavery. These Dr. Albert Barnes rebuked in a famous speech: "There is no power out of the Church that could sustain slavery for an hour if it were not sustained in it." But particularly among the smaller churches the living fire was fanned to a flame. The Christian principle of compassion and justice and brotherhood aroused such minds as Garrison's, Lovejoy's, Phillips', Johnson's to the conviction that the slave was a brother, that Christ had died for him, that no constitution could permanently support such an atrocious injustice as slavery. Garrison declared:

> "Emancipation must be the work of Christianity and the Church. They must achieve the elevation of the blacks and place them on the equality of the Gospels. . . . . I call upon the spirits of the just made perfect in heaven, upon all who have experienced the love of God in their souls here below, upon the Christian converts in India and the isles of the sea, to sustain one in the assertion, that there is power enough in the religion of Jesus Christ to melt down the most stubborn prejudices, to overthrow the highest wall of partition, to break the strongest caste, to improve and elevate the most degraded and to equalize all its recipients."

It was the Christian religion that sustained the great anti-slavery reformers in the United States, and aroused among the great mass of the folk the deepest opposition to slavery upon humane and religious grounds. This moral opposition ultimately brought about its abolition, even though at the cost of a great war.

*Abolition of Serfdom*

Nor must it be forgotten that not till the French Revolution were serfs set free in France, and not till the nineteenth century was this happy result achieved in Germany, Austria, Hungary, Denmark, Switzerland and Russia.

*Prison Reform*

The work inaugurated by John Howard to secure prison reform has been extended and deepened. Both his example and his writings[1] have inspired philanthropic effort to redeem the criminal and unfortunate. It was Christian love that animated and sustained him, and it was the Christian spirit in his followers[2] that led to the great reforms of the nineteenth century: the introduction of probation; grading and separating of prisoners;[3] the giving of educational facilities and religious services to men condemned; the abolition of degrading and senseless penalties and the general humanizing of all punishments; the use of reformatory, as well as deterrent, methods; the abolition of imprisonment for debt; the desire to win back the criminal rather than merely to punish him or even to safeguard society; the effort to develop and help the young rather than to inflict punishments after they have fallen into the criminal class; and many another gracious and helpful undertaking.

All these splendid achievements and reforms, with the extension and development of asylums, hospitals, reformatories and other institutions for the lame, the blind, the deaf, the idiots, the unfortunate of all kinds, the insane, dependent, delinquent, aged, all these compassionate efforts, and all measures to curtail excessive or cramping labor or to promote better conditions of work and more sanitary arrangements, and such Acts as the Lord's Day Act, that seeks to conserve both the spiritual and physical interests of the worker, all these are the product of that spirit which the Christian Church has sought to keep alive and to foster.

Nor have these efforts of compassion been made for man alone but for dumb animals as well, societies springing up on all sides, inspired by the very tenderness of the Master, that have sought to prevent cruelty and to encourage kindness.

*Position of Woman*

The Christian Faith has in every age operated to exalt the position of woman in society. In the Middle Ages chivalry added courtesy to the Christian attitude of reverence and respect. But in the common law of England the legal existence of a wife was suspended, or extinguished, during her marriage. Her fortune passed to her husband. She was placed almost absolutely in his hands as regards civil rights. She was not legally a person. She could not make a legal contract. The husband's and the wife's legal existences were merged into one, and that was the husband's, not the wife's.

1. His book, The State of Prisons in England and Wales, was first published in 1775.
2. Notably Neild, Mrs. Fry and the Prison Discipline Society.
3. Advocated by Jeremy Bentham.

In the nineteenth century the common law was modified in the Christian sense. Each human being has been more and more recognized in the Equity Courts of England as possessing a distinct personality and responsibility. Through Married Women's Property Acts the woman has been more and more recognized as the equal of 'the man. She was enabled to hold property as her own separate property. She could retain her own wages. In the same way in the United States after 1860 the rights of women have been greatly enlarged. In the Dominion of Canada, particularly in the Provinces, legislation in the interests of woman has been very advanced. The services rendered by women during the War have secured for them new positions of great dignity. They now have the vote, have entered Parliament, and have even been appointed to the Canadian Senate. They are Judges, Cabinet Ministers, and, in certain Churches, may become ordained ministers of the Gospel. The woman stands to-day on a legal, economic and social equality with the man. The Christian Faith, mediated through the Christian Church, has brought this to pass.

*The Home*

Another service the Christian Church has come more and more to render is to throw around fallen women the love and care of the environment of homes that are Christian. Not a few have been reclaimed to lives of sweetness and helpfulness. The Church has cared for the young and dependent, saving them from lives of shame. But greater than its work of redemption has been the work of upbuilding and prevention. And the Christian Church has done this through its increasing emphasis on home life, on the purity and stability of the marriage bond. There is great divergence of opinion in the various Christian Churches in the matter of divorce and the marriage of divorced persons. But all Churches are at one in finding the solution for this vexed problem in creating in the first instance a home on a Christian basis of mutual love and a recognition of mutual responsibility.

*International Relations*

Perhaps the most disheartening feature of our present survey of the social service of the Church is to ascertain how little Christian principles have influenced public relations between nations. Even when great advances have been made in Conventions and Agreements the actual intervention of war itself has too frequently led to a complete disregard of these on the part of one or both belligerents. And yet progress has been achieved. International law owes all too little to the Christian Church, but it does owe something to the permeating influence of Christian principles. We have already seen that Chivalry, the Truce of God, Arbitration Courts, were all achievements of the Church in the Middle Ages. But from the sixteenth century onwards new steps were taken. Henceforth it was forbidden to enslave prisoners of war. From 1648 it was the general custom of European nations to release all prisoners at the end of a war and without ransom. In the nineteenth century this practice was extended to other than Christian nations.

It was Grotius who in the seventeenth century began modern reforms in International Law. He declares:

> "For I saw prevailing through the Christian world a license in making war of which even barbarians would have been ashamed; recourse being had to arms for slight reason or no reason, and when arms were once taken up, all reverence for divine and human law was thrown away, just as if men were thenceforth authorized to commit all crime without restraint."

He expressed himself as in favor of Arbitrations "to prevent mischief far greater than going to law, namely: spoil, rapine, murther, yea, and sometimes desolation, which are the unhappy concomitants of war." He would have "constant diets and conventions of Christian princes" to compose all controversies and to force both parties to accept of peace upon equal and just terms.

Modern reforms have sought to limit the effect of war to combatants and to restrict damage to acts which were for the purpose of the War. In the same way privateering was regulated and then done away with on the high seas. The inviolability of private property on the sea was recognized, neutral commerce was protected, and war confined to belligerents. All public buildings for scientific and philanthropic purposes were to be respected, all works of art were forbidden to be carried off. Out of the Genevan Convention of 1864 and the work of the Red Cross Society were provided better care for the sick and wounded, even of the enemy. These provisions were all without exception terribly violated in the recent Great War. But when they were violated it was done for the first time in the history of the world with the reprobation of the whole world. A Christian conscience had been created and was aroused among all civilized peoples even in the matter of War.

It had been hoped also that there had been formed a stronger disposition to mediation and arbitration. Tribunals had been set up in the Peace Palace at the Hague to adjudicate upon international disputes. These had not been without their helpfulness, but in the crisis of August, 1914, all proved unavailing save the fatal appeal to the arbitrament of the sword. The lessons of that struggle are written in the experiences of over four years of sustained combat and in the no less heavy problems precipitated by the tremendous difficulties of the Peace Years. We may not look for a New Earth from the League of Nations nor from World Courts nor from Conferences on Disarmament. But we may hope for better things in the way of "Peace on Earth and Goodwill towards Men." The Christian Church will make its best contribution by its emphasis on its fundamental principles of love and brotherhood and by an aggressive programme of Foreign Missions. For Foreign Missions is perhaps the Church's most constructive work in the sphere of international influence.

In his *Gesta Christi*, 355, Brace has enumerated the following as constituting the influence of the Christian Faith or "Religion of Love" in limiting the evils of war:

"We have beheld it redeeming the lot of the prisoner of war from one exposed to massacre and slavery to that of the captive humanely treated under modern international customs. We have seen it ministering to the wants of the wounded and protecting all that belongs to their care even in the army of an enemy. We have found it prohibiting even the killing of an unarmed enemy, forbidding all useless destruction of life and property, all injury to women or defenceless persons, all objectless wasting of fields and fruits. We have seen it doing away with piracy and privateering, with the plunder of philanthropic and scientific buildings, with all private booty, and even urging the protection of private property on the sea."

*Foreign Missions*

It was the religious movement of the eighteenth century that led to the enthusiasm for foreign missionary endeavor which had been so striking a feature of church activity in the past century. Compassion for the heathen had its source in the same religious impulse that led to the liberation of the slave. The voyages of Captain Cook awakened a new interest in the men of all parts of the world.

The London Missionary Society grew up with a membership composed of men of all the Churches. It sent John Williams to the Pacific Islands. Darwin paid a glowing trubute to the work of the missionaries in this quarter: "They had abolished human sacrifices and the power of an idolatrous priesthood, a system of profligacy unparalleled in any part of the world, and bloody wars, and had greatly reduced dishonesty, intemperance and licentiousness." The very piece of rock on which the natives brained little children before eating them has now become a Christian font. Robert Moffatt went to Africa. Johann Krapf labored in Abyssinia, then at Mombasa, and produced a vocabulary of six African languages. Missionaries followed Carey and Henry Martyn to India. In fact, William Carey may be regarded as the English pioneer in the modern missionary movement. His great watchwords were: "Expect great things from God," and "Attempt great things for God." He completed the translation of the Bible in Bengali, and became the father of all modern Bengali literature. His labors were colossal in the forty-one years he spent in Bengal. He is the leader in modern missionary methods. David Livingstone gave his life to heal "the open sore of the world." as he called the devastating slave trade of Central Africa.

As the nineteenth century advanced the Churches took in hand the definite task of evangelizing the whole world. An increasing co-operation grew up among Protestant missions that led at length to a well-defined comity of effort. Since the days of Carey a tremendous advance has been made not only in the results attained, but also in the interest awakened, and in the methods employed.

Many different types of missionary endeavor have been employed, evangelistic, educational, medical. In times of famine and pestilence the Church has engaged in a noble relief work, and on a generous scale. It has called a native clergy into being. It has found for women a special ministry among women, in schools, in orphanages, in hospitals and among all kinds of sick and suffering. When Mrs. Caldwell, the wife of a missionary bishop in Southern India, began in 1853 to teach girls to read, their amazed parents exclaimed: "She will be teaching the cows next."

It is impossible here to make a survey of the Christian missions scattered over the whole world. But they are to be found in every country though only too often the equipment is inadequate, and the small staff unequal to the great opportunities presented. At the present time nothing less than a ferment is active throughout the East. "The work is so vast," writes Mrs. Creighton, "the opportunities so unrivalled, the call so urgent and clamorous as to tax all the resources of Christendom. It is true to say that never before in modern times has the most enlightened and progressive thought in the Christian Church been so interested in foreign missions." And again, "The missionary enterprise now, as ever, is the great adventure of the Christian Church. It is the source of hope and courage, the vision of the future to the believing Christian. Its annals are as full of exciting incidents as any romance, its ranks are rich with the names of heroes, and the record of its work brings new life and inspiration to those who, in the complications and disillusionments of the old world, are losing their ideals and their faith."

And these missions have played a great role not only in extending a knowledge of the Kingdom of God but also in spreading civilization. They have been pioneers in education and industry in heathen lands. They have built up splendid communities of useful men. A remarkable tribute to the transforming power of the Christian message and the social significance of missions is contained in the Inscription to Rev. John Geddie, Hero of the New Hebrides, in the church at Anelcauhat, Aneityum—"When I came to this land there was no man of light here, but when I left this land, there was no man of darkness in it."[1]

Missions have repressed the slave trade in Africa, and altars now stand where once were slave-markets and whipping-posts. They have done away with cannibalism and wholesale slaughter. They have opened up the countries of the world to trade and intercourse, and encouraged agriculture and all kinds of industries. They have put down drink, exposed atrocities as in the Congo, awakened the conscience of the world to the havoc wrought by opium, protected the rights of natives, worked for the abolition of enforced labor, and preached Christ and him crucified. Lord Lawrence once said: "Notwithstanding all that the English people have done to benefit India, the missionaries have done more than all other agencies." And Mrs. Creighton thus speaks of their contribution to culture: "Mis-

---

1. J. W. Falconer, John Geddie, Hero of the New Hebrides, Frontispiece.

sionaries have not only done much for civilization, they have also done much for science. All over the world they have been the first to reduce illiterate languages to writing, to make grammars for them, to provide them with translations of the Bible and other books. They have been foremost amongst discoveries and explorers of unknown lands, and their studies of the customs of primitive peoples have been a most important contribution to ethnology. Many of them have been distinguished as naturalists, geographers and scientific observers, and their letters home, from the days of the earliest Franciscan and Jesuit missionaries to the present time, are an important contribution to our knowledge of the world."[1]    And not the least achievement will be made by the Christian Church in the field of Foreign Missions when, as is now contemplated, the Mission churches will be transformed into Native Churches increasingly self-governing and self-supporting.

*The Church Not Bankrupt in Service*

Whatever other result the Great War had, however we may deplore the failure of the Church on that occasion to stem the tide of War itself, it left men in no manner of doubt but that the Church could rouse its members to defend the weak, to fight wrong, to face sacrifice, and to meet death. Nineteen centuries of social service have not exhausted the resources of the Church nor left it bankrupt to do good. They have rather created and developed a power and a will to serve in the spirit of Christian chivalry and sympathy and love. The teachings of the Christ are still valid and strong in their inspiration and impulses. Jesus had no specific political teaching to impart, but his principle of attaching value to human life works, and will work through all ages, to modify existing institutions in the direction of human betterment. The Christ released a moral force, that, during nineteen centuries, in spite of unions with state authorities, in spite of selfish hierarchical organizations, in spite of bigotry, corruption and ignorance, has achieved through the Christian Church certain definite results. It even gives evidence of increasing vitality as the centuries pass and as the Christian spirit is allowed fuller sway and dominion among men. It is not simply that the Christian Faith would teach us to think of the receiver of alms as well as the giver. It is not simply that the Christian Church lends its influence in support of honest trade, of war against wrong, of care of the weak, of the stewardship of wealth, and of the myriad of things which it does support and for which it does provide. It also guarantees that the Future will be kept humane and helpful because its own principles are supported by a Living Person, and that, the undying Christ. The end is not yet. He will in his own power and person never cease to awaken love. And whoever loves Him will, also, inevitably, love the whole brotherhood of men.

*Time Would Fail*

And what shall I more say? For the time would fail to tell the full story of services rendered in this Age as in every Age, only,

1. Missions, Their Rise and Development, 193.

perhaps, more conscientiously and more fully in this than in most Ages, in the work done in the Community by the local Church in the way of what has come to be almost regular routine. The preaching of the Crucified, the holding aloft of the torch of truth, the proclamation of the hope of a blessed future life, the challenge to better living, the denunciation of sin and injustice and wrong, the steadying influence and calming power of the enunciation of great principles and a love divine,—what this has meant in comfort, in holy living, in social good, no pen can ever write.

The pastoral work of the Minister of the Gospel, the cheer and blessing of the presence of the man of God, the kindliness in times of stress and loss, the sanctifying influence at the wedding festival, the comfort in the valley of deepest shadows, the coming and going in a Community of a friend who seeks only its good, who inspires the young and heartens the old, who gives honest counsel and unafraid to all,—this is a contribution that can never be assessed at anything approaching its true worth. Even the existence of the Church in a Community as a visible and permanent witness to things divine, the assembling of the people together on the Lord's Day, the symbol in their midst of an underlying and supporting unity of faith and worship, the demands that it has made in the way of voluntary sacrifice, the undying reminder that the issues of life are spiritual and eternal, that there is a God who lives and loves,—these things are beyond the price set in the market place or on the Exchange.

That for nineteen centuries the Church alone, in season and out of season, despite seeming falterings here and there, and mistakes at this or that time, the Church alone of all institutions in the world has sought man's good, has challenged his moral life, has supported his faith, has reminded him of the Better Country and shown the way, has spoken of God, has preached the story of the Cross,—this is *the* social service of the Church, and the gates of hell shall not prevail against it.

One does not usually go to *Punch* for a record of the social achievements of the Christian Church. But the lines which it published on the occasion of the death of Dr. Selwyn, first Bishop of New Zealand, might appropriately be applied to the transforming significance of the humble efforts of many a Christ-like worker on the Frontier "of whom the world was not worthy":

> "And there the Bishop stood, between the war
> Of clans and chiefs and settlers, all alone,
> Holding the Christian banner high and far
> 'Bove smoke of strife and noise of warriors blown.
>
> "Till savages were weaned from savageness,
> And white men owned a faith ne'er owned till then;
> And school and church rose in the wilderness,
> Fruit of the seed of Love,—Good will to men!"[1]

1. Quoted J. W. Falconer, John Geddie, Hero of the New Hebrides, 4.

## (c) CHARACTER OF THE SOCIAL ACHIEVEMENT

As one studies the social achievements of this period he is impressed by these facts:

1. The great contribution made by the Church at the end of the eighteenth century and afterwards was a larger spiritual power, a broader sympathy, and a stronger impulse towards practical effort.

2. Until near the close of the nineteenth century the Church did not itself as an organization furnish leadership for the solution of pressing social problems. It was content to confine itself largely to its own church work and to developing the men to attack these social problems.

3. From the close of the nineteenth century there has been distinctly a more aggressive attitude towards social questions on the part of the Churches. Many of them, while omitting no activity and overlooking no interest that formerly engaged their attention, have deliberatly adopted as an integral part of their policy "to Christianize the social order."

4. Through benevolent schemes and other means the Churches are seeking to meet the social needs of its own workers; through Home Missions and Social Departments, to meet the religious and social needs of the handicapped and unfortunate elements of society, and of the needy and frontier settlements of the Country; and through Foreign Missions, to meet the religious needs of unchristianized peoples, and to promote an international brotherhood of good will through the world, not merely a warless world, but the more positive implementing of the angel's message sung over the pasture-lands at Bethlehem.

5. Finally the Churches through federations and unions have sought to remove the reproach that they are unwilling to be socially-minded or to co-operate in aggressive social effort. The Federation of the churches of America has adopted what is practically a common programme for all churches. Unions of Churches, notably in Canada, Scotland, England, India, have prepared the way for still greater social achievements on the part of the Christian Church.

### QUESTIONS FOR DISCUSSION

1. How do you account for the fact that great social service—much of it a kind that was humane, if not distinctively Christian—was rendered by the Committee of Public Safety in France at a time when France possessed a worship that was anti-Christian? Ought these services to be reckoned to the credit of the Christian Church?

2. Are the "Quanta Cura" and the "Syllabus" social services rendered by the Church?

3. To what extent is the Church responsible for reforms in Factory Legislation? In the abolition of the Slave Trade and Slavery?

4. Was the battle waged for criticism by Professor Robertson Smith, a social service rendered by the Church?

5. What social services have Home Missions rendered to the Nation in Canada and the United States?

6. What social services have Foreign Missions rendered to the world since Carey?

7. Is the work done by the Y.M.C.A. and the Salvation Army a social service rendered by the Christian Church? Could this have been done within the organized Church?

8. Is Socialism better suited to render social service than the Christian Church? If not, why not?

9. What social services has the Church rendered in the nineteenth and twentieth centuries to the following: Women; Prisoners; the Defective; the Drunkard?

10. Why could not the Church have prevented the War with Germany?

11. What social service did the Church render in the Great War?

12. Which is making a greater contribution of social service in the world to-day, the Roman Catholic or the Protestant Churches? What is the difference in their conceptions of social service?

13. "The claim is often boldly advanced that the Labor Movement better interprets the spirit of Jesus than the Churches do." Discuss.

### Books for Advanced Study

John Morley, *Voltaire, Rousseau.* Shailer Mathews, *The French Revolution.* Seignobos' *Political History of Europe Since 1814* (MacVane). *The Progress of the Century* (Harper & Bros.). William Barry, *The Papacy and Modern Times.* J. MacCaffrey, *History of the Catholic Church in the Nineteenth Century.* F. K. Neilson, *History of the Papacy in the Thirteenth Century.* W. Walker, *A History of the Christian Church.* Mrs. Creighton, *Missions, Their Rise and Development.* J. R. Mott, *The Present World Situation.* C. H. Robinson, *History of Christian Missions.* J. H. Oldham, *The World and the Gospel.* Mrs. Carus-Wilson, *The Expansion of Christianity.* G. Smith, *Life of Henry Martyn.* G. Smith, *Life of William Carey.* J. S. Dennis, *Christian Missions and Social Progress.* W. H. P. Faunce, *The Social Aspects of Foreign Missions.* The Message of the Canadian Chaplains, O.S.M.F. to the Churches of Canada. Hutchins and Harrison, *History of Factory Legislation.* Brace, *Gesta Christi.* Ernst Troeltsch, *Protestantism and Progress.* Francis Herbert Stead, *The Story of Social Christianity.* Foster, *History of New England Theology.*

Chapter VIII

# THE PRESENT TREND AND THE PRESENT ISSUE

(a) The Present Trend

A Recent Development. Many-sided Social Programme. A Criticism. Co-operation. The Task of a Church. The Present Trend of Social Achievement.

(b) The Present Issue

(i) The Social Function of the Church. (ii) The Church in the Life of the Nation. (iii) The Church in the Life of the World.

## (a) THE PRESENT TREND

*A Recent Development*

After the evening cures in Capernaum, Mark tells us, Jesus withdrew to a solitary place to pray. There Peter excitedly sought him out—"Every one is seeking thee." Jesus replied—"Let us go elsewhere, to the neighboring towns. I must preach there also. For that was what I came out for." Instead of returning to Capernaum, he preached in their synagogues throughout all Galilee, and, adds Mark, "cast out devils." In spite of the conviction that the proclamation of the Kingdom was his real, or at least primary, work, Jesus, nevertheless, did "cast out devils." The early Protestant Churches, like Jesus, had the belief that the preaching of the Word, and not social service, was the real work of the Church as such. They were content to leave social endeavor to the State, which, so Protestant theologians were now teaching, was also an instrument of God. As a consequence, we see the Protestant Churches, in the period following the Reformation, proclaiming the Gospel to their members, we see the Christian spirit operating to convict men of sin, but we do not see a socialized Church working for a definite programme of reform. They assumed, as in the Middle Ages, that the State was a Divine Institution; but, unlike the Middle Ages, they assumed that it would find its authority and duties set forth in the Scriptures. This naïve faith in the State is seen in Geneva, Scotland and the Puritan Commonwealth, where Christian social effort actually did become the State ideal. As a consequence Protestant Synods pronounced on Articles and Creeds, but not upon Capital, Labor Class Struggles, unearned Increment, or Social Justice.

In the eighteenth century, deistic and atheistic philosophies arose, yielding godless Revolutions and secular States. A corrupt Walpole in England or the Committee of Public Safety in France, however beneficent the peace maintained by the former and the social reforms inaugurated by the latter, could not so easily be regarded by the Church as the arm of the Lord as could a Calvin or a Cromwell. The Church's confidence in the State was shaken.

At the same time, the Religious Revivals of the eighteenth century produced a new humanitarianism. Even so, the Churches, as Churches, did not embark upon the campaign of social reform. But, as in confronting actual need Jesus "cast out devils," so in the face of specific social need, Christian men, in the spirit of Christ, with a flame of zeal lighted at the altars of the new Revivals, attacked the problems and evils that confronted them. The Church itself did not as yet initiate measures of social reform. It was content to preach the Word. Nevertheless, it could not but rejoice that thereby it was able to inspire its members to inaugurate policies of social betterment. The effort to Christianize the whole social order has been only a comparatively recent development, an ideal programme set up by most of the Protestant churches, provoked to do so by the Industrial Revolution, the accentuation of wealth and poverty, the political economy in the state its favored wealth and industry, and the new Science which seemed to endanger the idea of the worth of individuals.

*Many-sided Social Programme*

To understand the drift of modern endeavor in the Churches, one must study not only its missionary enterprise, its educational work, its preaching, its pastoral service, its benevolent activities in providing for its aged and infirm ministers and for its widows and orphans, but one must also appreciate its many-sided social programme. To do this one should study, for instance, such a survey as is given in the Year Book of the Church and Social Service in the United States, prepared by Harry F. Ward for the Federal Council of the Churches of Christ in America. We note that when the Congregationalists, the United Brethren and the Methodists in 1906 were negotiating an organic union, one of the five Articles of the creed adopted was wholly devoted to the social duty of the Church: "We believe that according to Christ's law men of the Christian faith exist for the service of man, not only in holding forth the word of life, but in the support of works and institutions of pity and charity, in the maintenance of human freedom, in the deliverance of all those who are oppressed, in the enforcement of civic justice, and in the rebuke of all unrighteousness."[1] In the Men and Religion Movement of 1910 nothing was more remarkable than the response to the social service message and programme. In the past decades the social movement in the Churches has deepened its significance and widened its influence. "A social consciousness and a social conscience have been developed within the churches. Their social will is strengthening, and they

1. Article xx of the Basis of Union of The United Church of Canada is entitled "Of Christian Service and Final Triumph,"—"We believe that it is our duty as disciples and servants of Christ to further the extension of His Kingdom, to do good unto all men, to maintain the public and private worship of God, to hallow the Lord's Day, to preserve the inviolability of marriage and the sanctity of the family, to uphold the just authority of the State, and so to live in all honesty, purity and charity that our lives shall testify of Christ. We joyfully receive the word of Christ, bidding His people go into all the world and make disciples of all nations, declaring unto them that God was in Christ reconciling the world unto Himself, and that He will have all men to be saved and come to the knowledge of the truth. We confidently believe that by His power and grace all His enemies shall finally be overcome, and the kingdoms of this world be made the kingdom of our God and of His Christ."

are determined to make the gospel real, to carry it to its uttermost conclusion in the social order as in the individual life."

This Year Book describes in detail elaborate Church social service organizations with their general plan of work. There is a Federal Council with a Commission of more than one hundred social workers of the entire nation who represent the view-point of the churches. These maintain an intimate relation with educational institutions in the interest of training men and women for a social service which will have the distinctively spiritual point of view, with national agencies for social reform, with young people's organizations, and other groups similarly interested. They have inaugurated a campaign for one-day-in-seven for industrial workers. They have conducted several important investigations into industrial conditions. They have inspired the Churches to co-operative local social service. Each of the great Protestant Bodies of North America maintains a Church Social Service Organization. The Year Book contains a Directory of these. It also contains for each a statement of objectives and of means employed to reach these. Thus the objectives of the Social Service Department of the Northern Baptist Convention are as follows:

1. To make known the principles of social Christianity.

2. To interpret the Gospel of Jesus Christ in terms of human life and social redemption.

3. To arouse the spirit of social service in all our churches

4. To secure the co-operation of our churches with all other agencies doing social work.

5. To outline definite and constructive programmes for our churches in their work for community betterment.

6. To interpret the spirit and aims of the churches to the industrial workers of our land.

7. To show that the Christian Gospel leads to social effort and that true social effort is essentially Christian.

8. To suggest lessons in social service study for our people.

9. To represent the denomination in an official capacity at all meetings where Labor and Social Service are discussed.

The means adopted by the Department to realize its objectives are stated as follows:

1. By the discussion of social service work in the meetings of our churches.

2. By the consideration of the work of social service at associational meetings and state conventions.

3. By holding conferences and conventions at such times and places as seem necessary.

4. By distributing and publishing literature bearing upon this work.

5. By preparing social service study lessons and by correspondence courses.

6. By the utilization of a speakers' bureau.

7. By co-operating with the theological seminaries in the work of seminary extension.

8. By giving special attention to the country church in its relation to community service.

9. By conducting headquarters with a reference library and card index covering all phases of the work.

In this Year Book are found a chapter devoted to Publications and Bibliography with courses of reading on social subjects for ministers and workers, a chapter presenting suggestions for methods and programmes for local churches and groups of churches as worked out by the various denominational agencies, a list of co-operating agencies at work in the different fields which the church is called upon to enter, and a chapter containing some of the utterances of various church bodies concerning social and industrial questions. Thus one of the constituent churches of the present United Church of Canada, for instance, declared its belief in a programme:

> "For the acknowledgment of the obligations of wealth; for the application of Christian principles to industrial associations; for a more equitable distribution of wealth; for the abolition of poverty; for the protection of childhood; for the safeguarding of the working people from dangerous machinery; for compensation for industrial accidents; for the regulation of working conditions in other ways; for one day's rest in seven; for conciliation and arbitration in industrial disputes; for proper housing; for proper care of dependents and criminals and the prevention of crime and vice; for pure food and drugs; for wholesale recreation; and for international peace."

Among the themes on which the Churches uttered their voices are Industrial and Social Conditions, Social Justice, Capital, Labor, Industrial Democracy, Class Struggles, Wealth and Poverty, Unearned Increment in Land Values, Social Redemption and Peace. The Reformed Church in the United States put its social creed in the following words:

> "We believe that, in order to save others, those who are saved must, in accordance with the Christian law of love, do whatever in them lies to ameliorate the conditions, purify the environment and sanctify the relations in which men and women must live.

> "We believe that the work of saving the world hence implies the Christianizing of the entire social order, so that all the relations of life shall be controlled and governed by the Christian law of love.

> "We believe that such a Christian social order is indispensable to the full development of the individual."

The most recent reports of the Board of Evangelism and Social Service of The United Church of Canada show that beside its central concern for Evangelism the Board is definitely engaged in a varied social service and exercises a guidance and supervision of definitely redemptive and protective activities and agencies. It makes continuous surveys of the Dominion situation in the matter of traffic in alcohol. It makes a sustained effort to persuade every person, young and old, to adopt and declare a right personal attitude to liquor. It has participated in the successful agitation to have Parliament adopt measures to prevent the exportation of liquor to the United States declaring that, apart from being a scandal to Christian Canada, such exportation was a menace to international good will. The Board constantly draws the attention of the Church to the profound changes in all nations affecting the conception of the State and its functions, and the relation of the Church to the industrial order and to finance and industry. At the time of writing, the Board has Committees at work in various Provinces of the Dominion surveying the industrial field in Canada and preparing findings for a report on "The Christianization of Industry." The Board has also Redemptive Homes and Schools for Girls and Farm Centres for Boys. Its work for Juvenile Delinquency is not extensive but has been very successful. The Board has also taken over the obligations of the Armenian Relief Association of Canada and has cared for a considerable number of Armenian Orphans. The Board also engages in research work, especially regarding the effects of alcohol. It has promoted throughout the Dominion Study Groups for ministers, particularly on spiritual themes. It is characteristic of the modern trend of church life and work that the same Board should, at the same time, promote the evangelistic presentation of Jesus Christ and the claims of the Church and engage in an effort to organize, on a national scale, personal abstinence from liquor and a resistance to the nefarious traffic in narcotics.

In a recent report to the General Council, the Board of Evangelism and Social Service of The United Church of Canada thus defines its field of effort and its purpose:

"Rapidly changing conditions and the trend of modern thinking regarding moral and social forces, reveal the truth that responsibilities confronting the Church to-day bear very little resemblance to the same problems as they appeared twenty, or even fifteen years ago. This fact demands careful reflection in determining policies. It is more and more apparent that in this wide and varied branch of service, the Church must give its strength to educational efforts rather than attempt to secure reforms by direct political action. Facts are God's arguments. Hence the Board regards its duty primarily to be the discovery of facts, the revealing of spiritual values, and the presentation of these to the Church. By this means, there is reasonable hope to believe that an informed public opinion and a sustained political conscience may be created which will find expression through political channels and finally have its convictions, when necessary, enacted by law."

In the Dominion of Canada has been formed the Social Service Council of Canada. This is a Federal Council of Churches and other organizations for the promotion of social welfare. Among the organizations thus federated are Social Service Councils in each of the Provinces and in Bermuda and Newfoundland, the Council for Social Service of the Church of England in Canada, the Board of Evangelism and Social Service of The United Church of Canada, the Social Service Boards of the Baptist Conventions of Canada, the Salvation Army, the Y.M.C.A. and Y.W.C.A. National Councils, the Victorian Order of Nurses, the Canadian Prisoners' Welfare Association and the Federation of Women's Institutes The Social Service Council publishes a magazine entitled "Social Welfare." It holds annual meetings for reports and discussions. A review of its work for the year 1929-30 shows that it was responsible for a careful study of labor and living conditions in the steel industry of Canada, a report on "The Trend of Family Life and Marriage in our Times," a study of conditions in the Provincial prisons, and the granting of Social Service Fellowships to post-graduate students of the Universities. The Social Service Council is linked with the Christian Social Council of England (The Council of Churches in England for Social Questions) and through it with the Life and Work Movement inaugurated at the World Conference at Stockholm in 1925.

Canon Vernon, President of the Social Service Council of Canada, has recently defined its aims:

"In its emphasis on personality modern social work has, I am sure, the mind of Christ. While our Council and our churches need the burning and prophetic zeal of the days of our first love and our first enthusiasm, we dare not fail to avail ourselves of all the rapidly accumulating, rich stores of modern and scientific knowledge of our great 'Science and Art of Human Fellowship.' But we still need to live dangerously. I sometimes wonder whether social service has not become too popular and won its place on the map too rapidly. The best and purest age of the Christian Church was the period when it was dangerous to be a Christian, when the very name was despised, hated and unpopular, and it took real courage, a courage apt to be tested by persecution even unto death, to profess the name of Christ. The conversion of the Emperor Constantine, followed by the widespread conversion or pretended conversion of thousands, the recognition of the Church by the State, the growing popularity and wealth of the Church, made it easier and more popular to be a Christian than a heathen, and a loss of zeal, of self-sacrifice, of purity of ideal and of life too widely followed.

"Social service to-day is living in an era of popularity. The world accepts it. Employed social workers are, in the main, adequately remunerated. Vast sums are often collected by modern campaign methods to which our wealthy captains of industry readily respond. Is there not real danger in this change of the world's attitude? May not leaders of social work, for fear of losing the support of the rich too readily accept things as they are, and fall into the old social heresy of ministering relief even though it comes disguised as an angel of light and takes the form of the most approved modern case work, instead of following the more radical line of seeking the destruction of whatever demons and devils there are which corrupt the life of the individual, the country, the nation, the world? May we not sometimes forget that real social rehabilitation is impossible without spiritual restoration? May we not sometimes be content to offer social welfare work as an opiate to a sick community and a substitute for the wholesome surgery of social justice? We need to consolidate our positions, to present a bold and aggressive front against the forces of social evil, to risk unpopularity and to be content to live dangerously.

"The Social Service Council of Canada occupies a unique position of privilege, of opportunity, of responsibility. Its chief work, I firmly believe, is to stand as interpreter and mediator between all that is best and most worthwhile in modern social work and the great, and still largely uninformed, constituency of our churches. Our duty to modern social work is to understand, to interpret, to inspire with that Spirit of the Master, without which its wheels of elaborate machinery and developed method will in the long run prove futile. Our duty to the people of our churches is to interpret and explain the best ideals and the best methods of modern social work and to inspire them with a burning zeal to minister alike with Christian love and devotion and in the most approved way to the needs of others: at the same time, ever to keep in mind the vision of the new and Christian social order, in which life is more than livelihood, work well done more than wages, and service for others more than our personal gain."[1]

Enough has been written to illustrate the present trend of social service in the Christian Church in the Dominion of Canada and the United States. But a practical study of great usefulness and importance would be to assemble the most recent expositions of aims set forth in the highest Courts of as many Churches as possible on both sides of the Atlantic, and to note divergencies and common tendencies. Only by such an empirical study can one speak with confidence of the present trend.

*A Criticism*

Nor must we forget, in considering the present trend of social service, the criticism made against the Church of pursuing an antiquated and short-sighted policy in its social service. It is alleged that its members give relief from sentimental motives without personal knowledge of its effects. It is even asserted that they employ charity to make converts. Others claim that only a few

1. *Social Welfare*, May, 1930.

adopt discriminating methods, and that the spirit of co-operation as between the various churches and with other benevolent agencies is often lacking. In this connection it is important to listen to the late Professor Henderson on the Perils of Voluntary Charity:

"The regulative principles of relief methods have been discussed, and may be used here as critical tests. Violations of these principles are followed by serious results. Mendicancy and hypocrisy are fostered. A hungry person is greatly tempted to lie and profess any faith, and even a variety of creeds each day, if the hope is held out to him of thereby securing food, and especially drink. One tramp declared to a member of my class that gentlemen of his profession often support themselves all winter by 'working the missions.' This tramp knew one who boasted of having been 'saved' about fifty times. Such moral evils arise from neglect of co-operating with the Charity Organization Society. The smallest part of the damage lies in money lost on impostors; and the most serious evil is the hopeless degradation of the recipients who are encouraged to live by fraud. By using the aid of the Charity Organization Society such abuses are reduced to a minimum.

"Religious charity has a great advantage. If wisely conducted, it goes deepest into the spirit. Elizabeth Fry said that "Charity to the soul is the soul of charity." Religion teaches the almsgiver to regard the poor, not as objects of patronage, nor as mere animals who have no other needs than food and warmth; but as brothers, children of the same Divine Father, heirs of the eternal life, capable of endless development in all qualities of humanity. Religious teaching always has been, and ever must be, the most profound and enduring motive to beneficent gifts and services. There is no conceivable substitute for it."

*Co-operation*

As to the charge of failing to co-operate in the past, the Churches can only shamefacedly plead "Guilty!" But it is a happy sign that in recent years there has been a decided disposition to amend. In his *American Charities,* A. G. Warner gives the Church District Plan in Buffalo as the best illustration of a definite scheme of co-operation between a social service institution or charity organization society and the churches:

"The plan proposed to divide the city into districts, each district to be assigned a church. The Churches accepting a district agreed to care for every family not otherwise cared for by an individual, organization, or other church. When a family needing care had a definite church connection, that church was to be asked to provide the necessary visitor and such needed material relief as it could afford, calling on the society for the rest. If the family had no responsible church connection, it was to be referred to the church district which had agreed to provide a friendly visitor to work with the

\     society, and such material relief as it could afford. Further-
more, each church accepting a district pledged itself to feel a
special responsibility for the moral elevation of its district,
through friendly visiting to referred families and such other
agencies as settlements, clubs, classes, etc., as it could
establish."

*The Task of a Church*

The greatest social service of a Church will ever be to create
men, kindled with the passion for the good of their fellows,
strengthened by Divine might in their inner man. The sum total
of a Church's activities is their social service. To assess and weigh
that is beyond our power. But it is possible to pass in review the
labors of moral and social reform that a modern Protestant Church
undertakes. Thus The United Church of Canada possesses a special
Department called the Board of Evangelism and Social Service. One
Branch has to do with stimulating and recording the general progress
in Temperance sentiment and legislation throughout the Dominion.
The Church is kept informed of such new laws and amendments to
existing Statutes adopted by Provincial Legislatures and the Parliament of Canada as reflect the humanizing tendencies manifested
throughout the Dominion. Thus we are informed: "A genuine
desire to protect human life; anxiety to care for and provide for the
helpless and the young; a determination to encourage the recognition
of the spirit of justice among all classes; the need for severer
punishment for the violation of virtue are emphasized in the legislation of last year."[1]   The Church thus marks its interest in such
matters as minimum wages for women, education of the blind,
Mothers' Allowance Acts, the problem of venereal diseases, industrial conditions, children's protection, commercialized vice. The
Church in this way also maintains Social Settlements with Baby
Health Centres, Fresh Air Camps, Sunday Schools, Clubs, Mothers'
Meetings and other community activities: Redemptive Homes;
Homes for fatherless and motherless children. Other Departments
of this Board and of the Church make provision for Hospitals, for
School Homes, for work among the New Canadians, for Evangelism,
for Foreign Missions, for Education, for Publications. One needs
to read the Reports of the General Council to appreciate how many-
sided is such social enterprise. One has only to study the activities
of any local congregation to see this work in the actual process. The
Church has not given up the task of regenerating the individual.
But it believes that this work is not accomplished till it has linked
him to a task of social service, fighting against social evils, Christianizing all human relations, establishing social justice, outlawing War,
and crusading for God's Kingdom. "So we, being many, are one
body in Christ, and every one members one of another."

*The Present Trend of Social Achievement*

Social Service has in recent decades taken on a new point of
view and received a fresh impetus. And everything in Social Service

---

1. Report of 1921 of the Board of Home Missions and Social Service, Presbyterian
Church in Canada.

depends on impetus and point of view. The old poor relief, indiscriminate almsgiving, the dispensation of charity for the merit of the giver, the thought of a Church as a place where one received salvation or edification and himself gave nothing to some great purpose, these things are passing away. It is high time. We cannot any longer salve our conscience by pitching a dole to a needy brother. He must be taken into our heart and to his rightful place in the social organism. The new view of service looks to social justice, to the removal of unfair handicaps, to the establishment of proper opportunity for each to develop his life. There is a frank recognition that the Church, that all society, is vastly concerned when unjust handicaps or intolerable loads of exploitation or vice or disease crush or maim life.

The present trend is back to that meaningful point of view of the Master's, that individual life, however mean in aspect, is of infinite worth, that we must go out to seek that which is lost, to recover and make whole. Nothing that pertains to human interests is alien to the Church. "The home," says Edward T. Devine in *Social Forces,* speaking of the new view, "the factory, the school, the church, and the playground are all within its range. Disease, misery, and crime are seen, but seen in their true proportions, as a dark border land into which constantly new streams of light and energy are pouring with promise of ultimately taking possession." And it is the social service of the Church to outpour those new streams of light and energy.

And therefore men give themselves to the task in these days of protecting, as well as teaching, the young; of understanding and preventing disease no less than curing it; of restoring rather than merely punishing offenders; of considering the standard of living as well as regarding merely supply and demand in determining wages; of making an industry out of its profits bear the responsibility entailed by the deaths and injuries of its employees rather than ruthlessly imposing these on the family of the killed or disabled; of giving to all an education that will equip for life.

"It is the old view," says Devine,[1] "that those who found a charity or conduct a benevolent institution of any kind are from the mere fact of this association with charity to be looked upon with a certain degree of deference, their selfishness and eccentricities to be excused their motives to be accepted as sufficient justification for any follies and mistakes. It is the new view that effort expended in charity, as in any other direction, is to be judged by its result; that efficiency and comon sense are essential in the relief of the unfortunate as in any other equally important undertaking; that preparation and training and experience have their appropriate place in social work as in other serious callings.

"It is the old view that each agency for social betterment is a law unto itself. In the new view co-operation is the keynote. The old view emphasized the institution, the society; the mechanism by

1. Edward T. Devine, Social Forces, 10-13.

which is sought to do good. The new view is of the end to be accomplished, subordinating the agency, the method, and the worker to the end in view, to the family in trouble, to the individual who is in need, to the condition which is to be remedied. The new view is incompatible with institutionalism, with fruitless isolated labor, with working at cross purposes. The new view is democratic, co-operative, enthusiastic.

"The new view is that behind every form of degeneration, dependence, and injustice there is apt to be some intrenched pecuniary interest which it is desirable to discover and with which it is the duty of society to deal. It is the old view that the depraved man is the natural man, and that some families are inherently superior to others merely because of their better ancestry. It is the new view that there are no differences between the poor man and his normal neighbors which cannot be rapidly obliterated. The old view put the emphasis on the defects and weaknesses revealed by the family history. The new puts the emphasis on latent powers, new motives, and favorable conditions, on the release and guidance of energy, rather than its restraint.

"The new view of what? The new view of life—the new view of the common welfare; the new view of industrial and social forces; the new view of childhood, of womanhood and manhood; the new view of housing as the basis of domestic life; the new view of industrial occupations and the conditions under which they are carried on; the new view of misery and crime and disease as eradicable; the new view of charity, of reformation, of discipline, of human society; the new view of work, of recreation, of neighborhood; and, at last, the new view, prophetic though it be, of a social order in which ancient wrongs shall be righted, new corruptions foreseen and prevented, the nearest approach to equality of opportunity assured, and the individual rediscovered under conditions vastly more favorable for his greatest usefulness to his fellows and for the highest development of all his powers."

Jesus said: "I am come that they might have life, and that they might have it more abundantly." It is the life of the Kingdom that men even outside the Churches, often only too blindly, are seeking to attain. But the Church itself should give expert and sympathetic and constant guidance, seeking and saving that which is lost, leading men, however wayward, however fallen, however handicapped to the fulness of joy and service and existence in God's holy Temple of Life in which "ye also are builded together for an habitation of God through the Spirit."

"There never was a time," writes W. E. Hammond, "when the world, especially youth, had a greater need of Christ's spirit and teaching. Far from having completed its task, the church should enter upon a renewed ministry. What we mistake as evidence of a dying religion is simply the passing of complacent Christianity. . . . Once religion has again become intimately attached to the everyday affairs of life and is believed to possess vital significance, men will heed its appeal. Once the church focuses every ounce of its energy on the establishment of Christ's law of love throughout the world, there is every reason to believe that its voice will again be listened to, its leadership acknowledged, its challenge prove sufficiently virile to critical but adventurous youth, and its claim upon the loyalty and devotion of the unattached accepted by them."[1]

### (b)  THE PRESENT ISSUE
#### (i)  THE SOCIAL FUNCTION OF THE CHURCH

The modern trend of development raises the question as to the Social Function of the Church. Is it a part of the spiritual mission of the Church to seek to better conditions of life and work? Should the Church make actual provision to prevent the evils of the times, to meet the social needs of the age, to engage, as in the period of the Barbarian Invasions, in the establishment of hospitals, schools, rescue homes? Should the Church resort to legislation for social uplift? Should it directly take in hand to deal with social evils like drink, impurity and gambling, industrial problems, recreation, education, the press, unearned increment and a thousand like matters? The problem is acutely raised by the Church's policy, or lack of policy, in the matter of the educational and hospital problems in our own day. Should it be content to remain inactive, or to drift or, if it is to establish schools and hospitals, upon what principle, in what places, to what extent is this to be done? What should be the attitude of the Church towards Prohibition? In this matter there are wide differences of opinion betwen Churches in the New and Old World, nay, as between Churches in the same communities in both Worlds.

It would seem that the answer to all these questions is complex. To begin with, it is clear that, however much the Church interprets its task as to preach glad tidings and to send forth missionaries to the uttermost parts, still, if it will retain the spirit of Jesus, it can never escape the responsibility or the impulse to serve. The Church, too, must come not to be ministered unto, but to minister somewhere and somehow. It, too, must love much. In the second place, the interest of the Church in men must be as wide as human life itself. There can be no part of men's activities, relations or institutions that are merely "profane," "neutral," "common or unclean." Men with God's image in them and God's love seeking them are surely worthy of the Church's concern. This means that wherever there is a burden to be borne, a need to be met, a problem to be solved, the Church cannot remain aloof. Nor can it remain unconcerned when large sections of humanity still stand aloof from the church. In the third place, the New Testament lays down no code of social legislation, no command to do this or that in a particular set of circumstances —the Church must interpret its own task in the spirit of its Lord. In the fourth place, it is better to create an atmosphere of ministry, to inspire men to serve than itself to engage in the actual work officially.[2] And fifthly, the Church must ever be a trail-blazer, seeking out new

---

1. W. E. Hammond, The Dilemma of Protestantism, 149.
2. "The preacher is a man who is engaged in making himself unnecessary. And Christianity has been organized into the school and home and street." N. D. Hillis, *The Influence of Christ in Modern Life*, 27.

fields of service, cultivating them with care, and, then, as others are inspired to take up the tasks, content to have the moral courage to withdraw, leaving its blessing and its spirit, and to venture forth looking for fresh ways to serve. As a corollary of this truth, the Church must regard every social service institution, the State, charity organizations, all, not as rivals but as allies, and exhibit towards them the most appreciative sympathy.

The Christian Church, while finding no technical directions for social activity in the Gospel, believes that in the New Testament are to be found fundamental principles to inspire and govern service. The Church interprets its social function in the light of its being "the fulness of him that filleth all in all." It seeks to bear testimony to, and carry out, the spirit forever made known in the complete ministry of Jesus Christ. The Church has the following five-fold function in the sphere of social service—

1. It must exercise its age-long prophetic vocation and serve as conscience to Society. Christ was a conscience to his day. The Church must be no less than this in our day, and in every age. It must keep free from all entangling alliances that will hamper free and constructive social criticism. It must pursue no course that will prevent it from declaring the eternal verities or the claims of social justice. It must never permit ecclesiastical interests, economic considerations, social connections, political affiliations, a regard for its own past or present or future, to dull its sensitiveness to wrong or exploitation. It must be able and willing to reprove sin.

2. It must educate and inspire. The Church is evangelical. It must employ its power to awaken and to stimulate. It must make known to men the social ideals of the Kingdom, and not rest satisfied till they become part and parcel of human lives. It must remind the members of the community that they "work together in God's service," that they are "God's field to be planted, God's house to be built." The Church is interpreter, stimulator, guide. It must quicken all social impulses, interpret the Spirit of God, and inspire to service.

3. The Church must be pioneer, and never cease to be pastor. It must seek out fresh fields of helpfulness and have the courage to tread a new path of service. It must inaugurate and initiate. By all means it must avoid rigidity. It can never withdraw from service altogether.[1] And it ought never to withdraw from any service whatever, without first making sure that it has left its spirit there in those who carry on the work. It can never escape working, itself, for the unfit and the fallen, the weak and sinful. It must preach the Gospel to the poor, proclaim release for captives, set free the oppressed, if only to keep as a permanent possession the tender heart of its Lord. It must be pastor. And it must never do this work altogether by proxy. It must foster its social sympathy, itself taking care of "lost sheep" and mending broken lives. Jesus did this. The early Church did this. No true Church can or will avoid it.

1. In the United States in 1903 one-third of the benevolent institutions listed in the special census report, i.e. hospitals, day nurseries, permanent and temporary homes for adults and children, were connected with the church.

4. The Church must study, and it must seek rather to prevent than to cure. It is not enough to criticize, not enough to incite to serve, not enough to find new paths of ministry, and itself walk in these paths. It must do these things in a right way. It must deal with causes rather than symptoms, and prevent poverty, vice and suffering. Through some at least of its members and leaders the Church must study social problems, appreciate the underlying causes of social disorders.[1] and seek directly or through its members to better conditions of life. In a very real sense the Church must be a laboratory. It must not be content to have the poor with us always in order to cultivate in us the grace of charity. It must seek the good not of itself but of the poor, and seek to put away poverty and disease from the midst of men. As we have seen, it need not always do this thing itself in the whole entirety of the task, but it will arouse others to make this their aim in life. It is, then, we take it, a true impulse towards fundamental forms of service on the part of not a few churches that has been expressing itself in the multitude of "social surveys" in our day.

5. The Church will transform the helped into helpers. To rescue the perishing will not suffice. The Church must lift the fallen to lives of active social service. The Christian spirit is continually adapting, and is continuously adaptable. It will use every particle of human capacity and energy for the ever-changing tasks of the Kingdom. The process is not complete for the Church until the objects of its compassion have had kindled in them hearts of pity and love to seek and to save others who may be in need. The Church must believe that all of human kind are not only redeemable but, also, usable for, and in, the Kingdom. The spirit of ministry will impoverish unless it begets in those who are ministered unto, the passion and the power themselves to serve in their turn. The impulse to social service must be transmitted to all members of the social organism before the work is complete.

1. How complex a problem is thus opened up may be seen from an analysis of the causes of poverty given in A. G. Warner, *American Charities*, 37:

|  |  |  |
|---|---|---|
| Subjective | Characteristics | 1. Undervitalization and Indolence<br>2. Lubricity<br>3. Specific Disease<br>4. Lack of Judgment<br>5. Unhealthy Appetite |
|  | Habits producing and produced by the above | 1. Shiftlessness<br>2. Self-abuse and sexual excess<br>3. Abuse of stimulants and narcotics<br>4. Unhealthy diet<br>5. Disregard of family ties |
| Objective |  | 1. Inadequate natural resources<br>2. Bad climatic conditions<br>3. Defective sanitation, etc.<br>4. Evil associations and surroundings<br>5. Defective legislation and defective judicial and punitive machinery<br>6. Misdirected or inadequate education |
|  | 7. Bad industrial conditions | a. Variations in value of money<br>b. Changes in trade<br>c. Excessive or ill-managed taxation<br>d. Emergencies unprovided for<br>e. Undue power of class over class<br>f. Immobility of labor<br>g. Inadequate wages and irregular employment |
|  | 8. Unwise philanthropy |  |

We have stated the social function of the Church from the point of view of the Reformed Churches. It must not be forgotten, however, that there are two other main rival conceptions of the social function of the Church. The first of these we may designate as Plymouthism. The social function of the Church, according to this view, is wholly one of indifferentism—there are other and far weightier matters than any christianization of the social order. The other view is that of the Roman Catholic Church. It would pervade all life, have hospitals, schools, everything of its own, all dominated by its religious view of life. The Canon 1379 paragraph 2, of the new Canon Law, in speaking of the attitude of Roman Catholics to Universities, says—"If the public universities are not imbued with Catholic doctrine and surrounded with a Catholic atmosphere, it is most desirable to found in that country or region a Catholic University." Father Daly says—

"The Principle 'every Catholic boy and girl in a Catholic college and university' should be to us as sacred as in 'every Catholic child in a Catholic school.' One is the consequence of the other; both are the practical conclusions of our faith. This close connection between theories of education and the attitude towards problems of life is evident in history. . . . . . The tendency in our modern neutral universities is, without doubt, towards infidelity, or, to say the least, towards diluted Christianity. . . . . The great fallacy of the age, and particularly in this part of the country, is State Monopoly in educational matters. . . . . The right of Catholics in their own schools—primary, secondary, university, is a birthright we must always fight for. . . . . But what we strongly object to is the Arts Course, and particularly undergraduate work, even were the contentious subjects, such as philosophy and history to be given by Catholic teachers to Catholic students separately. . . . . The Catholic student in those most plastic years. . . . cannot help but imbibe ideas and doctrines opposed to his belief. . . . Through a Catholic University, and through it only, will the Church give its full contribution to the national life of Western Canada by creating Catholic leadership. . . . . On one of those mellow autumn evenings, of which the Prairie alone has the secret, the traveller, as his train steams into one of our Western Cities, will behold a stately cupola tipped with a golden cross—'What is that new building, yonder on the outskirts of the city?' he will inquire. The answer will be: 'That is the Catholic University of Western Canada.' "[1]

No one who has marked the progress of this Church in Saskatchewan can have doubts as to the interpretation which this religious body puts on the social function of the Church. A short visit to the Humbolt and Gravelbourg districts will suffice to reveal their social aims. This Church is never content to withdraw from

---

1. Father G. T. Daly, Catholic Problems in Western Canada, *passim* especially Ch. 11.

any service, trusting to the Christian spirit of uncontrolled men to work out the problems of life. It represents control.

The chief Protestant Churches stand between the two poles of domination and indifferentism. They put their confidence in free Christian men, fired by a social passion, capable of studying and solving social problems in the Christian spirit, their efforts to be augmented, where necessary, by the institutional Church. It is the Protestant Churches that are succeeding in making, even though indirectly, this twentieth century into an age of sacrificial social-mindedness.

The present leadership of the age has fallen too largely under the domination of two great movements—social humanitarianism and philosophic idealism. Both of these are signally failing to meet the demands of the present situation, for they do not accord first place to, nor put adequate emphasis upon, the worth of the individual. The Social Humanitarians too frequently content themselves with dealing with man, or with men, in the large, as a social phenomenon. The consequence is that the individual is submerged in the interests of the whole. On the other hand philosophic idealism makes a similar mistake in being satisfied to treat human nature, or the nature of the human, largely in relation to its ultimate significance. The tendency of the first movement is not only to ignore the individual in the interests of the group, but also to ignore that which gives the individual his deepest meaning, namely, Religion. The tendency of the second is not to ignore Religion—indeed it is to make the chief problem centre about the relation of human nature to the Divine. But its signal failure consists in dealing with just those practical considerations which are the implication of that ultimate relationship.

Jesus made the great synthesis. And the Christian Church is called and challenged to recognize this synthesis by a deeper interpretation of the infinite worth of the individual. That will be done when there is stressed on the one hand the religious significance of the individual, and, on the other hand, the true brotherhood by which only it can be expressed. Let the Christian Church set itself to this task and it will regain the leadership in a world sadly needing direction.

## (*ii*) THE CHURCH IN THE LIFE OF THE NATION

### *What the Past Has Taught*

The past has taught us that there are many relations between the Church and the State or the Nation that have been unsatisfying and even harmful. It will be necessary briefly to review the history of this relationship in order to appreciate to the full the great privilege which we enjoy in having the Church free to do its work.

The Christian Church did not begin as a national institution. It was a Faith that grew into a Fellowship and soon became a Force. At the outset it was not calculated to attract the attention of the State nor to influence all classes of the Nation. "Not many wise, not many mighty, not many noble" embraced the faith, according to the observation of Paul.

At a later date, Celsus sneered at a religion founded by a Carpenter, preached by fishermen, tentmakers and such like, and able to win the allegiance of only "the baker and the fuller." Till the end of the second century, the Christian appeal met with favor most largely among the slaves, the freedmen and the laborers. By the end of that century, the Church was more definitely organized. In the face of the fierce persecutions that assailed the faithful only a well-organized Church could have survived at all.

The Church met with courage the calumnies of its enemies, worshipped its God with a glad faith in the Catacombs under the Appian Way, waged war unceasingly against paganism, and inspired a high standard of literary production, and, of course, of Christian living. It was this Church that became the hope of the Roman Empire after being the object of its fiercest persecution. When Constantine cast about to find an ally for the State, he found it not in the Old Philosophy, nor the Old Paganism, nor the new organization of Diocletian, but in the hitherto despised and persecuted Christian religion. In the hour of its alliance with Constantine the Church became a kingdom of this world.

But unfortunately if the Church won its way in the world, the world also won its way in the Church. Many pagan elements entered. Many things were formally called Christian that partook but little of the character of Jesus. Social service, which had been largely personal and congregational, became highly organized and institutional.

This was a great experiment of the Church in the Nation. Even though much was accomplished, even though the Church became the refuge of the oppressed, established hospitals, saved learning, and raised the moral tone of society, yet the alliance was not altogether happy. It was too external, too formal. It did not involve a sufficient penetration of the common and national life by Christian ideals and Christian motives.

In the Middle Ages we witness the unedifying spectacle of the Church and State engaged in a fierce contest for supremacy. Emperor and Pope, feudal lord and bishop, strove through the weary years for mastery. In the end Gregory VII prevailed. But it was a fruitless victory for the kingdom of God. Though the parish church was the centre of every market town, though noble spirits like St. Francis of Assisi gave splendid examples of service, working for the lepers "till the bells of Umbria rang as he approached," yet the Church, as an institution, in the main, sought not to serve, but to dominate. It conceived itself to be an "instrument of salvation," not a fellowship of Christians striving to do the Master's will. In its strife with the State the Church forgot that it too must come, not to be ministered unto but to minister.

At the Reformation the revolt from Rome created great national churches. Scotland, England, Germany, Holland, Switzerland set up churches for themselves. These were State Churches. Whereas the Church had formerly sought to dominate the State, the State now endeavored, not without success, to determine the religion of its subjects. It was slowly and late that liberty of conscience and religious toleration came into being. There was much to be learned *after* the Reformation.

It is perhaps in the Reformed Church of Scotland that the problems of the relation of the Church to the State can best be studied in all phases of historical development. From the days of John Knox the question of spiritual freedom in its reference to the civil power has passed through various distinct stages. At first under Knox the Church was organized by its own action without regard to civil authority. Within a decade, in 1567, the Church became national, established. By the Act of 1592 the Church received recognition for "the liberty of the true Kirk of God."

Then came the Stuart struggles, bitter and prolonged, the upshot of which was the Revolution Settlement. This provided guarantees for the liberty of the Church of God and made the Confession of Faith statute law. And yet the legal decision that produced the Great Disruption of 1843 asserted that the Church was a "creature of statute," that it must obey the State in doing or in refraining from doing, spiritual acts.

This Disruption produced the Free Church with its glorious history. In more recent years came the Union of 1900 and the momentous House of Lords' Judgment in 1904. Sacrifice was involved before the Church finally asserted its liberty. But, in the memorable words of Principal Rainy, the principle was enunciated that "that Church will be free that dares to be free."

In the negotiations for the Union of the Church of Scotland and the United Free Church, so happily consummated in October, 1929, it became clear that the question of "spiritual independence," or the freedom of the Church from all secular authority in matters spiritual constituted a difficulty in the way of reunion. In the end the Church of Scotland formulated and adopted her own constitutional Articles, affirming her claim to spiritual freedom in language chosen by herself. The interposition of the State was limited to the recognition of these Articles as lawful, and the repeal of all statutory provisions which might be deemed to be inconsistent therewith. This policy was carried out. Articles were framed containing a bold and complete affirmation of the freedom of the Church in matters spiritual. The lawfulness of the Articles was recognized by Parliament in the Church of Scotland Act, 1921.[1]

This historical sketch is given to indicate that on its formal side the relation between the Church and the Nation has been a troublous and complicated one. In America we have no Established Church, and, so far as spiritual activity is concerned, no statutory control. The Church is free to do its work without let or hindrance. The State and the Church are neither rivals nor formal allies, and certainly not antagonists. The Church is free. Its function is primarily to create an atmosphere and a spirit. It may bring the leaven of its influence, the power of its ideals and life, to bear upon national problems and

---

1. The Edinburgh Scotsman, October 2, 1920. Article by Lord Sands, The Steps to Union.

national tasks. But it may bring only these. The first lesson that we must learn is that these will suffice for the work to be accomplished. *What is the Church's Work in the Nation?*

In order to appreciate the Church's work in and for Canada (which we select as an example) we should consider carefully certain determining factors that enter into the problem—

1. *What is Canada?* (1) Canada is a young country. Although the story of this land stretches back across four centuries, yet it is only in recent years that the Dominion has reached the maturity of nationhood. While large parts of the country are highly developed, extensive sections are still pioneer, and great stretches are quite undevloped. Though young, Canada enjoys the fullest self-government. Her destiny is in her own hands. The country needs moral leadership in its advance to maturity.

(2) Canada is a large country. Alberta is twice as large as the British Isles. British Columbia is larger than Italy, Switzerland and France. Ontario is larger than Germany. Quebec would make five United Kingdoms. Saskatchewan is equal in size to France, Belgium and Holland. The Dominion occupies the northern half of a great continent, stretching from sea to sea, with large reaches of coast region, mountain, prairies, lakes, rivers, and again more coast region. Its coast line is only less than half the whole circumference of the earth. Its area is one-third of the British Empire. The country needs breadth of vision to retain singleness of aim and purpose.

(3) Canada is a growing country. In the newer Provinces before the War one-tenth was being added to the population yearly. In 1913 there was an immigration into the Dominion of over 400,000. And yet, while Great Britain has a population to the square mile of 471, Canada has only 2. In some of the Western Provinces only one-tenth of the land is under cultivation. The natural resources of this land are relatively undeveloped, and, indeed, only too largely unknown. For many, many years Canada is bound to witness a tremendous growth. The country needs unselfish guidance to avoid exploitation and aggrandizement for the few, and for the many, to obtain a maximum of opportunity.

(4) Canada is a country with a mixed population. The first population was French. After the capture of Quebec and the War of Independence. settlers came from the British Isles, and the United Empire Loyalii' from the new Republic. Upon this foundation Eastern Canada ..as built. But in the past quarter of a century men have flocked hither from all regions of the earth, and the inhabitants of this Dominion are no longer homogeneous. Nearly half of the folk in the Central Prairies are non-Anglo-Saxon. The country needs a wide sympathy and an alert statesmanship to make the whole mass of our people truly Canadian.

2. *What is the Church?* There are many church organizations. There should be one Church organism—a fellowship that is vital, a faith that links us to the Unseen and Divine, a force that never wearies. It is the group of all the followers of Christ, "whate'er their

name or sign," that seek to live his life, to work for his Kingdom, and to realize his Presence.

3. *What is the Church's Work?* The Church's work is the work of the Master—not to be ministered unto but to minister. Service instead of selfishness. Purity instead of pollution. Friendship instead of feuds. Sympathy instead of suspicion. Peace instead of warfare. The high instead of the low. Enlightenment instead of ignorance. Health instead of disease. Christ instead of chaos.

## The Church in the Nation

We must now consider in what way the Church must do its work in the Nation.

1. The Church must serve its own community. The Church will not fail to look beyond Canada, for it can accept no commission less than the whole world. But the Church in this Dominion will remember that it owes a special duty to the Dominion itself. It must create a Christian atmosphere, a Christian tone and spirit that will be reflected in all the public acts and legislation of the country. Canada itself must be made Christian, not in any external way but from within. There is no other way to achieve this than to make its citizens Christian.

2. The Church must propagate its own life, express its own ideals and conserve its own forces.

The Church owes it to the Nation that the Church itself should persist. This means heavy and difficult mission work for the frontiers, the fostering of weak causes, the enlistment of recruits for service, and efficient working everywhere.

The Church owes it to the Nation to have the courage of its conviction. This means that its members should live the life of the Master in their homes, that the Church should raise up persons and create institutions to carry on the work of the Kingdom, and not hesitate to sacrifice its resources for the sake of reaching the fallen, the needy and the unsaved.

The Church owes it to the Nation to conserve its forces. Union, co-operation, concerted action as between churches is Christian.

3. The Church must ever be a pioneering force in the Nation. To support a hospital on the frontier or a nurse in a sparsely-settled region is Christian. But there comes a time when the district is developed and should be educated to the responsibility of caring for its own. The Church should then have the wisdom and the courage to withdraw, and to devolve this responsibility upon others. For the Church is an inspiring and educative agency and not simply an economy. Thus in the days after Constantine, hospitals, asylums, schools were inaugurated by the Church. The Church has since taught the civil power its responsibility for caring for these institutions.

4. The Church owes it to the Nation to fight for the helpless. It must always champion the dependent and the defective, strive to win the delinquent, and rescue the perishing.

5. The Church owes it to the Nation to make men. The Church is not interested primarily in political forms or economic measures or specific social programmes as such, but it is interested in justice, it is interested in freedom from oppression, it is interested in wholesome surroundings, for it is interested in men and women and little children. The Church brings the social test of human welfare to all panaceas and policies. And the Church is responsible to create in this Dominion men of sufficient moral calibre and character to be citizens with that righteousness which will exalt the Nation and that vision without which the people perish.

### (*iii*)    THE CHURCH IN THE LIFE OF THE WORLD

We have discussed the social function of the Church in modern times and the place of the Church in the life of the Nation. What social service should the Church render in the life of the world at large? The service should not be other than we have already indicated—to serve as conscience to educate and inspire, to seek out fresh spheres of service, to study, and to raise up helpers. The Church must do for the world at large what it must do for the Nation. "The days of hope are here once more," writes J. E. Davey,[1] "when we may have, not a temporal supremacy of State by Church authorities as tried in Rome, in Geneva, and elsewhere, but a vital permeation of the State in its actions and legislation by Christian ideals and forces." If we substitute the word "world" for "state" we have finely expressed the Christian aspiration. The Reformation was part of a movement that also created National States. It served to stress the relation of the Church to particular countries. At the Reformation the old World Church gave way to northern Europe to National Churches. The ideals of the old World Church were world-conquest and world-flight as embodied in the Papacy and Monasticism. It will not be in these directions that lies the hope of world-service for the Church.

Only in recent times has the Church again caught the world vision. This has been due to the Foreign Missions Movement, World Trade, World Travel, the spread of geographic knowledge, the application of Science, and the World War.

The International Missionary Council in Passiontide, 1928, met on the Mount of Olives, Jerusalem, to study and to articulate the world mission of Christianity. Dr. John R. Mott has stated the vital issues that were dealt with in a constructive manner in this challenging meeting—

"How may religious education, dealing as it does with the two subjects of widest and most fundamental concern—religion and education—be lifted into its proper place of central prominence, and this in time to meet the grave perils resulting from the rapid spread of purely secular systems of government education? What manifestation of the Christian life and what presentation of the Christian message are demanded in

Changing Vesture of the Faith, 168.

these days in the light of non-Christian systems of thought and faith? How afford to the present generation of youth, a fresh, convincing, and satisfying apologetic? How liberate a vastly greater lay force and relate it effectively to the great task of developing a dependable base for the world-wide mission and for the Christianization of the impact of the so-called Christian nations upon the non-Christian world? How secure and safeguard genuine religious liberty in the light of recent developments in different parts of the non-Christian world? How may the Christian Church get at the heart of the solution of the most alarming problem of to-day, that of securing right race relationships? Again, how ensure that, as modern industry spreads over Asia and Africa, and grave evils and perils which have been so manifest in Europe and America may be averted? How may wisest direction be given to the movement toward closer international co-operation and unity?"

Dr. Mott has briefly summarized the significance of the Conference:

"In some respects the most distinctive characteristic of Jerusalem might be expressed in the word 'sharing,' by which is meant that in the fellowship experienced in Jerusalem the Christian workers of the East and West shared their visions, insight, experience, burdens, hopes, and purposes. Moreover, a wider synthesis was achieved, a synthesis in which the individualistic and social conceptions of the Gospel of Christ are recognized as integral, mutually supporting, and indispensable aspects of Christ's all-inclusive mission; a synthesis in which many of the so-called secular organizations, movements, and forces, as well as those which bear the Christian name, are made tributary to the realization of the divine purpose, because we come to see more deeply and comprehensively that 'all are yours, and ye are Christ's and Christ is God's.' "

The Jerusalem Conference has called the churches everywhere to Prayer:

"1. *For a Missionary Spirit*—that the Church may see the whole world's need of Christ and may be ready for any sacrifice in order to make him known to all mankind.

2. *For a Spirit of Prayer*—that Christian people may learn to pray as Christ prayed and taught his disciples to pray; and that an ever-increasing number of interceders may be raised up until the whole church is awakened to prayer.

3. *For a Spirit of Sacrifice*—that the Church may be willing at whatever cost to follow and to bear witness to the way of Christ as she learns it.

4. *For a Spirit of Unity*—that the whole Church of Christ may desire and experience a new unity in Christ.

5. *For the Gift of Interpretation*—that the Church may learn to preach the eternal Gospel by word and life in terms that the men and women of this age will understand.

6. *For Courageous Witness in Moral Questions*—that the witness of the Church in the moral questions of our day may truly reflect the mind of God and may be known and felt throughout the world.

7. *For a Spirit of Service*—that a great number of men and women may offer themselves unreservedly to do Christ's work at home and abroad in our generation.

8. *For the Completion of Our Own Conversion*—for the removal of all hindrances in our own lives to the manifestation of God's redeeming love and power."

Basil Mathews, in his *Roads to the City of God*,[1] has pictured the return of the members of the Jerusalem Conference to their own work, a picture which may be taken to represent the Church in action in its world task:

"They have gone back to primitive African villages where the fetish rules by fear, where the industrial whirlpool drags the youth away into its engulfing waters, where crude alcohol from the West maddens and poisons and rots; but have gone back sure of new allies and certain of the Christ who has shown his power to lift the poorest and lowest to heroism and sainthood. They have plunged back again into the chaos and confusion of China, the agony of a nation in the long pangs of rebirth; but in the perspectives of Jerusalem they have caught some vision of the patient, persistent Providence of God. They are swept once more by the confused cross-currents of India's life, with its inter-communal clash and its political wrestling; but surer than ever, from the sheer experience at Jerusalem, that there are different paths from opposite sides up the steep slopes to a meeting-place on the shining plateau where God's City is built. They have returned to the modern Babylons of the West, Berlin and Paris, London and New York, Rio and Sydney, Cape Town and Toronto, and all the vivid, conquering, materialistic civilization for which they stand; but with a new and clearer picture of the nature of the hostile forces in the world, a fresh alignment of battle that will inspire effort and instruct strategy.

"All of them in all the continents see now, and see together, that there is no 'home' and 'foreign' in the mind of God, no geographically separated 'home base' and 'foreign mission field' in the thought of the Eternal; but one world inhabited by one humanity, all children of his, but not all knowing him. . . .

"Things that have for many been on the outer circumference have become central. Problems, tasks that have seemed secular, like the life of the industrial and agricultural world, have taken on a new and spiritual significance. All life is seen as sacramental, both instrument and organ of spiritual

1. Pp. 110-111.

values and realities. Having entered in a generous spirit into the strivings, sufferings, and hopes of all mankind, they have found fuller reasons for believing that Christ is able as the Son of the living God to cure the ills and save the lives of men everywhere."

Afresh the Church has been challenged to consider its world responsibilities. The spear-thrust of its activities is its policy of Foreign Missions. Its objective will be the angel-song of Bethlehem, "On earth peace, good will toward men!" Its marching orders remain in the Great Comission, "Go ye therefore, and teach all nations." Its strength is the promise of his presence, "I am with you alway, even unto the end of the world."

We grow impatient for the fulfilment of the vision. Let us remember the word of old, "Though it tarry, wait for it; because it will surely come, it will not tarry."[1] Leagues of Nations, Disarmament Conferences, Church Leagues to Promote Peace, Mission Conferences, and the whole complex of international relations are gradually socializing the world in a Christian sense. And this is a service of the Christian Church, "which is his body, the fulness of him that filleth all in all."[2] The great social service of the Christian Church is to bring every phase of human existence, every relation in the world of men under the sway of the ideals of the Christ.

"But now we see *not yet* all things put under him. But we see Jesus . . . crowned with glory and honor."[3]

QUESTIONS FOR DISCUSSION ON "THE PRESENT TREND"

1. Is the proper function of the minister of the Gospel "preaching" or "social service"?    State his function in your own words.

2. What qualifications has, say the Supreme Court of your Church, for pronouncing upon complicated social and economic questions?

3. "A social consciousness and a social conscience have been developed within the Churches."  Why was the development so late? What forces in recent years have contributed to this development?

4. How do we know that the social programme enunciated by your Church is consonant with the mind of Christ if your country is vastly different from Palestine and the twentieth century not at all like the first century.

5. "We believe that the work of saving the world implies the Christianizing the entire social order."  Does this mean that the saving of a man's soul is dependent on his environment?

6. To what extent should the Church claim credit for legislation, say on Temperance, passed by a Provincial or State Legislature?

7. What advantage has religious charity over that dispensed by a lay institution?  What disadvantages?

8. Is it the business of the Church to seek out the pecuniary interest entrenched behind injustice with a view to expose it?

9. Should the bestowal of charity be judged by its results on the recipient or by the motive of the giver?

1. Habakkuk, 2: 3.
2. Ephesians 1: 23.
3. Hebrews 2: 8-9.

10. Is the present trend of social activity of the Church towards giving up old forms or taking on new types of service?

11. If the social work in a town is done efficiently by a Charity Organization Society should the Church withdraw from all charitable activity.

12. Should the Church assail Capitalism?

13. The Bible exercises a civilizing influence on the language of many people. Is this a social service rendered by the Christian Church?

14. How do you account for the difference in attitude towards Prohibition on the part of various churches in the New and Old World?

15. What is the most fundamental social service that the Church can render in this age?

BOOKS FOR ADVANCED STUDY

E. T. Devine, *Social Forces*. A Year Book of the Church and Social Service in the United States. W. Rauschenbusch, *Christianizing the Social Order. Christianity and the Social Crisis.* H. F. Ward, *Social Creed of the Churches.* L. Abbott, *Christianity and Social Problems.* E. T. Devine, *Misery and its Causes.* W. Gladden, *Social Salvation.* C. F. Kent, *The Social Teaching of Jesus and the Prophets.* H. C. King, *The Moral and Religious Challenge of Our Times.* S. Mathews, *The Church and the Changing Order.* F. H. Lynch, *The New Opportunity of the Ministry.* F. G. Peabody, *Jesus Christ and the Social Question.* Graham Taylor, *Religion in Social Action.* W. E. Hammond, *The Dilemma of Protestantism.* F. E. Johnson, *The Social Work of the Churches.*

QUESTIONS FOR DISCUSSION ON "THE SOCIAL FUNCTION OF<br>THE CHURCH"

1. What social work is done by your own local Church? What are the special needs of a social nature that exist in your community?

2. What social work is done by your Church in the Nation?

3. Is the Church fulfilling its entire function when it worships?

4. Would it be wise for your minister to preach each year a series of sermons on the social and economic conditions of the Nation?

5. Is the "Saving of a soul" a "social work"?

6. Is the statement of the social function of the Church as given in the text complete? If not, wherein is it defective?

7. Make a list of the social service aims of your denomination as revealed in the reports of the proceedings of its highest courts during the past fifteen years.

8. Is the influence of the Church upon civilization becoming greater or is it becoming less as the years go by?

9. What special study of the needs of your community has ever been undertaken by your Church? What could it undertake?

10. What special programme has your Church for the City? What for the Country? Does it need these programmes?

11. Does your Church classify its young people as to their aspirations for life callings? What does it do to encourage them to attain these? Or is this any part of the work of the Church?

12. To what extent is your Church an institution of *Training?* In what respects does it compare favorably, and in what respects unfavorably, with a school?

13. The trend of education in America, particularly towards its western parts, in both Canada and the United States, has seen the Church withdraw more and more from contacts with School, College

and University in the interests of a "secular education free from sectarian influence." Is this a Social Service rendered by the Church?

14. There are "those who stand aloof from organized religion, convinced that the church is not making any notable contribution to the problems of the age. The charges include the industrial, international, and racial conflicts; its habitual opposition to new ideas; its inability to impart instruction adequate for moral guidance; its readiness to render unqualified and zealous support to the nation's wars, irrespective of their justification or aims, once war has been declared; its partiality and undue obsequiousness to wealth in the ordering of its message and policies." Discuss.

### BOOKS FOR ADVANCED STUDY

P. Carnegie Simpson, *The Life of Principal Rainy.* Father G. T. Daly, *Catholic Problems of Western Canada.* Rev. W. R. McIntosh, *Social Service, A Book for Young Canadians.* Albert F. McGarrah, *A Modern Church Programme.* H. F. Ward, *A Year Book of the Church and Social Service in the United States.* K. L. Butterfield, *Chapters in Rural Progress.* K. L. Butterfield, *The Country Church and the Rural Problem.* Gill and Pinchot, *The Country Church.* W. Gladden, *The Christian Pastor and the Working Church.* C. S. Macfarland, *Spiritual Culture and Social Service.* P. L. Vogt, *The Church and Country Life.* W. E. Hammond, *The Dilemma of Protestantism.* F. E. Johnson, *The Social Work of the Churches.*

### QUESTIONS FOR DISCUSSION ON "THE CHURCH IN THE LIFE OF THE NATION"

[NOTE: These questions and the list of books for advanced study have been prepared primarily with a view to the Dominion of Canada. Each Country or Nation has its own problems and questions and literature.]

1. What is the relation of the Roman Catholic Separate Schools to the Public or National School system in the various provinces of the Dominion?

2. What does the Canadian expect of the New Canadian?

3. What does the New Canadian expect of the Canadian?

4. To what extent is difference of language a problem in the Dominion? Have the Churches helped to solve or to intensify this problem?

5. What advance has been made in Temperance legislation in the Dominion during recent years? What contribution was made to this by the Church? What by the War?

6. What problem is presented by Race Track Gambling in Canada? If it were a matter merely of economic loss should the Church nevertheless be interested?

7. What does your Church do to help the Nation in the following matters: Rescue Homes, Settlement Work, Care of Dependants, Defectives, Delinquents?

8. What claim has the Indian upon the State and the Church in Canada?

9. What part should a Church take in a General Election? What part should an individual minister?

10. Did the regulations require that the Director of the Chaplain Service in the Overseas Military Forces of Canada in the late War must be a minister of the Church of England? Has any Church any precedence over another in Canada? In England? In Scotland?

11. What policy has your Church adopted towards the following people in our midst: The Ruthenian, the Hungarian, the Bohemian, the Icelander, the Doukhobor, the Mennonite, and others? If it has no policy concerning these or similar other Groups, should it have one?

12. What work can the Church do to prevent divisions in Canada proving a menace, particularly in relation to the following: The English and the French? The East and the West? The Urban and the Rural Populations?

BOOKS FOR ADVANCED STUDY

There is a great wealth of literature that relates to the Dominion. Every Public Library will be furnished with much that is good. The following is only a selection that has primary relation to some aspects of the History of the Church in Canada: Shortt and Doughty, *Canada and its Provinces,* 22 vols., particularly vols. 11 and 12, entitled *Missions, Arts, and Letters.* Wrong and Langton, *The Chronicles of Canada,* 32 vols. *The Makers of Canada,* 21 vols. Proceedings and Transactions of the Royal Society of Canada. Egerton and Grant, *Canadian Constitutional Development.* Rev. C. W. Gordon (Ralph Connor), *The Life of James Robertson, D.D.* Rev. Wm. McCulloch, D.D., *The Life of Thomas McCulloch, D.D.* E. H. Oliver, *The Winning of the Frontier.* John Maclean, *McDougall of Alberta.* Alexander Sutherland, *The Methodist Church and Missions.* Mrs. F. C. Stephenson, *One Hundred Years of Canadian Methodist Missions.* James Woodsworth, *Thirty Years in the Canadian North West.* J. T. McNeill, *The Presbyterian Church in Canada, 1875-1925.* Rev. L. Norman Tucher, *Western Canada.* Rev. George Bryce,, *John Black, The Apostle of the Red River.* Dean Harris, *Pioneers of the Cross in Canada.* Wm. Gregg, D.D., *History of the Presbyterian Church in Canada.* Father A. G. Morice, *History of the Catholic Church in Western Canada.* Father G. T. Daly, *Catholic Problems in Western Canada.* D. W. Duthie, *A Bishop in the Rough.* Katherine Hughes, *Father Lacombe, The Black-Robe Voyageur.* Robert Machray, *Life of Archbishop Machray.* J. S. Woodsworth, *Strangers Within Our Gates.* Margaret K. Strong, *Public Welfare Administration in Canada.* *The Canada Year Book; Social Welfare;* University Magazines, and many others.

QUESTIONS FOR DISCUSSION ON "THE CHURCH IN THE LIFE OF THE WORLD."

1. "Practical service and inner renewal are two equally valid and mutually supplementary poles of the truly and totally religious life." Do you agree? Or are these two purposes mutually independent or even exclusive?

2. "The right of private judgment, procured at stupendous sacrifice and suffering, has for hosts of Protestants so far lost its original moral and spiritual content as to provide sanction for all manner of unsocial conduct, irresponsibility, and unbridled license, much to the danger of civilization." Discuss.

3. "Sectarianism has created a big demand for ministers." Is this loss or gain, if true?

4. "The newly acquired knowledge has so revolutionized men's religious outlook and beliefs that it has affected the individual's religious experience and the church's programme." Discuss.

5. "One may well question the justice of religious Superintendents and Secretaries (and Professors) who live comfortably while the minister and his family on the pioneer field endure all manner of hardships and privations. Is it not time the Church faced some of these

questions before she undertakes to eliminate the evils of the industrial world?" Discuss.

6. "Many a Protestant who deprecates denominational rivalry contributes to the orgy he condemns by supporting half a dozen rival societies whose professed aims are similar and competitive." Discuss.

7. "We need to eliminate the root causes that produce impoverishment, war, vice, and vicious contributing evils." How can it be achieved?

8. "Conditions which a few generations ago failed to disturb the finest souls now make the ordinary man uneasy. Exploitation, oppression, ignorance, abject poverty, war, physical suffering, all of which left the saints of bygone days unperturbed, agitate our own generation and demand the removal of these intolerable handicaps." Is this true? If so, how do you account for this?

9. "War and the heartless exploitation of backward races are being denounced with a seriousness and vigor peculiar to our own age." To what extent is the Church responsible?

10. "The same consciousness that is critically scrutinizing the secular institutions and conventions of our times has not allowed to go unquestioned what the Church has long held and taught as sacred. Jesus' explosive utterance, 'The Sabbath was made for man and not man for the Sabbath,' eloquently voices the modern temper towards things 'sacred'. Is this a challenge to the Church's suitability, or to its right, to perform social service?

11. "The modern tendency is to sever the tie of marriage the moment it ceases to contribute to the happiness and well-being of those involved." Has the church a social service to render by giving instruction in this matter? What should that instruction be?

12. Has the Church ever yet had the courage faithfully to grapple with the problem of Divorce? Discuss the Church's responsibility in treating such themes as Eugenics, Divorce, Companionate Marriage.

13. Should the Church withdraw from its hospital work in China as soon as each local Chinese Province establishes hospitals of its own? Should the Church ever withdraw from any work or institution without a guarantee that the main motive and spirit of those henceforth responsible for the work will be Christian? Is it ever possible to secure such a guarantee?

14. Does the Church discharge its full world-responsibility through its Board of Foreign Missions?

15. What is the ideal relation of the Church to the University?

16. Is the Church giving adequate sympathy and leadership to the Trade Unions enterprise?

17. How far, if at all, is Christian Socialism the solution of modern ills?

18. Is the antagonism of certain economic thinkers to the Christian Church, on the ground that it has supported Slavery, Feudalism, and now Capitalism, justified?

19. Should the Church ever commit itself to a current economic order, philosophy of life or scientific theory? Or does the Church exist by its own right?

20. Has the Church a definite responsibility in the matter of Unemployment? Have the ministers and leaders of the Christian Church the requisite equipment in economic, social and political knowledge to make a contribution to the solution of this problem? Is a benevolent Christian spirit enough for this complex task?

21. Should Christian people provide their own "Service Clubs"?

22. "The seven deadly sins of the age are: Politics without principles; wealth without work; pleasure without conscience; knowledge without character; commerce without morality; science without humanity; worship without sacrifice." So far as you know the Church, is it definitely doing battle with these sins? Consider each in turn.

23. "The primary purpose of Christianity is to produce Christian personality and a Christianized world order." Is this a complete and satisfactory statement?

24. "Humanitarianism can never be made a successful substitute for religion." Why not?

25. "It is safe to assume that multitudes now standing aloof from organized religion would be more inclined to listen to the Church's voice, once convinced that its chief mission and purpose is to force the issue of the application of Jesus' principle of love to every phase of human endeavor and relationship." Discuss.

26. Has the modern "public" school proved a failure because of its lack of religious instruction and because of its secular spirit? Should Protestantism turn from the "public" schools to a system of "parish" schools directly controlled and inspired by the Church?

### BOOKS FOR ADVANCED STUDY

Books on the Jerusalem Conference: The Complete Report in eight volumes; The World Mission of Christianity. Basil Mathews, Roads to the City of God.